El Alamein

Halting an Impending Holocaust in the Middle East

Kelvin Crombie

First published in 2012.

Contacts details:
Kelvin Crombie, PO Box 565, Mundaring, WA, 6073, Australia
Email: kjcrombie09@bigpond.com

Crombie, Kelvin
El Alamein: Halting an Impending Holocaust in the Middle East

ISBN: 978-0-9873630-1-5

Artwork:
Cover by Dao Wanwiper, Minutemanpress, Midland, Western Australia.
Typesetting by Mike Lockhart, Print Publishing, Perth. Western Australia.
Printed in Great Britain by Imprint Digital, Exeter.

Visuals:
Front Cover:
Rommel with the 15th Panzer Division, from www.topedge.com/panels/ww2/na/rommel.html. Unsuccessful efforts were made to locate the source of this photograph.
Captain Charles Upham in battle dress after the campaign of Greece and Crete c1941, Wairoru Army Museum, New Zealand, DA 6981.
New Zealand troops on training at the Western Desert, Wairoru Army Museum, No. DA 2099.
General Bernard Montgomery, Wairoru Army Museum, DA 10815.
Back Cover:
Montgomery Bible, Christ Church Museum, Jerusalem.

ACKNOWLEDGEMENTS

This book would not be possible without the people who made the history in the first place. Thanks and honour go to them, and especially to those soldiers who volunteered to go and fight far away from their homes in order to ensure the light of freedom was not extinguished.

There are many who have written about this subject matter over many years, and I want to acknowledge these historians and researchers. I have accessed both primary and secondary sources to write this book, and each of these sources was possible because someone dedicated time and energy to putting them together. One exceptional source of primary material was the documents from the German Foreign Office, and thanks must goes to those people who translated these documents into English.

In addition there have been the personal memoirs and histories of Winston Churchill, Viscount Montgomery and Field Marshal Rommel. I tried to use their writings as much as possible.

Then there are the personal reflections of various Allied soldiers, written either by themselves, as in the case of Ron Turrel, Bob Holt and Arthur Leggett, or by others, as in the case of Charles Upham and Thomas Derrick.

Apart from the primary sources, many thanks go to those who wrote the numerous secondary sources that I accessed. By far the most import such secondary source was the invaluable book *Nazi Palestine* by German researchers and academics Klaus-Michael Mallmann and Martin Cuppers, of which more will be said in the Introduction.

I would like to thank Dr Sabine Dumschatt in particular, at the Bundesarchiv (Federal Archive) in Berlin who made life a bit easier for a non-German speaker like myself, and my daughter Orit, as we endeavoured to access primary materials in the German sources. To my cousins by marriage, Christoph and Annemarie Grueneisen, in Heidelberg who also assisted, both with research and translation. Also to Dolores Ho from the New Zealand Army Museum, Waiouru, who was extremely helpful. Other archives and libraries too have been helpful including, the Australian War Museum, Canberra; the Bundesarchiv in Berlin; and CMJ Archives, Christ Church, Jerusalem.

Then special thanks go to the many who encouraged me with this project, and by reading through and correcting the material, including Rev. Dr. Cyril Pritchard, Peter and Kathy Booth, Peter Cuthbertson, Craig Beech, Anne Edgar, Steve Lieblich, David Pileggi, Grant and Jill Crombie, Eileen Alvis and my wife Lexie.

A number of people have also loaned materials, including photographs and among these are Noel and Barbara Bell, Ross Olive, Edward and Mary Pritchett, Helen Ardente, Jill Ross, Kim Weatherston and Merv Squire. Thanks to any others who I have inadvertently omitted from this list.

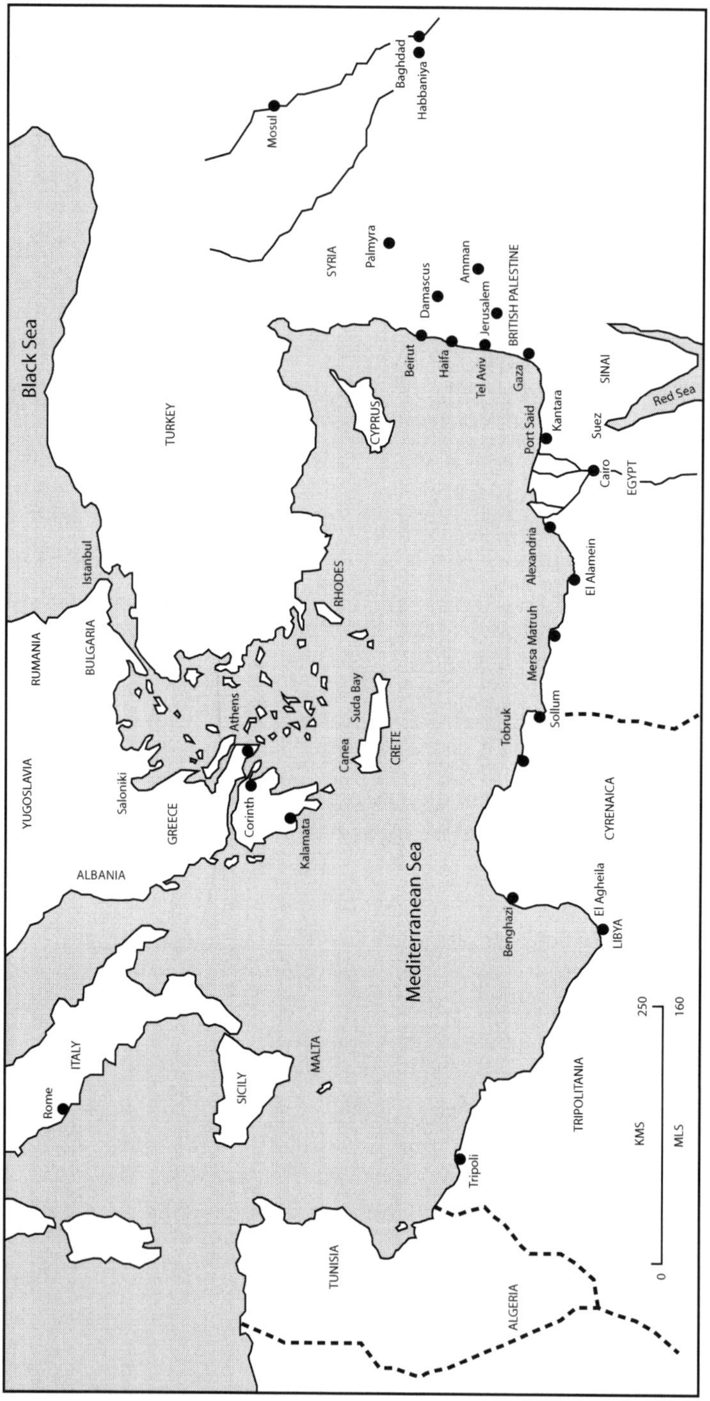
Black Sea
TURKEY
Mosul
Baghdad
Habbaniya
SYRIA
Palmyra
Damascus
Amman
Jerusalem
BRITISH PALESTINE
Beirut
Haifa
Tel Aviv
Gaza
CYPRUS
SINAI
Red Sea
Suez
Kantara
Port Said
Cairo
EGYPT
Alexandria
El Alamein
Mersa Matruh
Sollum
Tobruk
RHODES
Istanbul
RUMANIA
BULGARIA
YUGOSLAVIA
Saloniki
GREECE
ALBANIA
Athens
Corinth
Kalamata
Suda Bay
Canea
CRETE
CYRENAICA
Benghazi
El Agheila
LIBYA
Mediterranean Sea
ITALY
Rome
SICILY
MALTA
TRIPOLITANIA
Tripoli
TUNISIA
ALGERIA
KMS
MLS
0
250
160

TABLE OF CONTENTS

INTRODUCTION

IS THERE A CONNECTION BETWEEN EL ALAMEIN AND THE HOLOCAUST?

My initial acquaintance with the two aspects of this subject – the battle of El Alamein and the Holocaust - began while growing up on a farm in a remote area of Western Australia. It came due to a boyhood interest in the North African campaign of 1940-1942, and particularly the two iconic battles of Tobruk and El Alamein.[1] The 'Rats of Tobruk' were among my heroes.[2]

This interest was furthered through reading the weekly instalments of Purnell's *History of the Second World War Encyclopaedia* from London, which were often devoured prior to and even in place of any home work.

There was one particular instalment which really grabbed my interest, and this related to 'Hitler's Final Solution to the Jewish Problem.' At the age of between ten to twelve I was struck by the images of the concentration and death camps, and was left with a huge question which just floated around in my young brain: 'Why? Why were these Jewish people, including little children, being murdered in such a way?'

Quite remarkably an Israeli family came to live on a nearby farm for two years during that period, and their presence played a large role in shaping my desire to go to Israel.

So, at the age of twenty-one I left Australia in 1978 to go to Israel, not realising at the time that those two themes would criss-cross my path consistently for the following thirty years.

Prior to arriving in Israel I spent a year savouring the hedonistic delights of Europe. Time was also spent surveying aspects of World War Two, especially in the Soviet Union, Poland (particularly looking around the former Warsaw Ghetto area), and East and West Germany. The time in Germany was spent visiting various sites in Berlin and in Bavaria, including Hitler's Eagles Nest retreat at Obersalzberg near Berchtesgaden; and Dachau Concentration Camp.[3]

No normal human being can ever visit a former concentration camp and be left emotionally unmoved. That childhood question returned: 'Why.' Now an added question began to join it, 'How.' How did Germany get to that point of perpetrating the Holocaust?

1 Two uncles had also served in the region during this period, and one of them died at Tobruk in 1941.

2 One famous 'Rat of Tobruk' was Thomas Derrick VC, DCM of the 2/48th Battalion 9th Australian Division. My father fought in Tarakan in Borneo alongside Derrick and other heroes from Tobruk and El Alamein, and was nearby when he was mortally shot in 1945.

3 On subsequent trips to the region I also visited Theresienstadt, Treblinka and Auschwitz-Birkenau Concentration Camps.

Finally in 1979 I made it to Israel and lived on a kibbutz (collective farm) in the north of the country. This kibbutz had been established by Jewish soldiers from the *Palmach* and South African Jewish men in 1947. The *Palmach* was a specialised Jewish fighting force set up in 1941 to ward off an impending invasion of Palestine by the German-led Army. The South Africans were all former soldiers from the British-led Eighth Army in North Africa, and had fought at El Alamein.

Those Jewish South African soldiers returned to British Mandated Palestine after the War and together with the *Palmach* soldiers, established kibbutz Mayan Baruch.

There was at least one Holocaust survivor on the kibbutz, while many members lost entire families in the Holocaust. A deeper awareness of this terrible tragedy was gained when visiting the Holocaust Museum (*Yad Vashem*) in Jerusalem.

After a year on the kibbutz I moved to Jerusalem and became involved in various types of work and activity. One of these was looking after an elderly Jewish man who had been knocked senseless by Nazis on *Kristallnacht* in 1938.[4] Thereafter his family managed somehow to escape Germany and went to Argentina.

Many years later the sister came to live in Israel with her mentally incapacitated brother, whom she devoted herself to care for. The sister needed a break, and I was asked to be the main carer for some time. Near to this man's bed was a photograph of him as a vibrant young Berliner – until the Nazis cut him down.

For about a year and a half I worked as a nurse's aide in a psychiatric and geriatric hospital in Jerusalem. This work also involved assisting one of the senior staff, who herself had fled Nazi Germany in the 1930's, working twice a week in the enclosed psychiatric section where many Holocaust survivors were located. These people were the so-called lucky ones, they had managed to escape the gas chambers: but afterwards they just were not able to escape the mental repercussions of that great tragedy.

These and numerous other accounts and impressions slowly brought me to a point of realising that this was not a TV documentary, this was not stories and photographs in war-time books and magazines - this was real. These things actually happened to real flesh and blood people like me. But … why did these things happen?

Work as a guide-historian

From 1986 I began working as a guide-historian and researcher at Christ Church, an evangelical Anglican Church, inside the Old City of Jerusalem.[5]

It was here where the first western, British and Protestant activities in the land of Israel began in the 1830's[6], and as such the area was visited by many Israeli academic and

4 A Nazi inspired pogrom against the Jewish people in Germany and Austria in November 1938.

5 Christ Church is owned by CMJ (Churches Ministry among Jewish People). This society was established in 1809 in London, and one of its first vice-Presidents was William Wilberforce, and a long-term President was Lord Shaftesbury.

6 Location of the first Protestant church in the region, as well as the British Consulate and in 1842 it was the seat of the Anglican bishop. The first Anglican bishop in Jerusalem was a former Jewish rabbi, named Michael Solomon Alexander.

educational groups studying the beginnings of modern history in the land. My task as the guide was to explain to these visitors the history of the location, and the belief system of its founders. As these groups were often led by professors of history, much study was required related to British involvement in Jerusalem, and indeed the entire Eastern Mediterranean.

This research led me to 1798 as a beginning point, the year in which Napoleon invaded Egypt in order to ultimately oust Britain from India, and ended with the conclusion of the British Mandate in 1948. This study permitted me to see the bigger picture of British involvement in this region, and it was into this bigger picture that the Australian, New Zealand, Indian and South African soldiers fitted during two small time frames, 1915-1918 and 1940-1942.

This bigger picture had eluded me while growing up in Australia, due mostly to national parochialism. For the first time I was now able to better understand the role of my own country in the region and the geo-political dynamics behind the establishment of modern Israel.

Discovering the' Montgomery Bible'

The parent organisation which owned Christ Church was CMJ, and during its two hundred years of existence had amassed a sizeable collection of artefacts which were mostly tucked away in an attic in their UK headquarters. One artefact, at least as far as this topic is concerned, stood out: the 'Montgomery Bible'. On one occasion in the late 1980's while visiting CMJ's UK office I was joined by an Israeli professor named Alex Carmel.

Alex informed me that once many years before he had been shown a special Bible belonging to General Montgomery. On this visit I was determined to discover this special Bible, and finally one staff member recalled seeing it tucked away in a filing cabinet. So we opened the cabinet and there it was. It was a sight to behold – a beautifully made Hebrew Bible, with silver and mother of pearl on the cover.

Although only quite small, this artefact punched far above its weight. The sentiment behind this Bible was of tremendous historical value, and was expressed in the inscription on the accompanying parchment. Written in both Hebrew and English were these words:

> Field Marshall Viscount Montgomery, the gallant leader of the victorious British forces, by whose hand God has placed salvation in Zion in the days of El Alamein.
>
> Presented in token of gratitude of Palestine Jewry by the Vaad Leumi, the National Council of the Jewish people in Palestine.[7]

Accompanying the Bible was also a letter written by the Bishop of Rochester, Christopher Chavasse, to CMJ. After receiving this Bible (an official gift from the Jewish leadership in

7 *Vaad Leumi* translates as National Council, and was the government of the Jewish people in Palestine before the state of Israel was established on 14 May 1948.

Palestine), Field Marshal Montgomery gave it to the Bishop of Rochester.[8] Then in 1946 Bishop Chavasse, a prominent supporter of CMJ at that time, presented it to CMJ in order for them to sell. Thankfully they never did sell it – and there it was tucked away waiting to be 'discovered' in the late 1980's.

That little Bible went back to Israel with me where it became a major exhibit in the Christ Church Museum. Thereafter when an Israeli group visited, and particularly if the group had older people, I would speak about the Bible and the reason why it was given, basically saying:

> The Jewish leadership of the land of Israel in 1942 recognized that their salvation was due to the victory at El Alamein wrought by British and Commonwealth soldiers as well as Free French, and others soldiers from Greece, Poland and even Jewish soldiers from the land of Israel.

This presentation was often within the context of a wider perspective of Gentile involvement in the region, including the First World War, and the role of British and Anzac forces in capturing the region from the Turks.[9]

It wasn't just Israelis who were hearing this perspective: hundreds of groups from overseas were also exposed to the story line. [10]

Researching and writing the subject

It was now becoming quite clear to me that the battle of El Alamein was extremely significant not only in the context of the Allied war effort, but to the survival of the Jewish people in the Middle East, particularly in Palestine.[11] I began compiling information to write a specific book about this perspective, and the research also included visiting El Alamein for the 50th anniversary event in 1992.[12]

The research also included speaking to many Israelis who lived through that period of time. Two interviews probably stand out, not so much by the content, but in view of the standing of the people. These were Prime Minister Yitzchak Rabin, and General Uzi Narkiss, the man who led the capture of Jerusalem in 1967.

8 Chavasse was a friend of Montgomery's father, who had been an Anglican bishop in Tasmania, where incidentally, General Montgomery spent his childhood years. Chavasse was the twin brother of Noel Chavasse who won two Victoria Crosses in the First World War.

9 Anzac is an acronym for Australian and New Zealand Army Corps, and between 1916-1918 Anzac soldiers fought in the Middle East as mounted infantry, the Australian Light Horse and the New Zealand Mounted Rifles. They served primarily under the overall command of General Allenby.

10 One group from Britain was the 'Parliamentary Wives' led by Suzie Sainsbury. One year Tessa Montgomery (wife of Lord David Montgomery, who was the son of the Field Marshal) was present, and was quite excited hearing the history associated with the Montgomery Bible. Later in London I met David Montgomery, who also was unaware of this heirloom and of the special story attached to it.

11 At that time there were about 70,000 Jewish people in Egypt and 500,000 in the land of Israel, British Mandated Palestine at the time.

12 While on the same trip I travelled up to Sollum on the Egypt-Libya border and located my uncle's grave.

Two of Israel's most outstanding generals said virtually the same thing as everyone else I had spoken to: the Allied victory at El Alamein saved the Jewish *yishuv* (settlement) in Palestine from a catastrophe.[13]

After close to a decade of research *Anzacs, Empires and Israel's Restoration 1798-1948* was published in 1998. Although quite an effort was made to access quality source material, I was never able to locate any primary sources which clearly stated that it was a Nazi-German policy to murder the Jewish people in the Middle East.[14]

It was only in the year 2010 while writing an abridged version of the above stated book,[15] that I became aware of the ground-breaking research of Klaus-Michael Mallmann from the University of Ludwigsburg and Martin Cuppers from the University of Berlin. Then in 2012 I attained an English version of their book, entitled *Nazi Palestine.*

These two German scholars had located the source material confirming that the Nazi leadership had in fact planned to annihilate the Jewish communities in the lands conquered by German forces in the Middle East. Their discovery of the primary sources validated the secondary evidence I had managed to collate over the previous twenty-five years, especially the spoken testimony of many Jewish people who 'just knew' what the Nazis intended to do once they entered into Egypt and Palestine. Although there were several key opportunities for this to happen, the crucial time was from July till November 1942, and would result from an Axis victory at – El Alamein.

An impression from Leipzig

While attending a conference in Leipzig in the former East Germany some years ago I visited an exhibition which 'just happened' to be on at the same time. This huge exhibition, entitled *Verbrechen der Wehrmacht: Dimensionen des Vernichtungskrieges 1941–1944* (Crimes of the German Wehrmacht: Dimensions of a War of Annihilation 1941-1944) was very controversial as it revealed the role that the German Army (*Wehrmacht Heer*) had played in carrying out atrocities throughout Nazi occupied Europe.[16]

The exhibition included hundreds of graphic photographs and documents, revealing clearly that many ordinary German soldiers had been involved in carrying out killings and atrocities.

Until that point it was generally thought that such atrocities were only carried out by the SS and other entities within the German system which were totally committed to the Nazi racist ideology.

13 The discussion with Rabin came as a result of accompanying Lord Gerald Balfour to a meeting with him in 1992, while the interview with General (res) Narkiss was part of a documentary, *The Battle for Zion*, produced by Peter Darg. Narkiss is probably best known for walking alongside Moshe Dayan and Yitzchak Rabin in the famous photograph entering into the Old City of Jerusalem in June 1967.

14 Not speaking nor reading German was an obvious disadvantage.

15 Entitled *Anzacs & Israel: A Significant Connection.*

16 It was organized by the Hamburg Institute of Social Research, and after running from 1995-1999 it had to be revamped after accusations that some of the photographs were not accurately described. The revamped exhibition ran from 2001-2004 and is now permanently based in Berlin.

There were thousands of Germans at that exhibition, young to old, filing silently through the many rows of exhibits. I was struck by how little noise there was and by the looks of shock and disbelief on the faces of many. Most of those people, I am sure, were saying to themselves and to each other, 'How could this be? Surely these were not ordinary soldiers from our nation who did all these terrible things?'

Sadly, order or no orders, Hitler had many executioners willing to carry out his racist and hate-ridden ideology, not just in Germany but throughout Europe. Racism and particularly anti-Semitism was spread into almost every corner of the continent, and if he had managed to get into Britain, then there would also have been willing executioners there as well.[17]

Having said the above it is important to also qualify and state that there were many in Germany who did not support Hitler and the Nazi ideology, and those who opposed it endangered their own lives. Many courageous German people found themselves alongside Jews, gypsies, pastors, communists, homosexuals and other so-called undesirables at Dachau, Buchenwald, Bergen Belsen and Sachsenhausen concentration camps. Two prominent evangelical German pastors, Martin Niemoller and Dietrich Bonhoffer readily come to mind.

During my years in Israel I had met and become acquainted with many German people who were very remorseful about what their nation had perpetrated, and had come to Israel to work with Holocaust survivors, or to say sorry in some other way – even though most of these people were born after the War.

Most of the people filing through that exhibition centre in Leipzig that day, however, probably would not fit into that category. Most of these people were ordinary Germans who, having previously been under the Communist system, had only just recently been exposed to this perspective.

The impression gained from viewing those participants was another part of the chain for me – it was almost like I was not looking at German people in those lines, I was looking at humanity itself.

El Alamein: Halting a possible Holocaust in the Middle East

Several years ago I realized there would one day need to be a reprint of *Anzacs, Empires and Israel's Restoration.* Then the thought came that as 2012 was the 70th anniversary of the battles of El Alamein, then I could forego doing a reprint and instead do a rewrite of the World War Two section and incorporate some extra material including the important findings of Mallmann and Cuppers as well as documents from the German Foreign Office.

The timing of this project though may be significant, as there seem to be some interesting similarities today to what was happening back in the period between 1933-1945, and particularly 1940-1942.

17 Racism and anti-Semitism are not just European phenomenon – both are world-wide.

So as I have set out to write up this narrative[18] I have endeavoured to look for the dynamics which lay behind the Middle Eastern campaign of 1940-42; and to determine if the Holocaust would have been introduced into the Middle East if the German-led army had been victorious at El Alamein.

It is now time to allow the narrative to begin.

18 I will admit from the outset that this narrative has many gaps – there is just so much that could be written and not the space to write it all.

CHAPTER 1

THE WRITING ON THE WALL

The Nazi Party comes to power

On 30 January 1933 Adolf Hitler was appointed chancellor of Germany. Although not attaining a majority in the elections, Hitler's Nazi party was the strongest of the many parties running in the elections. Hitler, who was not necessarily an advocate of democracy, used the democratic system of the Weimar Republic to ascend to power.[1] He and his racist party came to power (it could be said) by default.

Once in power Hitler, though, slowly began to destroy the very system that got him there – democracy. In its place he instituted an autocratic system of government, he himself becoming the *Fuhrer*, or dictator. The unwritten constitution of this new Nazi-led Germany became the ideals he had written in his manifesto, *Mein Kampf*.[2]

A key component of Hitler's manifesto was his belief in the superiority of the German (Aryan) race, and that all other races were to be in servitude to the Germans. In addition there was his belief that the German nation needed to have *Lebensraum* (Living Space). On one occasion he stated, 'we National Socialists must hold unflinchingly to our aim in foreign policy, namely, to secure for the German people the land and soil to which they are entitled on this earth.'[3] In one entire chapter of *Mein Kampf* he explains in more depth how he anticipated to achieve this goal on behalf of the German nation – it would primarily be at the expense of Russia and the Slavic people.[4]

Of all the non-Germanic races (or ethnic groups) whom Hitler deemed as inferior, the Jewish people were the lowest. Hitler in fact detested them.[5] While living in Vienna as a young ardent German nationalist, and seeking to understand the world around him, his negative attitudes towards the Jewish people were formulated. He devoted one entire section of *Mein Kampf* to this formative period, and concluded this section:

> ... to my deep and joyful satisfaction, I had at last come to the conclusion that the Jew was no German.

1 The Weimar Republic was formed in 1918 (the constitution was formulated at Weimar), replacing the German Empire established in 1871 by Kaiser Wilhelm I.

2 While incarcerated in Lansgsberg Prison in 1924 for his involvement in instigating the Munich *Putsch* (attempted *coup d'etat*) Hitler wrote up his belief system, moulded as it was upon his own life experiences. Many of his core beliefs were also expounded by the German Workers Party, founded in 1920, which he joined, and which was then transformed into the National Socialist German Workers Party (*Nationalsozialistische Deutsche Arbeiterpartei* - NSDAP) and thereafter known as the Nazi Party.

3 Hitler, A. *Mein Kampf*, p. 596.

4 Hitler, A. *Mein Kampf*, pp. 586-610.

5 Hitler, A. *Mein Kampf*, pp. 52-57.

Only now did I become thoroughly acquainted with the seducer of my people.[6]

Hitler was an avowed racist and anti-Semite.

Anti-Semitism leads to the rise of Zionism

Hitler of course was not alone when it came to hating Jewish people. Anti-Semitism had been around a long time and much of European and Western society had been affected by it. The institutional Church had been a major conduit of what could be termed 'ecclesiastical anti-Semitism' since the second century AD, with some of the influential Church Fathers espousing very strong anti-Semitic attitudes.[7] Unfortunately even the great Reformer Martin Luther towards the end of his life espoused some very strong anti-Semitic attitudes, especially in his book *On the Jews and their Lies*.[8] Then in the modern period, the period of the enlightenment, a new form of anti-Semitism took root in Europe: nationalistic anti-Semitism.

This was the anti-Semitism which basically said, 'If you don't look and think like the rest of us, then you really aren't one of us.' It was this attitude which undergirded Hitler's anti-Semitism. It was this type of anti-Semitism which greatly affected a Hungarian Jewish journalist named Theodore Herzl who worked for a Vienna newspaper in the late nineteenth century.

Herzl was in Paris in 1895 to cover the trial of Alfred Dreyfus, a Jewish Frenchman accused of treason, and he was shocked when he heard the cry 'Death to the traitor' or 'Death to the Jews'. Later he realised there was foul-play, just because Dreyfus was a Jew.[9] If such deep-seated hatred of the Jewish people could exist in enlightened western Europe, Herzl thought, then there really was only one solution for the Jewish people – they had to leave Europe.

This realisation led to the formation of the Zionist movement in 1897 which had a vision to establish a Jewish State in Palestine, the ancient home of the Jewish people.[10] Herzl's mandate was to seek a European power which could sponsor this vision and assist the Jewish people in attaining legal recognition from the Ottoman Turkish Empire. Germany

6 Hitler, A. *Mein Kampf*, p. 57.

7 Not only did such Church Fathers as John of Chrysostom write vitriolic anti-Semitic material in his *Eight Homilies Against the Jews* in 387 AD, but Emperor Constantine and others involved in shaping the doctrine of the Roman Church laid the foundations for a theology which we term today 'replacement theology' or 'supercessionism', that is, the Church is the New Israel, and that God has revoked his covenant with the nation of Israel because they as a nation rejected Jesus. The Jewish people became an accursed people. Needless to say this theology is totally un-Biblical.

8 Published in 1543.

9 This is the traditional account, but Marvin Lowenthal provides another perspective on how Herzl's attitude developed. See Lowenthal, M. *The Diaries of Theodor Herzl*, (New York, 1956), p. xix.

10 Jewish people had been living in the land of Israel (known as Palestine or southern Syria after 135 AD) ever since Biblical times. Even following the defeat by the Romans in 70 AD and 135 AD and the exile of most of the Jewish people to Rome and their subsequent spread throughout the Roman Empire, Jewish people still continued to live in the land (except several brief interludes). Since the early 1800's more Jewish people began returning there - even establishing agricultural colonies, like Europeans were doing all over the New World.

was initially seen to be this power, but when Kaiser Wilhelm II turned it down in 1898, the Zionists looked to Britain.

Many Jewish people before Herzl held a similar perspective. In the wake of growing nationalism in Europe after the Napoleonic period, and especially after the 1848 Revolutions, Jewish intellectuals saw there would be no place for Jewish people in many European societies, as they were 'a nation apart' or 'a nation within a nation.'

Following the issuing of nationalistic edicts in Russia in 1881 many Jewish people there realised they could no longer exist peacefully as 'a nation apart' in Russia. Small groups of intellectuals called *Chovevei Zion* (Lovers of Zion) emerged, dedicated to establishing a Jewish national presence in Palestine.

In 1882 the Russian Government unleashed terrible pogroms against the Jewish people in Russia, forcing hundreds of thousands to uproot and leave. While most went to the New World (the United States, Canada, South Africa, Australia) some went to Britain and other European countries, and some went to Palestine. Those Jewish people who remained in Russia were secluded to an area which became known as the 'pale of settlement.'

There was, therefore, a nascent Zionist movement when Herzl established the Zionist Organisation in 1897. Thereafter while entities such as the *Chovevei Zion* and Baron Rothschild legally purchased land in Palestine and established agricultural colonies there, Herzl and others such as Chaim Weizmann worked for attaining legal status.

Initially they thought that Germany would assist them in obtaining a legal charter from the Turks to establish such a Jewish national entity in Palestine. When Germany rejected the Zionist proposal in 1898, the Jewish nationalist movement turned to Britain. Britain at that time, however, was pre-occupied elsewhere, and was more concerned with maintaining a strong relationship with France (which had ambitions for the province of Syria) and Turkey.

There was, nevertheless, tremendous sympathy in Britain for such a concept as a Jewish homeland or State, due primarily to the influence which the Bible had held in Britain for some three hundred years, ever since the times of the Puritans and the evangelicals. Numerous devout Christians, be they Baptists, Congregationalists, Presbyterians, Anglicans, Brethren and others, subscribed to the belief in the restoration of Israel.

Israel's restoration becomes a reality

An ideal opportunity arose during World War One. Turkey chose to fight with Germany against Britain. From 1915 till 1918 soldiers from the British Empire (Australia, New Zealand and India) fought against the Turks in Gallipoli, the Sinai, Palestine and Syria. Already at the time of the Gallipoli Campaign it was clear that if Turkey was defeated by the Allies, then the Turkish Empire would be dismantled. The question in 1915 was, 'Who would administer this vast area?'

Britain, France and Russia then began negotiations to determine what would be the future status of the Arabic speaking regions of the Turkish Empire pending Turkey's defeat. Britain and France came to an agreement in 1916 known as the Sykes-Picot Agreement. With this agreement it was stated that much of the region of Syria would be included within a French zone of interest. The area of Palestine would be the subject of special negotiations.

From the British perspective it was very important that the future status of Palestine be aligned with its own geo-political objectives – to ensure the trade route between Britain and its eastern empire (India, Australia, New Zealand, Malaya (Malaysia), Ceylon (Sri Lanka), Singapore, Hong Kong etc) was secure. Central in this geo-political consideration was the Suez Canal.

The British also made overtures during the early years of the war to King Hussein of the Hejaz concerning the possibility of the Arabs rebelling against their Turkish overlords. There was already a vibrant Arab nationalist movement in Syria, primarily based in Damascus. During 1916 the new British high commissioner in Egypt, Sir Henry McMahon continued informal discussions with King Hussein (the so-called McMahon-Hussein Correspondence) and in return for Arab assistance in ousting the Turks the British would assist in establishing an Arab Kingdom in Syria. From late 1916 a small armed force led by Hussein's son Feisal and assisted by Colonel T.E. Lawrence, began to be formed in the Hejaz to hassle Turkish troops in Arabia and later in the region of Transjordan.

Despite some supposed ambiguity, Palestine, being a place of special interest, was not included in the area proposed for any future Arab Kingdom in Syria. No individual British diplomat at that time would have committed Palestine to any entity.

Following the defeat at Gallipoli the Allied troops returned to Egypt. The Turks now planned a major offensive to either capture or destabilise the Suez Canal. The British then established the Egyptian Expeditionary Force (EEF), comprised of British infantry and cavalry and Australian and New Zealand (Anzac) mounted infantry. The vanguard of the EEF was on many occasions the Desert Mounted Corps, commanded by General Harry Chauvel.

Within the context of protecting the Suez Canal the EEF captured the entire Sinai in 1916. A new British government took office in late 1916 comprised of David Lloyd-George as prime minister and Arthur Balfour as foreign minister. Both these men did not want see the province of Syria and especially Palestine fall into potential belligerent hands at the conclusion of the War. It was too close to the Suez Canal.

They therefore sanctioned the capture of the entire province of Syria. Simultaneously they then began seeking the best political solution for Palestine. Negotiations then began in mid-1917 with the Zionist leadership pertaining to the establishment of a national Jewish entity in Palestine. On 31 October 1917 the British War Cabinet unanimously voted to establish in Palestine a national home for the Jewish people. This decision hereafter was called the 'Balfour Declaration.'

On that same day General Chauvel oversaw, under the overall command of General Edmund Allenby, the capture of Beersheba, the first major Allied victory in the capture of the entire province of Syria from the Turks. In December Jerusalem was captured, and then on 1 October 1918, Damascus was captured. One of the Allied units involved in the capture of Damascus was the Arab Northern Army commanded by Prince Feisal. On 3 October 1918 General Allenby met with Feisal in Damascus and explained to him, as per instructions from London, the future administration of the province of Syria: a combination of French and Arab rule.

By the end of October 1918 the mostly British Empire force had reached the northern border between Syria and Turkey proper – and then Turkey surrendered. The military goal had been accomplished. The following years would witness the outworking of these results in the political realm.

At the San Remo Conference held to determine the surrender terms with Turkey, the League of Nations offered a mandate to Britain to administer Palestine, and incorporated the Balfour Declaration into the mandate, whereby the British Government was to prepare Palestine to be a national home for the Jewish people. A mandate was also offered to Britain to prepare Mesopotamia (thereafter Iraq) for future independence; and they offered France a mandate to prepare Syria for future independence.

The nationalistic aims and desires of both the Jewish and Arab people were set to be accomplished, within the context of the imperial desires of both the British and the French. The outworking of these goals and aims would not be a straightforward process.

Haj Amin el-Husseini – the Mufti of Jerusalem

On 31 March 1933 the German Consul-General in Jerusalem, Heinrich Wolff, received a distinguished visitor. He was Haj Amin el-Husseini, the Mufti, or Muslim spiritual leader, of Palestine, and Chairman of the Supreme Muslim Council. Haj Amin was not just the senior Muslim cleric in Palestine, he was highly esteemed throughout the Arab and Islamic world and regarded as one of the champions of the Arab nationalist movement. As a devout Muslim, Haj Amin had a similar attitude towards the Jewish people as did Hitler.[11]

Haj Amin came to congratulate Herr Wolff on the victory of Adolf Hitler. He was expressing his personal sentiments, and the sentiments of many other Arabs and Muslims for the victory of Hitler and the Nazi Party. [12]

Haj Amin had something in common with Adolf Hitler. He was an avowed anti-

11 The founder of Islam, Muhammad, believed he received a revelation that he was Allah's final messenger to mankind. He shared his 'revelation' with the Jewish people in Arabia, but they rejected him and his message. As a consequence Muhammad thereafter massacred many Jewish people in Arabia, and subjected others to slavery. This attitude is expressed in *Surah* 9:5 of the *Koran*, and has been called '*The Verse (Surah) of the Sword*', 'Kill the Mushrikun [unbelievers] wherever you find them, and capture and besiege them, and lie in wait for them in each and every ambush. But if they repent … then leave their way free.' *Sura* 9:5, as quoted in Gabriel, M. *Islam and the Jews*, (Lake Mary, Florida, 2003), p. 103. Anyone who did not accept the teaching of Muhammad was either killed by the sword, or had to accept a position of servitude (*dhimmitude*) under Islam. In other words, Jews (and Christians) could never be equal citizens in an Islamic state, but only second-class citizens.

12 Mallman, K. and Cuppers, M. *Nazi Palestine*, ibid, p. 37. Mallman and Cuppers offer numerous examples of Arab support in Palestine for Nazi Germany in pages 29-43. In addition there are numerous examples in *Germany and the Middle East 1835-1939,* edited by Jehuda Wallach, Tel Aviv, 1975.

Semite and an avowed opponent of the Jewish national home in Palestine. Haj Amin had activated a riot in Jerusalem in 1920 to oppose the Balfour Declaration being endorsed by the League of Nations at the San Remo Conference.[13] This riot left five innocent Jewish people dead and dozens of others seriously wounded. He was sentenced to ten years imprisonment by the British authorities, but then amazingly this sentence was commuted shortly afterwards when the High Commissioner Herbert Samuel wanted to appease the Muslim community – so he installed him as the Mufti of Jerusalem. The British authorities also established the Supreme Muslim Council, and made Haj Amin the chairman.

From then on Haj Amin used his two positions of authority to foster anti-Jewish and anti-British sentiment. In 1929 he again instigated murderous assaults against Jewish communities throughout Palestine, the worst being in Hebron where 66 innocent Jewish people were brutally murdered.

Haj Amin was also a strong supporter of Arab nationalism, and saw no place for any European imperialist presence in the Arab world, especially not the British and the French. Haj had two main objectives therefore, to destroy the Jewish national home in Palestine, and to oust the British and the French from the Middle East.

When it came to his desire to oust the British (and the French) it would be another six years before he and Hitler were united on that issue. Yet concerning hatred of the Jewish people, he and Hitler were on the same wave-length from the very beginning, and there would come a time when they became fused in order to bring about their common goal: to destroy the Jewish people. Ironically, though, it was Hitler's anti-Semitic policies soon after coming to power in 1933 which initially created some challenges for Haj Amin.

Institutional anti-Semitism begins in Germany

Only two months after the Nazis came to power their anti-Jewish attitude was evident. On 1 April 1933, the day after Haj Amin visited Consul-General Wolff, the Nazi Party instituted boycotts against the Jewish people throughout Germany. One man who experienced this was Dr. Heinz Karo from Berlin, who said:

> "April 1, 1933. This was the first time we had ever seen violent anti-Semitism in Germany. Nazi guards stood wherever there was a sign indicating a Jewish doctor or lawyer, or by every Jewish shop, telling the other Germans, our 'brothers': 'Don't go in! They're Jews! Don't buy! They're Jews!'"[14]

Suddenly throughout Germany Jewish people, who until this time had been fully accepted as citizens of German society, were now classified as second-class citizens.

13 At the conclusion of the First World War the nations gathered at Versailles to determine the peace terms. For various reasons the peace conference with the former Ottoman Turkish Empire would only be in April 1920 at San Remo.

14 Lossin,Y. *Pillar of Fire*, p.199. The term anti-Semitism is a term primarily aimed at hatred of the Jewish people rather than hatred of any Semitic person (the Arab people are also Semitic).

While many Jewish people thought this was just a temporary aberration in Germany and that it would soon go away, others saw the writing on the wall, and chose to leave Germany. While some of these went to the New World, some went to neighbouring European countries such as Holland, and some went to Palestine. Nazi Germany did not care where the Jewish people went, so long as they left the boundaries of the German Reich.[15]

Further conflict in the land of Israel

At that point the authorities of the British Mandate in Palestine had imposed a limit, whereby Jewish migrants could only enter if the economic infrastructure of the country could absorb them, and any more than this number needed to have assets of at least 1,000 pounds.[16]

The German Jewish refugees who were permitted to enter Palestine brought with them a tremendous pool of talent, made up of numerous doctors, academics and other professionals. These political refugees very quickly began having a positive influence upon the welfare of all the people of the land, Arab as well as Jew.

Although the emigration of Jewish people suited Germany's policy (she wanted the Jews to leave), conversely, Germany did not want them to take all of their resources with them. The Reich Government therefore devised a plan whereby they could retain some of the Jewish capital (Germany faced an international boycott at that time) and also encourage Jewish people to leave with some of their own resources. On 25 August 1933 an agreement was reached between the Anglo-Palestine Bank and the German Ministry of Economics, known as the Haavara (Transfer) Agreement.

Not all the people of Palestine, however, wanted these Jewish refugees in their midst. Encouraged by Haj Amin al-Husseini, violent anti-Jewish riots erupted throughout the land. As they had done on several previous occasions, in 1920 and 1929, the British authorities caved into the violence, and restricted Jewish immigrant visas in 1934.

Despite this restriction, the numbers of Jewish people entering Palestine, mostly from Germany, nevertheless remained constant, in part due to the Haavara Agreement. In 1933 there were about 30,000 Jewish immigrants, in 1934 some 42,000 and in 1935 some 61,000.

The Nuremberg Laws

Each year in September the Nazi Party held a huge rally at Nuremberg, at which was displayed much anti-Semitic material. One of the major displays was Martin Luther's *On the Jews and their Lies!* At the 1935 Nuremberg rally Hitler had purposed to give a dramatic foreign policy speech. His foreign minister, Baron Neurath, however, persuaded him to drop this speech as it was too provocative at a time when Germany was still trying to

15 The 'Nazification of Germany', as William Shirer named an entire chapter of his classic book, *The Rise and Fall of the Third Reich*, affected not just the Jewish people, but every strand of German society, from the youth to the Church. Many democratic minded and law–abiding Germans also suffered because of the racist policies of the Nazi regime.

16 Mallman and Cuppers, ibid, p. 45.

portray itself as pursuing peace.

Instead, and somewhat in haste, Hitler decided to introduce his race law defining who was and who was not a Jew, which was called, *The Laws for the Protection of German Blood and German Honour.* These laws, outlined in five sections, effectively stripped Jewish people of their German citizenship and their means of living an ordinary life in Germany and forbade any form of social interaction between German Aryans and Jewish Germans. Any Jewish person caught violating any of these laws and restrictions was to be sentenced to hard labour and imprisonment.

This was the Nazi attempt to establish a Law to justify its intolerant attitude towards the Jewish people. Following the release of these Laws on 15 September 1935 hundreds of Jewish people were interred as inmates of Dachau and other such camps now established in Germany.[17]

Many others now saw the writing on the wall, and left for the United, States, Canada, Britain and even Australia - wherever they could obtain visas. While some went to neighbouring European countries hoping to ride out this wave of insidious anti-Semitism, most on this occasion had no choice but to go to Palestine.

Consequences in Palestine

This increased Jewish immigration stimulated another round of Arab violence, and dozens of Jewish people were murdered. In addition the Arab leadership, spearheaded by Haj Amin, called for a general strike which began in 1936.

The British authorities could not manage the violence, so they sanctioned the formation of a special Jewish police force, the Jewish Supernumery Police. Many of these men had received military experience during the First World War and were also members of the Jewish self-defence force, the *Hagana.*

This round of violence once again forced Britain to send out a commission of enquiry, as they had done after the serious riots and massacres of 1929. This Commission, headed by Lord Peel, interviewed many people from both sides, including Haj Amin el-Husseini. Haj Amin insisted upon receiving full Arab independence, and when quizzed by the Commission on the solution for the Jewish people in Palestine, he intimated that they would be liquidated.[18]

The following year the findings of the Peel Commission were published and became public in July 1937. The Commission called for the division of Palestine into a Jewish State and an Arab State which would be linked to Transjordan.

Although rejected by some of the Jewish Zionists, especially the Revisionists,[19] it was

17 From 1933 the Nazi Party established a number of special camps where those who opposed them were interred. Dachau was established near Munich in March 1933, less than two months after Hitler came to power. Sachsenhausen, located near to Weimar, was established in 1937. Buchenwald, located north of Berlin, was established in 1936. Many of the SS (*Schutzstaffel*) officers were trained there.

18 Lossin, Y. *Pillar of Fire,* p. 235.

19 Revisionist Zionism was established by Zev Jabotinsky in 1924.

accepted by the mainstream of the Zionist leadership, especially David Ben Gurion and Chaim Weizmann. Although accepted by a few moderate Arab leaders, however, it was rejected outright by the Arab mainstream, including Haj Amin el-Husseini. To most of the Arab and Muslim leaders there could be no Jewish State in Palestine at all, no matter how small.[20]

Italian imperial expansion into Africa

While the Arab leadership was working to destroy the slightest possibility of there being a national home for the Jewish people in Palestine, and while the Nazis were stripping all vestiges of human decency from the Jewish people in Germany, Benito Mussolini was in the process of carving out an Italian Empire. In 1935 Mussolini invaded and conquered Abyssinia in east Africa, forcing the pro-British ruler, Emperor Haile Selassi, to flee to Jerusalem for refuge. The Italian invasion was an ominous development for Britain, as it placed the Italians near the sea route from Britain to her eastern empire via the Red Sea.

This act by the Italians was closely observed by the Arab nations of the region. The Arab nationalist movement was agitating to establish either independent Arab nations, or even a Great Arab Kingdom in the region administered by the British and the French. This current act of aggression, coupled with Italy's colonisation of Libya in 1911, created a certain degree of mistrust between the Arab nationalist movement and the Italians. It also caused the new king of Egypt, King Farouk, to enter into a treaty with Britain (the Anglo-Egyptian Treaty), in order to protect his nation from a possible Italian invasion.

While the King of Egypt was protecting his nation in this way, Italy sought to protect its new found status, and in October 1936 entered into an alliance with Germany, which laid the foundations for a formal alliance, *The Pact of Steel* in 1939. With this agreement, Germany recognized the Mediterranean region as Italy's particular sphere of interest.

The Arab Revolt

Following the issuing of the Peel *White Paper* Haj Amin el Husseini, declared war, not only on the Jewish people, but also on the British authorities. At the Mufti's instigation Lewis Andrews, the British Governor of the Galilee, was assassinated on 26 September 1937.[21] The British authorities immediately disbanded the Arab Higher Committee and sought to arrest Haj Amin. The Mufti of Jerusalem, however, eluded them and fled to Syria.

From Syria Haj Amin encouraged an Arab revolt, which thereupon spread throughout the land. The local situation now was taken over by other radicals. This revolt made life

20 Muslim leaders after Muhammad spread Islam throughout the Middle East and North Africa. Later Islamic clerics divided the world into two spheres, one known as *dar al-Islam* (the home or abode of Islam) and the other as *dar al-Harm*, the area not under the rule of Islam. The land of Israel was regarded as part of *dar al-Islam* and as such it would be impossible for a non-Islamic society to have independence there. There are no distinct references in either the *Koran* or *Hadith* to these divisions. For more on the relationship of Islam to the land of Israel and the Jewish people I refer you to the writings of Professor Bernard Lewis, especially *The Middle East and the West*, (New York, 1964), and Mark Gabriel, *Islam and the Jews*.

21 Andrews was born in Sydney in 1896 and served with the Australian Army in World War One.

extremely difficult for all the people in Palestine, and forced the British authorities to call for reinforcements. [22]

One unit which was despatched was the Manchester Regiment, commanded by Bernard Montgomery, son of the former Anglican bishop of Tasmania. Montgomery had been born in Ireland but lived his formative years in Hobart. Another specialist they brought in was Orde Wingate. Wingate established a Jewish force to combat the Arabs, named the 'Special Night Squad', and took under his arm many young Jewish men who were later to lead the Israeli Army, men such as Moshe Dayan and Yigal Allon.

Arab support for Hitler and Nazism

The deteriorating relationship between the Arab leadership in Palestine and the British authorities led to a simultaneous increase of interest in, and support of, Hitler and Nazism by the Arab nationalists. This interest was abetted by the increasingly open anti-Jewish actions of the Nazi regime.

Iraq became independent from Britain in 1932, although a treaty was signed between the two nations guaranteeing Britain certain privileges. Shortly after gaining her independence Iraq established full diplomatic relations with Germany. The first German ambassador, Dr. Fritz Grobba, thereafter became a strong advocate of Arab nationalism. After 1933 there was widespread support for Germany and Nazism in Iraq. One Iraqi newspaper wrote, "Germany must be proud of its Fuhrer, and Iraq offers Germany it's most cordial congratulations and salutes the German nation and its Fuhrer."[23]

Thirty Iraqis were invited to Germany in September 1938 where they were hosted by the Hitler Youth and were met by Hitler himself. When they returned to Iraq a youth movement was established, run along similar lines as the Hitler Youth.[24]

The situation in Egypt was slightly different from Iraq, in that although Britain had granted independence to Egypt in 1922, considerable numbers of British troops were still based in the Suez Canal region, and Britain still had limited involvement in Egypt's foreign policy.[25] Despite having gained their independence, though, many in Egypt were disappointed with their system of government. Professor Shimon Shamir stated:

In foreign affairs Liberal-Nationalism failed to achieve the national goals - expulsion of

22 Ironically the community most affected was the Arab community. Many were subsequently killed by the British Army, while several thousand were actually killed and murdered by fellow Arabs, as an opportunity now arose for exacting personal vendettas under the pretext of a nationalist war.

23 DG Baghdad to RMVP, 25 August 1934, BAB, R 43 II/1420, quoted in Mallman and Cuppers, ibid, p. 30.

24 See Mallman and Cuppers, ibid, p. 35. Uriel Dann, 'Iraqi-German Relations between the Two World Wars', in *Germany and the Middle East, 1835-1939,* edited by Jehuda Wallach, (Tel Aviv, 1975), p. 200.

25 The region of the Suez Canal has been geo-politically important for Britain since Napoleon invaded the region in 1798 in an attempt to cut Britain off from India. When a French consortium built the Suez Canal in 1869 Britain became very concerned about the link to India and the eastern empire. In 1875 the British Government purchased the majority shares of the Suez Canal Company. British troops were landed there in 1882 to ensure the region was not taken over by any belligerent entity.

British troops and unification with the Sudan. On the other hand, Nazism appeared as a model for an effective and powerful regime and for a political orientation which might counteract British (and French) supremacy in the region.'[26]

From the very outset Nazism created an impression in Egypt. A series of pro-Hitler articles appeared in a newspaper as early as 1933, and thereafter the interest in Hitler and Nazism continued to grow. Shamir again stated:

> The 1930's witnessed the emergence of radical movements which propagated a great variety of anti-Liberal concepts, from Islamic Fundamentalism to Socialist Revolution. These movements offered a channel of expression for the alienated social classes, called for a drastic reformation of the social and political order, and tended towards paramilitary patterns of organization. Most of them were, directly or indirectly, inspired by the Fascist and Nazi parties of central Europe.[27]

Ironically one of the vehicles of this interest in Nazism in Egypt was the Muslim Brotherhood organization.[28] By the end of the 1930's and as a result of the Mufti inspired Arab revolt in Palestine, the Muslim Brotherhood had a sizeable following in Egypt, and it's slogan was "Jews out of Egypt and Palestine."[29] But, as Shamir stated, 'Many other political movements were influenced by Nazism.'[30] These included the 'Young Men's Muslim Association', the 'Wafd Party' and 'Young Egypt', a party which impacted the lives of some of Egypt's future leaders in their political orientation, most notably the future President of Egypt, Anwar Sadat. In addition, Shamir states:

> ... the leaders of Young Egypt adopted the racist and anti-Semitic doctrines of Nazi Germany as well. Hitler's racist policies were lauded ... Anti-Semitism was even more important in the party's program. Writing in the party's organ Ahmad Husayn had this to say of the Jews: *"They are the secret of this moral desolation which has become prevalent in the Arab and Islamic worlds. They are the secret of this religious and moral decay, up to the point where it has become correct to say: 'Search for the Jew behind every depravity'."*[31]

The 'Young Egypt' party's anti-Semitism was expressed by boycotting and harassing the Jewish community in Egypt, and supporting the Arabs in Palestine in combatting the

26 Shamir, S. 'The Influence of German National-Socialism on Radical Movements in Egypt' in *Germany and the Middle East, 1835-1939,* edited by Jehuda Wallach, (Tel Aviv, 1975), p. 201.
27 Shamir, S. 'The Influence of German National-Socialism on Radical Movements in Egypt' in *Germany and the Middle East, 1835-1939,* edited by Jehuda Wallach, (Tel Aviv, 1975), p. 202.
28 Founded in 1928 by Hassan al-Banna, a friend of Haj Amin el-Husseini. See Mallman and Cuppers, ibid, p. 33.
29 Mallman and Cuppers, ibid, p. 33.
30 Shamir, S. ibid, p. 202.
31 Jankowski, J. P. *The Young Egypt Party and Egyptian Nationalism 1933-1945,* Ph.D. dissertation, (University of Michigin, 1967) pp. 122-128, 356, quoted in Shamir, S, ibid, p. 207.

Jewish people.[32] Although the German Government had little direct contact with any of the Egyptian parties, yet there was a circle of pro-Axis politicians who were in close contact with the 'Young Egypt' party and 'supported it politically and financially.' 'The Military officers,' Shamir further states 'who formed an espionage ring to serve the German intelligence – including among their members Anwar al-Sadat … and many of the officers themselves were apparently inspired by the ideas of 'Young Egypt.'[33]

Nazi sympathies were also held by many in Syria and Lebanon, especially after the French granted limited independence to Syria in 1936. It was only after that period that Germany had any real involvement with Syria. The limited independence was due to a failure by the French Government and Syrian nationalists to reach a complete agreement. As a result of the failure of the Syrian nationalists to achieve their complete goals an environment was created for numerous radical movements. Of these Professor Itamar Rabinovitch wrote:

> The radical movements and their membership were clearly influenced by German National Socialism and Italian Fascism. The outward trappings, the militant nationalism, the patterns of organizations, the Fuhrer-prinzip, the spirit of anti-Western liberalism, the emphasis on youth and dynamism can be clearly related to these outside influences.[34]

Even Saudi Arabia was not exempt from this influence of Nazism. Mallman and Cuppers mention how in 1939 Ibn Saud, the new ruler of Arabia and a close friend of Haj Amin, had stated:

> All Arabs and Mohammedans throughout the world have great respect for Germany, and this respect is increased by the battle that Germany is waging against the Jews, the archenemy of the Arabs.[35]

Despite this statement, Ibn Saud did, however, maintain close links with the British.

Although these sentiments of support for Hitler and Nazism may not have been held by all the Arab people in the countries of the Middle East, there was no doubt a large and increasing number who did maintain sympathies for Hitler and the Nazis, and supported their anti-Jewish rhetoric and actions. The combination of these two attitudes was not a good omen at all for the future in the region. [36]

In general, though, despite Grobba's influence in Iraq, Berlin did not prioritize developing a strong German political network within the Arab world. This was primarily due to

32 Shamir, S. ibid, p. 207.

33 Shamir, S. ibid, p. 207.

34 Rabinovitch, I. 'Germany and the Syrian Political Scene in the late 1930's', in *Germany and the Middle East, 1835-1939,* edited by Jehuda Wallach, (Tel Aviv, 1975), p.197.

35 Annex to report by DG Djidda, 18 February, 1939, ADAP, series D, Vol. 5, p. 680, in Mallman and Cuppers, p.34.

36 For more specific information on this subject I recommend Mallman and Cuppers, *Nazi Palestine*, pp, 29-43.

Germany's desire to concentrate upon northern Europe; the close scrutiny of the Mandate powers, i.e. Britain and France; a desire of Germany to maintain good relations with Britain; and a reluctance, especially after May 1939, to interfere in a region which the Italians saw as their sphere of activity.

German interest and involvement in the emigration of Jewish people to Palestine was caught up in this bigger picture. Before, and especially after the issuing of the Nuremberg Laws, Germany wanted to get rid of its Jewish population. If other countries were reducing the numbers of Jews they would accept, and if many could go to Palestine, then all the better as far as the Nazi regime was concerned.

This attitude, however, was not accepted by all in the Reich Government. The German Consul-General in Jerusalem, Doehle informed the Foreign Ministry on 22 March 1937 that by abetting this emigration of Jews to Palestine, and thereby encouraging the growth and development of the Jewish national home there, Germany 'had done little to strengthen and support the Arab's sympathies for the new Germany,' and he even inferred that this could make the Arabs Germany's opponents.[37]

The ambiguity of this situation was that although many Arab nationalists saw in Hitler and Germany a natural ally in their struggle against Britain (and France) and for solving the Jewish 'problem', Hitler during this very same period held the delusion that he would enter into a lasting relationship with Britain, and that Britain would acknowledge him as the dominant power in Continental Europe. With this in view he was unwilling to overly interfere in the internal affairs of Palestine.

Hitler's position though did not preclude German contacts with the Arab nationalist representatives. In 1937 Adolf Eichmann of the Jewish Affairs Department was on his way to Palestine to ascertain the state of affairs there, and one of his scheduled meetings was with Haj Amin. Eichmann's meeting however was called off due to the security situation.[38]

As the possibility of Germany being accepted by Britain diminished by 1938, there was no further need for German reticence to keep out of the internal affairs of Palestine, and indeed of the Arab world - except where it might conflict with its commitment to Italy whose special sphere of interest was the Mediterranean region.

37 DGK Jerusalem to AA. Mar. 22, 1937, PAAA, R 104791, quoted in Mallman and Cuppers, ibid, p. 45.
38 Mallman and Cuppers, ibid, p. 47.

Chapter 2

The Imminence of War

German aggression –the *Anschluss*

Hitler's vision of a German Reich which united all the German peoples became more tangible when, on 12 March 1938, he sent German troops into Austria and annexed it to Germany the following day. This event was known as the *Anschluss* – 'joining together'.

Many, but by no means, all Austrians welcomed this event. One particular group who did not welcome it was the Jewish community. They had every reason to be concerned. Within days of the *Anschluss* the Jewish people began to be harassed. Many Austrian citizens became willing accomplices to the Nazis and SS in performing these anti-Jewish actions. This unfortunately was hereafter to be a normal occurrence: wherever the German Army invaded they were followed by the SS who came to institute the Nazi program, and often used local collaborators. This Nazi program called for the destruction of all non-desirables, and at the top of the list of Nazi undesirables were the Jewish people.

It was at this point that a new organization was formed, which operated under the authority of the SS[1], named the *Einsatzgruppen* ('task force', the full name being *Einsatzgruppe der Sicherheitpolizei und der SD*). Their primary task was to take over offices formerly belonging to the Austrian state, or as Timothy Snyder states in his profound book *Bloodlands*, it was to 'pacify the rear areas after military occupation.'[2] In time the responsibilities of the *Einsatzgruppen* expanded, and they became specialised murder squads.

Immediately upon the annexation of Austria, most of the Jewish people there wanted to leave. But to where could they go?

The Evian Conference

Following the *Anschluss* and the subsequent dire consequences for the Jewish people, President Roosevelt of the United States convened a meeting in the French resort town of Evian in July 1938 to discuss the issue of the Jewish refugees.

The assembled nations, including all of the western democracies, expressed sympathy for

1 Following his release from prison Hitler redeveloped the Nazi Party. As part of this re-organisation he created a special bodyguard unit, later known as *Schutzstaffel* (SS), headed by Heinrich Himmler. This unit was comprised only of the true Party faithful, who rigidly adhered to the Nazi ideology as espoused in Hitler's writings. Officers in the SS had to prove pure Aryan ancestry as far back as 1750, and had to prove they were not Jewish. Himmler himself was an avowed anti-Semite. Himmler and other Nazi leaders were involved in the occult to varying degrees. Occultism had a deep hold or elements of German society especially from the late 1800's. See, Roland, P. *The Nazis and the Occult,* (London, 2007); and Nicholas Goodrich-Clarke, *The Occult Roots of Nazism: The Ariosophists of Austria and Germany 1890-1935,* (London, 1985).

2 Snyder, T. *Bloodlands,* (London, 2011), p. 126. See also *Einsatzgruppen*, www.wikipedia.

these Jewish refugees, but few were willing to offer much tangible assistance. The Jewish Agency from Palestine had several observers present, and one of these, Golda Meir, later stated:

> The Australians even went so far as to explain why not. Australia, they said, had no anti-Semitism. If Jews are brought in, anti-Semitism might develop.[3]

In fact the Australian representative at that Conference, the Minister for Trade and Commerce, Colonel White, stated '…it will no doubt be appreciated also that, as we have no real racial problems, we are not desirous of importing one…'[4]

With only a few exceptions the western democracies closed their doors on the Jewish people. As a result of this decision, hundreds of thousands of Jewish people were locked in the prison that was Nazi-occupied central Europe. There was only one exit door for them: Palestine. And even there the British were slamming the door tighter and tighter against them.

The Nazis observed how none of the western democracies showed much genuine compassion for the welfare of the Jewish people. They thereupon knew that no-one was seriously going to challenge them if they enacted even more severe policies against the Jewish people.

Hitler and the Sudetenland

The support that Hitler received from many Austrians for his bold action in annexing Austria caused him to then champion the cause of ethnic Germans living in other countries. He then made claims to annex the Sudetenland, the predominately German-speaking region of Czechoslovakia.

This situation almost brought Europe to war in the middle of 1938. Ultimately Mussolini put forward a proposal (actually prepared by the German Ministry of Foreign Affairs) that Germany annex the Sudeten region and would make no further territorial demands in Czechoslovakia. No representative of the Czech Government was present.

The meeting was attended by British Prime Minister Chamberlain, French Premier Daladier, Mussolini and Hitler. Chamberlain then pressed Hitler to sign an agreement concerning this promise, which he did. The so-called Munich Agreement of 29/30 September 1938 was thereupon declared by Chamberlain as the instrument to bring peace in our time. German troops then marched into the Sudetenland. As in Austria, the *Wehrmacht* (German Army) was followed by the *Einsatzgruppen,* whose task was to do as they did in Austria, to take charge over the infrastructure of the former Czech state, and

3 Lossin Y. *Pillar of Fire*, p. 247.

4 www.kooriweb.org/foley/essays/essay. The main reason there was no racial problem in Australia was that the British founders had either murdered or killed off by other means many of the indigenous Aborigines, and had in most instances secluded the descendants of those survivors into outlying areas. The Aboriginal people at that time also did not have Australian citizenship, and were classified primarily as 'Flora and Fauna.'

to pacify areas which the army had taken.

This event was carefully observed by people all over the world. A British official spoke of the attitude of the general public in Egypt at this time as one of:

> ...bewilderment mixed, on the one hand, with anxiety and, on the other, with a pleasant anticipation of the weakening or destruction of Anglo-French influence in the Arab world. There was, however, no panic whatever, for the public did not realize the imminence of war.[5]

Kristallnacht and Hitler's speech in the Reichstag

After having evidenced the lack of true compassion for the Jewish people by the western democracies of the world, the Nazi Party then moved to its next level of anti-Jewish action. In the evening of 10 November 1938 the Nazis began a violent rampage of destruction against the entire Jewish community in Germany, in what became known as *Kristallnacht*, the Night of Broken Glass.

During this blatant act of barbarism over ninety Jewish people were killed, hundreds injured, and at least 30,000 were arrested and sent to the concentration camps. There were by this time a number of special concentration camps, where various undesirables were interred, such as Dachau, Buchenwald and Sachsenhausen. These camps became a blueprint for the development within just a few years of camps for the systematic annihilation of the Jewish people.

Besides the human tragedy, at least 1,000 synagogues were either partially or wholly destroyed during *Kristallnacht*, while countless Jewish-owned businesses and homes were attacked and many were destroyed.

This event clearly revealed the Nazi intentions. Thereafter, no Jewish person in Germany and Austria felt secure. Those who could leave now left. Some managed to get to other European countries, some to Britain, and a few were fortunate enough to make it to the United States. But everywhere the gates were closing.

Hitler then gave a speech in the Reichstag on 30 January 1939, in which he again highlighted his attitude towards the Jewish people. He stated:

> Europe cannot find peace until the Jewish question has been solved... If the international Jewish financiers, in and outside Europe should succeed in plunging the nations once more into a world war, then the result will not be the Bolshevization of the earth, and thus the victory of Jewry – and with it victory for the Jews, but the annihilation of the Jewish race in Europe![6]

Until this point every declaration which Hitler had made he fulfilled. But did he really

5 Kirk, G. *The Middle East in the War*, (Oxford University Press, 1952), p. 31.

6 Stein, Dr, S.D. *Statements by Hitler and Senior Nazis concerning Jews and Judaism*, www.ess.uwe.ac.uk

mean to physically annihilate the Jewish race in Europe? Future events would answer that question.

Britain virtually dissolves the concept of a Jewish national home

Shortly after Hitler's speech in the Reichstag the British Government convened a conference in London and invited leaders from the entire Arab world, as well as Jewish delegates from Palestine. This Conference was known as the Round Table Conference and was held at St. James Palace in London.

When the Conference began on 7 February 1939 the Arab delegates (from Egypt, Iraq, Saudi Arabia, Transjordan, Yemen, and three representatives from Palestine, Jamal el-Husseini, George Antonius and Musa al-Alami) refused to sit around the same table as the Jewish delegates. Separate meetings were therefore held.

The discussion carried on for five weeks. The Arab delegates were adamant that the original McMahon-Hussein Correspondence included Palestine in the proposed Arab Kingdom, while the Jewish delegates remained steadfast upon the promise as contained in the Balfour Declaration, and insisted on large scale immigration.

In the midst of the Conference Australian Prime Minister Lyons sent the following communiqué to British Prime Minister Neville Chamberlain:

> ...we regard the situation in Egypt, Palestine and in fact the whole Near East as being of great importance to Australia owing to its relation to vital imperial communication...We feel it will be highly dangerous to estrange the Moslem world at the present time by any decision over Palestine which might be regarded as unduly favourable to the Jews ... We feel that all the partition schemes put forward are impracticable and politically unwise and the best solution might be some settlement which maintains relatively the present status quo with safeguards to prevent Jewish predominance.[7]

This sentiment spelled out very clearly the official attitude of the Australian Government, although it did not express the opinion of all Australians. One of these was Harry Chauvel, who commanded the Desert Mounted Corps in the Middle East between 1916-1918 and who was a witness to General Allenby clearly informing Prince Feisal in Damascus on 3 October 1918 of the impending relationship between France and the Arab nationalist movement in Syria.[8]

On 15 March 1939 the British Foreign Secretary, Malcolm MacDonald informed the delegates of the British Government's decision: Jewish immigration would be limited to 15,000 per year for the following five years, (of whom 25,000 would be refugees). At the conclusion of that period Jewish immigration would be conditional upon Arab consent.

7 Australian Archives, Canberra: A981/1 Palestine 8 part 5. Quoted in Chanan Reich, *Australia and Israel*, p. 10.
8 See Chanan Reich, *Australia and Israel*, p. 11.

At the conclusion of a ten-year period there would be a Palestine State, which, naturally enough, would be dominated by Muslims (although measures would need to be taken to ensure the security of the Jewish minority!) In addition land purchases by Jewish people would virtually become illegal.

Naturally the Jewish leaders were distraught by this proposal, as it virtually nullified the original promises contained in the Balfour Declaration, and Chaim Weizmann responded that the Jewish people were not able to accept this unworkable proposal. Both parties then left the Conference to discuss and debate about their next move.

The Cabinet then further discussed the Palestine question on 20 April 1939, and according to the Minutes, Prime Minister Chamberlain impressed upon the members that it was important 'to have the Moslem world with us.' 'If', he continued, 'we must offend one side. Let us offend the Jews rather than the Arabs.'[9]

The reason behind this rather sinister explanation was that in a possible upcoming confrontation with Nazi Germany it was imperative to have as many friends as possible. The Jewish people would fight for the Allied cause come what may, but the Arab and Muslim world was very uncertain and unpredictable and every effort would need to be made to placate them – even to the detriment of the Jewish people.

The findings of the Round Table Conference became public on 17 May 1939. The Jewish leaders, naturally, were extremely disappointed. Just at the time when tens of thousands of Jewish people wanted to flee the dangerous situation in Europe, the very place to which they could go, Palestine, was closed to them.

Many non-Jewish Britons were also very upset. Winston Churchill delivered a damning condemnation of this decision in the House of Commons on 23 May 1939. As eloquent as Churchill was on the subject, his speech never swayed the House. They voted the *White Paper* into being, although the minor points, particularly concerning the Land Regulations, were still to be worked out.

The situation by September 1939

On 16 March 1939 Hitler sanctioned the invasion of the remainder of Czechoslovakia, in clear violation of the Munich Agreement of September 1938. The nation was divided into various smaller entities, part of which became the Protectorate of Bohemia and Moravia, governed by the deputy commander of the SS, Reinhard Heydrich. The Jewish people living in the former Czechoslovakia now came under the same conditions as their brethren in Austria and Germany.

It was now clear to all that Hitler had no intention of maintaining peace and had every intention of expanding the boundaries of the Reich. It was obvious that Poland would be a future objective of the expansionist Nazi regime. In the following months efforts were made by the Poles to prepare themselves for an inevitable invasion, and to

9 Cabinet Palestine Committee, 20 April 1939, Cabinet papers, 24/285, quoted in Gilbert, M. *Churchill and the Jews*, (Simon and Schuster, 2007), p. 157.

shore up international backing. Britain gave a firm guarantee of support to Poland on 31 March 1939, as too did the French Government, that if there was any act against Polish independence then Britain (and France) would come to Poland's aid. This guarantee was formalised on 6 April 1939 when the Polish foreign minister visited Britain.

The following day, 7 April 1939, Mussolini's armies invaded Albania, and within just a few days the Italians had captured the entire country, and thereupon annexed the small nation into Italy. This event sent shock waves through the Balkans region. On 13 April 1939 Britain entered into similar agreements with both Greece and Romania as she had made with Poland. General Archibald Wavell was then appointed as Commander-in-Chief in the Middle East on 28 July 1939.

Germany too was firming up its political alliances. On 22 May 1939 Germany and Italy formalised their alliance in the 'Pact of Friendship and Alliance between Germany and Italy' (commonly referred to as the 'Treaty of Steel'). The Pact contained a number of open clauses and several hidden clauses, but basically it maintained that either nation would come to the aid of the other in the event of a war.

Then on 23 August 1939 Germany formalised an agreement with the Soviet Union. The German representative was Foreign Minister von Ribbentrop and the Russian representative was Molotov their Foreign Minister. Although officially termed the 'Treaty of Non-Aggression between Germany and the Soviet Union' it was thereafter referred to as the Ribbentrop-Molotov Agreement. This agreement stated that in the event of an invasion of Poland then Germany would gain the western half and Russia the eastern half.

When this Pact became known, the British and Polish signed a new agreement, on 25 August, the 'Polish-British Common Defence Pact'.

By the end of August 1939 Europe was in a similar position as it had been in August 1914: the nations were aligned one against the other. War was imminent.

CHAPTER 3

WAR – THE FIGHT FOR JEWISH SURVIVAL BEGINS

Germany invades Poland

Utilizing a deception Hitler induced a situation whereby he sent German troops into Poland on 1 September 1939. The *Luftwaffe* heavily bombed Polish troops and even cities, and then the powerful German Army (*Wehrmacht)* streamed over the border.

In accordance with their agreement with Poland, the British and French Governments issued Hitler with an ultimatum to withdraw from Poland. When by 3 September this ultimatum had not been met, both governments declared war on Germany.

The fate of some three million Jewish people was now sealed. Many fled eastwards, but the majority, like the remainder of the Jewish people living under Nazi rule, were now trapped. Some Jewish people from those territories did manage to escape and made their way to the Black Sea where, despite the British restrictions and blockade, they boarded ships by which the Jewish authorities in Palestine 'illegally' brought them into Palestine.

With the declaration of War, the Jewish people now knew who their real enemy was. David Ben Gurion, the chairman of the Zionist Executive, stated, "We will fight with the British against Hitler as if there were no White paper; we will fight the White Paper as if there were no war."[1]

The Commonwealth joins in – New Zealand

As in August 1914 so too in September 1939 the dominions of Britain also declared war, and declared their allegiance to the 'Mother Country.' The Prime Minister of New Zealand, Michael Joseph Savage stated:

> Both with gratitude for the past, and with confidence in the future, we arrange ourselves without fear beside Britain. Where she goes, we go, where she stands, we stand … we march forward with a union of hearts and wills to a common destiny.[2]

Enlistment in the New Zealand Expeditionary Force began on 12 September, and this force was to be commanded by Major-General Bernard Freyberg, VC. One of the early recruits was Arthur Helm, who stated:

> All classes and creeds and all conditions of men were among the volunteers … Some

1 Ben Gurion, D. *Israel: A Personal History*, (New York, 1971) p. 54.
2 King, M. *New Zealanders at War*, p. 168.

looked upon it as a great lark, others enlisted from a genuine sense of duty, a few others to escape their responsibilities, or to try and make a fresh start after a life of drudgery during the depression years.[3]

Another who signed up immediately was Charles Hazlitt Upham from Christchurch. Upham's biographer Kenneth Sandford wrote of the reasons why this unassuming young New Zealander enlisted:

> … the darkening months of 1939 saw Upham thinking more and more deeply about events on the other side of the world. Slowly he evolved his own ideas of where lay the rights and wrongs. Once he had convinced himself, his mind was made up for a lifetime.
> With the call for volunteers in September 1939, he lost no time in putting his name on the lists. His career, his own future, his life ahead with Molly – none of these could be assured, he reasoned, unless the menace in Europe was quickly halted.
> He enlisted out of conviction that the Nazis had to be stopped.[4]

Shortly afterwards Upham found himself in Burnham Camp near Christchurch as part of the first draft for the New Zealand 2nd Division,[5] and ultimately found himself in A Company, 20th Battalion. Upham's commanding officer at Burham camp was Colonel Howard Kippenberger.

Kippenberger wanted to locate suitable candidates among the recruits for his NCO's (Non-Commissioned Officers). He was informed that Charles Upham was one such possible candidate. While he was considering whom he should commission, he was informed that despite a clear order that there was to be no leave on the first weekend, an officer informed Colonel Kippenberger that there was one soldier who was adamant he needed to take leave. That man was none other than Charles Upham.

Somewhat bemused, Kippenberger invited him in. Initially Private Upham was unwilling to explain why he wanted leave, except for 'private reasons.' But when Kippenberger insisted, Upham finally informed the commanding officer:

> 'I sold a man a car…He owes me 12 pounds.10s. on it and he says he's not going to pay it. If I don't get my money I'm going to take it out of his hide.'[6]

Colonel Kippenberger instinctively knew he had his man. His leave was granted. When he came back he informed Colonel Kippenger, that yes he met the man, no he did not get his money, and yes he gave the man a hiding. Colonel Kippenger indeed had his man. By

3 King, M. *New Zealanders at War*, p. 168.
4 Sandford, K. *Mark of the Lion*, (London, 1962), p. 24.
5 The 1st New Zealand Division had served with distinction in Gallipoli, France and Belgium during World War One.
6 Sandford, K. ibid, p. 27. '… take it out of his hide' is an expression meaning, 'give him a beating.'

December Charles Upham, now a Sergeant, was in the first group of New Zealanders to sail to war.

- Australia

Australia's Prime Minister, Robert Menzies stated on the radio on 3 September:

> 'Whatever the inflamed ambitions of the German Fuhrer may be, he will undoubtedly learn, as other great empires of freedom have learned before, that no empire, no dominion, can be soundly established upon a basis of broken promises or dishonoured agreements…
>
> I know that in spite of the emotions we are all feeling, you will show that Australia is ready to see it through. May God in his mercy and compassion grant that the world may soon be delivered from this agony.'[7]

Recruitment in Australia began immediately and on 15 September 1939 the Australian Government announced that it would raise an expeditionary force of 20,000 men, as well as air and naval forces. The initial Australian land force would be the 6th Division, Second Australian Imperial Force, to be commanded by General Sir Thomas Blamey.[8]

One of the first to join was fifteen (nearly sixteen) year-old Bob 'Hooker' Holt, who wrote:

> …I hot-footed it to enlist, giving my age as 21. My people protested vigorously, but upstart that I was, I informed them that if they pulled me out I would leave home and enlist under a bodgie name. With that they bowed to the inevitable and gave me their blessing – more or less, anyhow.[9]

Holt joined the 2/3rd Infantry Battalion, completed his initial training, but then had the misfortune to get a poisoned arm just at the time when the first echelon of Australian troops left for war. When the battalion moved out on 9 January and boarded the *Orcades*, he was, he stated, 'the most despondent A.I.F. man in Australia.'[10] Several months later, on 15 April, he finally managed to sail off to war.

Another to join was Arthur Leggett from Perth. Leggett has some initial troubles, though, as he was only 5 feet 3 inches tall, one inch below the minimum. Luckily Captain Sandover of the Cameron Highlanders appeared at the right time, and knowing Leggett from a previous occasion, put in a good word for him, and suddenly Private Leggett had

7 *Menzies Speech: Declaration of War*, www.aso.gov.au.

8 Blamey had also been a Gallipoli veteran and had served as Chief-of-Staff for General Monash in France in 1918. One of the first to enlist was the author's uncle, John Crombie, who was then working on a farm near Sale in Victoria, and joined the 2/7th Battalion.

9 Holt, B. *From Ingelburn to Aitape*, (Lakemba, 1981), p. 3.

10 Holt, R. ibid, p. 14.

grown an inch and the 2/11th Battalion had another soldier![11]

- South Africa

The South African situation was somewhat complicated due to the prevailing attitude of the white South African population, many of whom were either decidedly anti-British or even pro-German. Distinct from Australia and New Zealand, whose indigenous populations were very small, and whose white population was almost exclusively of British origin, South Africa had an overwhelming black and Coloured population, while the white population had a Dutch-German (Afrikaans) and British origin.

One future South African soldier, Ton Turrel gives an insight into the somewhat complicated South African situation. A year or so before the outbreak of war Turrel was at a Scout Camp which was near to a farm belonging to Mr. Freese, and, he recalls,

> ...around the time of that camp, Hitler was making history with the Sudeten troubles in Czechoslovakia and the Austrian Anschluss. I had to go to the farmhouse for some reason one day, and found our host's living room full of Nazi swastika flags![12]

The prime minister of the Union of South Africa on 1 September 1939 was J.B.M. Herzog, originally from the National Party, which was more pro-Afrikaner and anti-British. The other prominent leader was Jan Christian Smuts originally of the more pro-British South African Party. These two major parties had amalgamated in 1931 to become the United Party. A third influential leader was Daniel Malan, a strong advocate of Afrikaner nationalism, and he and many of his supporters were decidedly pro-German.

The United Party was constitutionally bound to Britain, and Britain was bound to support Poland due to the Polish-British Common Defence Pact. When therefore Herzog opted for neutrality following Germany's attack upon Poland, the United Party had no choice but to depose him from his position. Smuts was installed as Prime Minister.

The South African Army could only be comprised of whites, and because many of the white population were Afrikaner and anti-British, volunteers were called for.[13] Later, however, non-whites were recruited into various service units, but very few were permitted to carry arms.

One of the South Africans who joined up was Ron Turrell. Turrell wrote how on 3 September he was at the home of friends in Durban, and as midday approached they turned on the radio to listen to the speech by Prime Minister Chamberlain. Turrell wrote that following Chamberlain's message:

11 Leggett, A. *Don't Cry for Me*, (Oldbury, 2006), p. 89.

12 Turrel, R. *It's Only Me*, (Durban, 1980), p. 148.

13 According to the Wikipedia entry on South Africa's military history during World War II, there were only 320,000 men eligible for enlistment. Ultimately some 334,000 South African's enlisted for active service, 210,000 of these being white, 77,000 being black and 46,000 were coloureds and Indians. See www.wikipedia.org.militaryhistoryofsou thafricaduring worldwarII.

> ...the set was turned off, and Bill, Mary and I look at each other, in a silence that seemed to last several minutes, each trying to assess what impact the news which we had just heard would have on our lives. We had little doubt that the effect would be profound enough, but we could hardly have guessed that we were living through the end of an era.[14]

Ron Turrel then joined the South African Corps of Signals, attached to 2nd South African Division, and shortly afterwards found himself at camp at Voortrekkerhoogte and experienced all the regular trials of being a rookie at a military camp. Turrel's journey was to take him from this camp all the way to another camp – in Germany.

Shortly after the initial flurry of declarations and enlistments Chamberlain said in a speech in the House of Commons, that there were, '...many practical demonstrations of loyal cooperation of the Empire. Australia and New Zealand have announced their intention to despatch at an early date land forces trained in those dominions for overseas service.' He also alluded to a report from the Secretary of State for Air of 'the help our air service is receiving from Canada, Australia, New Zealand and South Africa.'[15]

- India

In his speech Chamberlain also especially mentioned the situation in India, and stated, 'There is no lack of men ready to answer any call. The production of essential war materials is steadily growing. We greatly appreciate India's contribution to the war effort...'[16]

India was similar to South Africa in that the population of British origin was small. The vast majority of the population was indigenous. Although much of the country was under British administration, some (known as the princely states) were self administered.

At the outbreak of the war there was also a strong independence movement in India, of which Mahatma Ghandi was part. Although many of the independence leaders opposed Nazism, they nevertheless were opposed to India being at war without any indigenous Indian voice in the decision.

Due to India's vast size and resources, it became during the course of the war a major manufacturing nation for the war effort, and provided some two and half million soldiers for the Allied war effort.[17]

Italy opts for neutrality

While the nations of the British Empire (Commonwealth) and the French colonies joined with the Allies in the declaration of war, Germany's major ally, Italy initially did not. Despite the strong relationship already forged between *Il Duce* and *Der Fuhrer*, Italy did

14 Turrel, R. *It's Only Me,* Durban, 1980, p. 149.
15 Speech of Neville Chamberlain, 14 December 1939, in *Hansard,* 14 December 1939, Vol. 335, cc. 1342.
16 Speech of Neville Chamberlain, 14 December 1939, in *Hansard,* 14 December 1939, Vol. 335, cc. 1342.
17 *India in World War Two,* www.wikipedia

not join with Germany either in the invasion or on 3 September. Mussolini stated to Foreign Minister Ribbentrop that 'Italy had not been ready at the outbreak of the war on September 3' and that he had been 'sincerely grateful for the telegram in which the Fuhrer had told him that he would not require Italy's military help in the Polish campaign.'[18]

Mussolini explained that due to her commitments in Libya, the Aegean Sea, Albania and Africa (meaning eastern Africa – Abyssinia), if Italy joined the war at that initial stage she 'would have had to conduct not only a two-front but a multiple-front war.'[19]

Repercussions in the Middle East

One of the many repercussions of the declaration of War in the Middle East occurred in Iraq. The German Mission in Baghdad was asked to depart on 6 September 1939 by the pro-British foreign minister, Nuri as-Said. This move was not endorsed by all members of the Iraqi Cabinet, and the Iraqi Government did not declare war on Germany. This would mean, that in the event of a direct confrontation, the Iraqi Army would not be required to fight against any German forces.

Many Iraqis were pro-German but not necessarily pro-Axis, that is, they distrusted the Italians. They did not want to see the British ousted and the Italians take their place as an imperial overlord.

A result of the official decision was that a number of pro-Axis leaders agitated behind the scenes to ensure that Iraq would not be induced to be involved alongside the British. To assist them at this time the Iraqi Government, led by the 'Golden Square' invited Haj Amin to come from his place of exile in Syria to live in Baghdad. Haj Amin arrived in October 1939 and remained and used this as a base for his anti-British and anti-Jewish propaganda for the following twenty months.

The other major Middle East entity was Egypt. The Egyptian Government also cut off diplomatic relations with Germany, and in addition 'sequestered German property, and interned all German subjects who could not establish an anti-Nazi record.'[20] Egypt, like Iraq, did not declare war on Germany, which perturbed the British, for it would mean the same as in Iraq: if German forces were ever on Egyptian soil, the Egyptian Army would not be required to fight against the Germans.

For the time being when war was in Europe there was quiet in Egypt. All that would change once war encroached into the Middle East.

New task for the *Einsatzgruppen* - murder squads

Shortly after the *Wehrmacht* invaded Poland they were followed by the *Einsatzgruppen*, or task forces. The main object of these specialised task forces was to control the local civilian

18 Conversation between the Reich Foreign Minister and the Duce in the presence of Ambassador von Mackensen and Count Ciano on March 11, 1940, Document No. 669, in *Documents on German Foreign Policy 1918-1945,* Series D, 9 (Her Majesty's Stationery Office, 1962), ibid, Vol. 8, pp. 900-901.
19 Conversation between the Reich Foreign Minister and the Duce, ibid, p. 902.
20 Kirk, G. ibid, p. 34.

population, Jewish and non-Jewish. This included the purging of all real and potential Polish leadership, and Jewish leaders. This purging was named Operation *Tannenberg.*

The task of the *Einsatzgruppen* in Poland is explained by Snyder:

> It was in Poland that the Einsatzgruppen were to fulfill their mission as "ideological soldiers" by eliminating the educated classes of a defeated enemy. (They were in a sense killing their peers: fifteen of the twenty-five Einsatzgruppe and Einsatzkommado commanders had doctorates). In Operation Tannenerg, Heydrich wanted the Einsatzgruppen to render "the upper levels of society" harmless by murdering sixty-one thousand Polish citizens. As Hitler put it, "only a nation whose upper levels are destroyed can be pushed into the ranks of slavery." The ultimate goal of this decapitation project was to "destroy Poland" as a functioning society.[21]

In the first weeks of the invasion some 15,000 Poles (including numerous Jewish people) were executed by the *Einsatzgruppen.*[22] The head of the Reich Main Security Office, SS Lieutenant General Reinhard Heydrich issued a set of instructions for the *Einsatzgruppen* on 27 September 1939. When relating to the Jewish population, the instructions stated that the Jews were to be concentrated in specific locations until such time as a "final goal" for them would be instituted. The instructions stated:

> A distinction must be made between:
> 1. the final goal (which will require a lengthy period) and
> 2. the stages toward the achievement of this final goal (which can be carried out on a short-term basis)

These instructions then continued, stating:

> ...The following instructions and directives serve simultaneously the purpose of encouraging the chiefs of the *Einsatzgruppen* to reflect on the practical issues.
>
> The first preliminary measure for achieving the final goal is the concentration of the Jews from the countryside in the larger cities. It must be speedily implemented ... as few concentration points as possible should be established so that only those cities are designated which are either railway junctions or at least on a railway line. As a matter of principle, Jewish communities of under 500 are to be dissolved and transferred to the nearest concentration city.
>
> It must be ensured that the economic exploitation of the occupied territories does not

21 Snyder, T. *Bloodlands*, p. 126.
22 *Einsatzgruppen*, www.deathcamps.org/occupation.einsatzgruppen.

suffer as a result of these measures.[23]

Irrespective of whether or not the Nazis at this stage had purposed to physically annihilate all the Jewish people, the fact is that the stage was set for depriving the Jewish people of German occupied Poland of all their rights, and relocating them to concentration points in larger cities. These concentration points became, very shortly afterwards, over-crowded ghettos.

The plight of the Jewish people throughout Nazi-occupied Poland worsened daily. Concerning the actions of the *Einsatzgruppen* against the Jewish population, Snyder wrote:

> The Einsatzgruppen were more successful in missions against Jews, which required much less discrimination. One Einsatzgruppe was tasked with terrorizing Jews so that they would flee east from the German occupation zone to the Soviet side. As much as possible was to be accomplished in September 1939, while military operations were still taking place. So in Bedzin, for example, this Einsatzgruppe burned down the synagogue with flamethrowers, killing about five hundred Jews in two days…In Przemysl between the sixteenth and nineteenth of September Einsatzkommandos shot at least five hundred Jews. As a result of such action, hundreds of thousands of Jews fled to the Soviet occupation zone.[24]

The surviving Jewish people were traumatised. Those who did not flee to the Soviet zone were now trapped, and with no opportunity for escape. Unfortunately, for most of those who did manage to flee, they were safe for only a short time.

Jewish concerns

Despite the immense anger in Palestine at the issuing of the White Paper, the beginning of the Second World War saw the temporary end to local violence, as the focus was placed upon the common enemy of both Britain and the Jewish people - Nazi Germany and its allies. Following the invasion of Poland, and especially as news leaked out about Nazi atrocities, the Jewish leaders in Palestine began agitating for the British to permit the enlistment of Jewish volunteers.

Prime Minister Chamberlain also brought Winston Churchill in from the 'cold' and placed him in charge of the Admiralty. Churchill met with Chaim Weizmann on 19 September, who informed him that 75,000 Jewish men and women in Palestine had registered with the authorities for national service, and he asked Churchill to assist in getting them armed. Churchill responded that they should be armed as this would allow the British soldiers

23 Quoted in J Noakes and G Pridham (eds.) *Nazism 1919-1945: A Documentary Reader*. Vol. 3 Exeter: University of Exeter Press, 1988, pp.1051-1053, and this excerpt is taken from Dr. S. D. Stein, *Statements by Hitler and Senior Nazis Concerning Jews and Judaism*, www.ess.uwe.ac.uk.
24 Snyder, T. *Bloodlands*, p. 127.

there to be released.[25]

Chaim Weizmann summed up the Jewish position in 1939:

> In the fight against the Nazi monster no one could have had a deeper stake, no one could have been more fanatically eager to contribute to the common cause, than the Jews. At the same time England, then the leader of the anti-Nazi coalition, was keeping the gates of Palestine closed against the unhappy thousands of men, women and children who were making their last desperate effort to reach the safety of the National Home.[26]

Weizmann continued pressing the British Government in London for permission to raise a Jewish fighting force able to serve under their own flag. While Winston Churchill supported the idea, the Government did not, as they believed the Jewish people would then hanker for political favours after the war.[27] In Palestine however, the authorities finally agreed to establish the 'Auxiliary Military Pioneer Corps' (AMPC), which was for service units only and not for combat. Although the Jewish leadership was disappointed with this outcome, there was no problem at all in finding Jewish volunteers.

The British, however, in their attempt to be even-handed, also encouraged the enlistment of Arab 'volunteers'. The Arabs enlisted somewhat reluctantly when compared to the enthusiasm of the Jewish volunteers. In February 1940 this 500 strong Corps left for France to serve with the British Expeditionary Force there.[28]

Churchill (with Weizmann's backing) continued to agitate 1) to have the proposed Land Regulations repealed, and 2) to arm the Jewish people in Palestine in order to release the regular British soldiers there. At a War Cabinet meeting on 12 February 1940 Churchill went so far as to state that an equal number of Arabs could also be armed. He could not understand the logic behind maintaining a garrison in Palestine one-quarter the size of that stationed in all of India – when it could be replaced by armed Jewish soldiers.[29]

His arguments on both accounts, as well as those of others, made no headway. The British Cabinet was set on its course, a course which during the War in the Middle East right up to November 1942, was to prove wrong, as the sympathies of the majority of the Arab nationalist leaders seemed to be more with Nazi Germany than with Britain.

1940 – The sons of the Anzacs arrive

The first contingent of Anzac troops left in January 1940 en-route for the Suez Canal. The New Zealanders were to be based in Egypt, while the Australians were initially to be

25 Gilbert, M. *Churchill and the Jews*, p. 163. Weizmann had a similar meeting on 17 December 1939, just prior to his departure to the United States. See Weizmann, C. *Trial and Error*, Vol. 2, pp. 418-19.

26 Weizmann, C. *Trial and Error*, (Philadelphia, 1949), Vol. 11, p. 417.

27 Gilbert, M. *Churchill and the Jews*, pp. 163-72.

28 Lossin, Y. ibid, p. 287.

29 War Cabinet Minutes, 12 February 1940: Cabinet Papers, 65/5, as quoted in Gilbert, M. *Churchill and the Jews*, p. 170.

based in seven camps in Palestine, two near Gaza, and others at Deir Suneid, Beit Jirja, Barbara, Julis and Qastina.

One Australian who arrived in Palestine before the troops was a young doctor named Edward "Weary" Dunlop,[30] who was based at the Fast Hotel in Jerusalem. This hotel would soon become the Australian Soldiers Club. Dunlop's task was to prepare the medical infrastructure at these camps before the arrival of the 6th Australian Division which was due on 12 February.

When the first Anzacs arrived in the region, Dunlop was there to meet them. While he accompanied the Australians off to their camps in Palestine, the New Zealanders moved to their camps in Egypt. Among them was Charles Upham. The 'Kiwi's' found themselves walking in the exact footsteps of their fathers from the 1st New Zealand Expeditionary Force from 1914.

The local population in Palestine, particularly the Jewish people, were ecstatic that the sons of the Anzacs had arrived. They had heard all the stories about the men of the First World War on their big horses, with their big hats, their big smiles and their big bent for humour and pranks,

The Hebrew press and English language *Palestine Post* were full of editorials and comments about their arrival, with the *Palestine Post* leading the way with brazen front-page headlines, and accompanying editorial on 13 February:

ANZACS BACK AGAIN

To the dominion forces will fall a vital share in the common effort...To maintain peace in this region, to erect a barrier against a German advance into the Balkans, or a Russian threat into the Middle east, and to buttress the position of Turkey – these are the objects which have brought to the Middle East, for the second time in a quarter of a century, the volunteer troops of Australia and New Zealand...[31]

The Hebrew daily, *HaBoker* (The Morning) wrote on 15 February 1940, under the headline:

Our Greetings to the Australian Army

The Jewish population of Palestine heartily welcomes the Australian Army who came for the second time in the last twenty five years ... They arrived yesterday to this country, not as an armed force putting fear and awe in the hearts of the civilian population, pushing aside the civil authorities, and showing off their armed strength and its superiority ... They came as regiments of blossoming youth, jovial and smiling. Upright and brave fellows overflowing with the joy of life and from whose eyes shines the love for strangers, the sufferance of neighbours, and pity for the weak, the old and the children. For these

30 Dunlop later became one of Australia's most esteemed soldiers earning great distinction by his bravery in the Japanese POW camps in Thailand.

31 *Palestine Post,* 13 February 1940, p. 6.

young men come from a far and wonderful continent, which has not been contaminated yet by the evil and horrid propaganda of the Dictators, who pretend to bring happiness to Europe. Their souls are still pure and their faith wholehearted …[32]

Once the new garrison forces had settled into their camps they were permitted to enjoy their first outing on 22 February, and some 600 of them 'invaded' Tel Aviv and 400 'invaded' Jerusalem. These two cities would never be the same for the remainder of the war. In Tel Aviv the soldiers adopted the young Yemenite Jewish children who peddled shoe laces. Some soldiers bought out all of their stock and in the process won the hearts of these poor children. Of another group of soldiers in Jerusalem, the *Palestine Post* reported:

> One group of men hired mules and started a "race" along Jaffa Road, causing much amusement to the passersby who cheered them, especially when the animals turned out to be intractable.

By the time these soldiers left Jerusalem again at 6.30 in the evening, wrote the *Palestine Post* the people were 'lining the pavements along Jaffa Road to see them off, and cheers and goodbyes were exchanged.'[33]

Thereafter the troops were released on furlough of four days at a time. Hostels for the soldiers were established in all of the major cities. In Jerusalem this was the Fast Hotel, near to Jaffa Gate, which overlooked the road which connected the New City with the Old City and named the Australian Soldiers Club.

Only fifty soldiers were allowed to visit Jerusalem at any one time, and this was probably a wise decision, as Jerusalem, less so than Tel Aviv, was a more religious and serious city. Yet the holy sites were visited by all the soldiers. Many of these soldiers visited the CMJ's Christ Church and signed the visitors book afterwards.

A young Jewish student who lived in Tel Aviv at the time was Yitzhak Toussia-Cohen, who recalled:

> The Australians were all very jolly and they compensated for the lack of warmth experienced from the British authorities. They loved to drink, but were very popular with the children, for they used to throw coins into the air for them to catch.'[34]

Despite their pranks and larrikinism, the locals continued to deeply appreciate the Australian and New Zealand soldiers. The Hebrew newspaper *HaSha'ah (The Gate)* wrote:

32 *HaBoker*, 15 February 1940, quoted in *The Aussies in Tel Aviv*, Gestetner. Copy in author's possession.
33 *Palestine Post*, 23 February 1940, p. 2.
34 Story related to me by the late Yitzhak Toussia-Cohen.

The Australians in Town

> Yesterday there again arrived a few hundred Australians, 'from somewhere in the country', to visit Tel-Aviv, they filled the town with gaiety, as is their custom, and drew the attention of the crowds...The visitors arrived at about noon, and after a short while, you could notice them everywhere...The main streets ... were crowded with onlookers watching the pranks of the Australians. Some of them hired a horse and cart and went for a ride through the town, others again took rides on private cars. One group bought a box of vegetables and distributed same among the needy. Another group regulated the traffic. Hundreds of children followed the Australians wherever they went and had a good time together...[35]

Amongst those children and teenagers who thoroughly loved the Australians was Uzi Narkiss, the man who later as General Uzi Narkiss commanded the capture of Jerusalem in 1967. Narkiss had many stories to tell about these soldiers, but his proudest moment was when he managed to 'borrow' an Australian hat, which was, it has to be said, a favourite past time of many.

Narkiss did not believe he stole the hat, just 'borrowed' it, as the Australian army, so he believed, was rich, and they could afford more.[36] A young Alex Carmel, son of German Jewish immigrants in Haifa, also remembers the Australians in 'their big hats.' Carmel preferred stamp collecting instead of slouch hat collecting. He recalls going onto the streets of Haifa when he saw the Anzac soldiers and asking for stamps, and recalls receiving stamps 'with a Kiwi on it.'[37]

Even though the Kiwi's were based in Egypt, many of them came up into Palestine on furlough, while others, such as Charles Upham, went through specialized training of various kinds in Palestine. Upham's special training was for use of the Bren-gun. Another to learn the use of the Bren-gun was 'Hooker' Holt, who only began his course after he had endured the long sea-voyage, a period in hospital and then fourteen days in the Jerusalem Prison for insubordination, and then back to the hospital. Perhaps he and Charles Upham ended up being on the same course together!

While the Australians and New Zealanders were arriving in the Middle East, the first South African troops departed from Durban destined for East Africa as a garrison force, just in case Italy joined the war at some stage. Ron Turrell was there to see them off. Later, on 13 August 1940 the South African units were constituted as the 1st South African Division under General George Brink.

35 *Ha-Sha'Ah*, 12 March 1940, quoted in 'The Aussies in Tel Aviv', by Gestetner, 1940.
36 Information gained from interview with the late Uzi Narkiss, May 1997.
37 Information gained from interview with the late Alex Carmel, May 1997.

Disclosure of the Land Regulations associated with the White paper

Ironically, while colonial soldiers were bringing some gaiety into the land of Israel, an event occurred on 12 February 1940 which was one of the most difficult blows yet to the Jewish people during the period of the British Mandate. While many were still reeling from the shock of the White Paper, and even held out hopes that in view of the current situation it would be repealed, the British Government finalised the Land Transfer Regulations, associated with the White Paper.[38]

This British Cabinet decision effectively cancelled out the Balfour Declaration of 1917. At a time when the survival of the Jewish community in Europe was in the balance, Britain closed the last door for any Jewish people able to escape the death trap of Europe.

When these Land Regulations were made public on 28 February 1940 thousands of Jewish people took to the streets in Palestine in protest and several were killed by the British authorities. This was possibly one of the hardest days for many in Jewish leadership. David ben Gurion may have said that they would fight the White Paper as if there was no war, and would fight the war as if there was no White Paper, but this, this was very painful for the Jewish people in Palestine and indeed everywhere. It was like the carpet had been whisked away from under their feet.

Yet, they had to concentrate upon the main object at this point, and the main object was the defeat of Nazi Germany. At this time when the British had just crushed the last hope of a Jewish national home in Palestine, when soldiers of the Empire congregated in the Middle East, and when the Jewish people in Poland were entering into a fight for their survival, Weizmann continued to press for a Jewish Division, complete with its own flag and insignia.

One British politician who supported this vision was Winston Churchill. Soon he was in a position to forward this vision.

38 Another episode which irked the Jewish community was the arrest in October 1939 of forty-four Jewish men, including Moshe Dayan, for ten years imprisonment in Acre prison, for carrying a few weapons.

Chapter 4
Italy joins the War

Italy prepares for war

The German move into Norway on 9 April, and the accompanying defeat of the British forces there, further excited the attention of the world. Mussolini now became more determined to enter the war alongside Germany. He sent Hitler a message of encouragement on 11 April 1940 and, after stating details of the situation in the Balkans region, he wrote:

> I assure you that from tomorrow, the 12th, the Italian Fleet will be entirely on a war footing while I am speeding up the "tempo" of the other armed forces…
>
> As to the Italian people, although they desire a delay in order to be better prepared, they are now aware they will not be able to avoid entering the field.[1]

Mussolini still did not feel he was sufficiently prepared to enter into conflict on two fronts, which would have happened if he declared war on Britain and France at that stage. Events soon overtook him though.

Hitler invades the West – calls for Jewish soldiers in Palestine

On 10 May 1940 the soldiers of the Third Reich invaded France, Belgium, Luxembourg and the Netherlands. The same day Neville Chamberlain resigned as prime minister and Winston Churchill took on the position which he was destined to fulfill.

Everyone understood what was at stake. Hitler's *Blitzkreig* or 'lightning strike' was crushing all opposition before him. If these four nations, and especially France, fell, then Britain would bear the brunt of the assault. Home defence was now the top priority. It was imperative to bring as many regular British troops home as possible.

At that point there were some 20,000 regular British troops based in Palestine. The newly arrived Australian soldiers there, as well as the New Zealand soldiers in Egypt, were raw recruits and still in the midst of their basic training. The eleven regular British battalions, however, were needed in Britain. Churchill stated his sentiments on 23 May 1940:

> The main and almost the sole aim in Palestine at the present time is to liberate the eleven battalions of excellent regular troops who are now tethered there. For this purpose the Jews should be armed in their own defence, and properly organised as speedily as

1 Mussolini to Hitler, 11 April 1940, Document No. 92, ibid, vol. IX, p. 131.

possible. We can always prevent them from attacking the Arabs by our sea power which cuts them off from the outer world, and by other friendly influences. On the other hand we cannot leave them unarmed when our troops leave, as leave they must at a very early date.[2]

The logic of Churchill's case was not enough to overturn stubborn resistance in his own Cabinet, especially from the Secretary of State for Colonies, Lord Lloyd. He like others, feared that showing favouritism to the Jewish people in such a manner was bound to have adverse effects upon the Arabs. Once again the welfare of the Jewish people was being sacrificed in order not to upset the Arab leadership.

Italy attacks France

The German forces quickly overwhelmed the French Army and soldiers of the British Expeditionary Force (BEF), and the remnants were pushed hard against the northern French coast near the port of Dunkirk. The British Government ordered the evacuation of the BEF, which began on 25 May and which lasted until 3 June 1940.[3] During that period 338,226 Allied soldiers were evacuated, including 139,997 French, Polish, Belgium and Dutch soldiers. Many of those who managed to evade the German ring later fought in North Africa.[4]

When it was apparent that France (and Britain) were close to defeat, Mussolini informed Hitler, on 30 May 1940, that Italy was slowly getting ready for war.[5] He informed Ribbentrop on 2 June that he was concerned that the British would attack him from Egypt, and had consequently ordered the transfer of 'an armored unit from Albania to Libia.' Mussolini further stated that he 'did not expect an attack so much from Tunis as from Egypt, as the English would doubtless attempt an advance from there for reasons of prestige.'[6]

When it was apparent that the French were to be defeated, and that the Italians would not have to face a French attack from either France or French-controlled North Africa (primarily Tunisia which was adjacent to Libya), Mussolini declared war on France on 10 June 1940.

While the remnants of the French Army continued to fight the invading German Army, the Italians invaded France from the south on 20 June 1940. They achieved nowhere near the goals which Mussolini desired, and were soundly defeated on many occasions by the much weakened French Army.

2 Letters of 23 May 1940: Churchill Papers, 20/13, quoted in Gilbert, M. *Churchill and the Jews*, p. 173.
3 Many troops (and civilians) were evacuated from other locations as well. Leading Seaman Edward Pritchett was at St. Nazaire and witnessed the sinking of the *Lancastria* on 17 June 1940 in which some 4-5,000 people lost their lives. This was initially suppressed by the British authorities, and was the biggest single maritime disaster in British history. Pritchett was later involved in Operation *Vigorous* – getting supplies to Malta, and was on the ship, *HMS Airedale* when it was sunk on 15 June 1942.
4 See Churchill, W. *Their Finest Hour*, p. 115.
5 Mussolini to Hitler, 30 May 1940, Document No. 356, ibid, Vol. IX, p. 483.
6 The Ambassador in Italy to the Foreign Minister, 2 June 1940, Document No. 371, ibid, Vol. IX, pp. 503-4.

Wavell strikes first

This wasn't Mussolini's only disappointment. At the time of France's collapse the Italians had about 215,000 troops in North Africa, while the combined British and Commonwealth troops in Egypt amounted to about 50,000 men. The main westward Allied position was at Mersa Matruh. General Archibald Wavell was Commander-in-Chief for the region, and to whom was entrusted responsibility for this region as well as British possessions south of Egypt. On 7 June 1940 Wavell brought Major-General R. O'Connor to Egypt and placed him in command of Western Desert Force (the vanguard of the Army of the Nile) to prepare for an anticipated Italian attack from Libya.

On 11 June 1940, the day after Italy entered the war, men from Major-General O'Connor's Western Desert Force cut the wire separating Egypt and Libya and made a daring dash into Libya and captured some Italian soldiers who were caught completely unawares. Then they attacked the frontier Italian fortresses of Fort Capuzzo and Maddalena, and captured over 200 Italian soldiers. Several days later they raided further into Libya, causing considerable damage and capturing more Italians including an Italian general.

Mussolini was incensed with this situation and ordered his commander in the province of Cyrenaica, General Graziani, to win some victories. Soon afterwards preparations began, including the construction of a road from Tripoli through to Benghazi, then onto Tobruk and ending at the Libya-Egypt border near Sollum. Thereupon the 10th Italian Army began moving slowly eastwards. All the main ports and bases were restocked with provisions, especially Benghazi and Tobruk. Italy was now preparing to attack Egypt.

The fall of France

France ultimately surrendered to Germany on 22 June 1940, and on 25 June 1940 France and Italy signed an armistice. The Armistice between Germany and France allowed for a German zone of occupation which encompassed all of the French ports along the Atlantic and the English Channel. The remainder of inland France was to be governed by the French from the city of Vichy. The Vichy Government was also involved in some of the administrative governance of the zone under German military occupation.

In an attempt to keep the vast French colonial empire from succumbing to the control of the Free French government-in-exile led by General Charles de Gaulle, the administration of the French colonies was entrusted to the Vichy Government. This, as time would show, was not a straightforward situation, as many French soldiers in those colonies were not at all enthusiastic about the defeat of France and the subsequent armistice with Germany. Syria, although having received a degree of independence in 1936, now came under the jurisdiction of the Vichy Government.

One of the stipulations of the Armistice was for the retention of a small French military presence in the colonies, for internal security and to prevent attack by the Allies. In Lebanon and Syria the 'Army of the Levant'[7] had about 50,000 men at the time of the

7 Also called the 'Army of the Orient.'

surrender. An Armistice Commission was also set up and was led by the Italians to ensure the conditions of the Armistice were adhered to, and much of the weaponry of this French Army was interred.

Mussolini's North African plans

At the time when Italy entered into the war the Italian Foreign Minister Count Galeazzo Ciano informed Hitler of Italy's military intentions. Apart from his European aspirations, Mussolini conceived of an expanded Italian empire in the Eastern Mediterranean and Africa. Hitler responded to Mussolini on 13 July 1940, 'Count Ciano has informed me that Italy is getting ready for an attack on Egypt and the Suez Canal. Any such strike, Duce, is an enormous gain.'[8]

A few days later the German Ambassador in Rome, Von Mackensen, informed Berlin that Italy asked for:

> ... a wide land connection between Libia and Ethiopia, whereby a large portion of the Sudan would fall to Italy, while the rest of the Sudan would fall under Egyptian sovereignty. With Egypt, Palestine and Syria, bilateral treaties would be concluded by which Italian influence in those areas and Italian interest in their raw materials, particularly cotton and oil, would be secured. Italy hopes to be able to conclude such a treaty with Iraq, too, and is determined to accord Egypt every consideration in matters of her sovereignty and independence.[9]

Mussolini dreamed of an Italian Empire. The Italians had two colonies in the region, one in Libya to the west of Egypt and one in Abyssinia to the south of Egypt. Egypt was clearly in his sights. If and when he attacked Egypt, the raw colonial recruits were there to meet him. Holt recalls of this time:

> After Italy entered the War we dispersed our tents and dug them into the ground... Route marches and manoeuvres were the order of the day.[10]

Jewish soldiers from Palestine

The British Government's opposition to the enlistment of Jewish forces changed when Germany invaded France, and especially following the defeat of France. While Weizmann kept pressing for a Jewish Division, Churchill continued with his call for the formation of a Jewish fighting force. Finally on 15 July 1940 the British War Cabinet agreed to the immediate formation of a battalion of six companies of soldiers from Palestine, to be attached to the Buffs Regiment, and thus thereafter known as *Buffs*. But, as usual, they

8 Hitler to Mussolini, 13 July 1940, Document No. 166, ibid, Vol. X, p. 211.
9 Ambassador Von Mackensen to the Foreign Ministry, Rome, 17 July 1940, Document No. 193, ibid, Vol. X, p. 252.
10 Holt, B. ibid, p. 19.

wanted an equal number of Jewish and Arab recruits, and these troops would be in non-combat units.

Few Arabs wanted to join, particularly because much of their leadership, especially the exiled Haj Amin, was pro-Nazi. Later, when these companies were enlisted, most of the Arab recruits deserted. This factor was carefully concealed from the general public.[11] By September 1940 fifteen battalions of Jewish volunteers from Palestine had been formed – amounting to some 20,000 Jewish volunteers.[12] One of the first recruits was Moses Mosenson from Kibbutz Naan. He wrote to his wife and daughter on 5 August 1940:

> Here I am in the training camp. There is barbed wire around it and a stranger is on guard at the gate. The way home is both barred and distant; how far away Naan seems to me now!
>
> I was sworn in some days ago … [13]

And again on 11 August 1940, 'Everything is still new and strange, full of expectance for whatever will happen next…I do not cease to be surprised when I put on my military uniform…'[14] On 12 August 1940 he wrote, You'll probably be surprised to hear that your father has begun to go to school…This is a school for soldiers. This school is at Sarafand and thousands of boys from all parts of the country are here. They are studying to be soldiers.'[15] Mosenson and his fellow Jewish soldiers moved out to Egypt on 24 October 1940.

Although this was a start, Weizmann and other Jewish leaders continued to press for armed Jewish soldiers. Weizmann wrote to Churchill in August 1940:

> In a war with the magnitude of the present one, it is impossible to say what the strategic disposition of the British fleets and armies may be before victory is attained. Should it come to a temporary withdrawal from Palestine – a contingency which we hope will never arise – the Jews of Palestine would be exposed to wholesale massacre at the hands of the Arabs, encouraged and directed by the Nazis and the fascists. This possibility reinforces the demand for our elementary human right to bear arms, which should not morally be denied to the loyal citizens of a country at war. Palestinian Jewry can furnish a force of 50,000 fighting men, all of them in the prime of their strength – no negligible force if properly trained, armed and led.[16]

11 Lossin,Y. ibid, p. 297.
12 Gilbert, M. *Churchill and the Jews*, p. 176.
13 Mosenson, M. *Letters from the Desert*, (New York, 1945), p. 3.
14 Mosenson, M. ibid, p. 6.
15 Mosenson, M. ibid, p. 7. In a following letter on 8 September, Mosenson spoke of a man named Dov who came from Vienna and who managed to survive a year in Dachau concentration camp before finally after much travail entering into Palestine. (see Mosenson, ibid, page. 9)
16 Weizmann, C. *Trail and Error*, Vol. II, p. 424.

Churchill took this matter seriously and then wrote to General Ismay (for Wavell) on 12 August 1940:

> I do not consider that proper use is being made of the large forces in Palestine. The essence of the situation depends on arming the Jewish colonists sufficiently to enable them to undertake their own defence, so that if necessary for a short time the whole of Palestine can be left to very small British forces. A proposal should be made to liberate immediately a large portion of the garrison, including the Yeomanry Cavalry Division.[17]

At a luncheon with the Prime Minister in September 1940, Weizmann again presented the idea of a Jewish Division, and according to him, Churchill was 'friendly about the idea, and was interested in the details, and we worked out there and then a five point program, the outline of which I had brought with me and which I was to submit immediately in a memorandum to Lieutenant General Sir John Dill, Chief of the Imperial General Staff.'[18]

Weizmann wrote about these five points:

> The first point on the program called for "recruitment of the greatest possible number of Jews in Palestine for the fighting services, to be formed into Jewish battalions or larger formations." The third point … called for "officers cadres, sufficient for a Jewish division in the first instance, to be picked immediately from Jews in Palestine, and trained in Egypt." The fourth point dealt with a Jewish "desert unit," the fifth with the recruitment of foreign Jews in England.
>
> The second point was ominous for us, if only as an indication of the difficulties we were to encounter in being permitted to serve. "The Colonial Office insists on an approximate parity in the number of Jews and of Arabs recruited for specific Jewish and Arab units in Palestine. As Jewish recruitment in Palestine is certain to yield much larger numbers than Arab, the excess of Jews is to be sent for training to Egypt or anywhere else in the Middle East." On this point Mr. Churchill yielded to the Foreign Office; on all others he was unreservedly co-operative. I was, on the whole, satisfied with the results; so were the others at the luncheon.[19]

Churchill may have been sympathetic and supportive, but such was not the case within the echelons of the British political and military establishment, including General Wavell, and it was a full four years until this vision of having armed Jewish soldiers was implemented with the formation of the *Jewish Brigade* in September 1944.

Due to British official intransigence against more Jews volunteering for the army, the

17 Prime Minister to General Ismay, for General Wavell. 12 August, 1940, in Churchill, W. *Finest Hour*, p. 426. In the same letter he also stated he could not understand why the Australia and New Zealand soldiers were not being given a role in the 'defence of Egypt.'

18 Weizmann, C. *Trail and Error*, Vol. II, p. 424.

19 Weizmann, C. *Trial and Error*, Vol. II, pp. 424-5.

numbers of Jewish men and women who enlisted in the *Haganah* increased dramatically. Ironically, the Special Operations Executive (SOE) of the British Army, did not feel constrained by the dictates of the British civil administration, and often cooperated with the *Haganah*.[20]

Formation of Long Range Desert Group

While endeavours were being made to establish Jewish fighting units, a new unit was being birthed in Cairo. On 23 June 1940 Major Ralph Bagnold approached Wavell with a proposal to establish a specialised unit to work behind Italian lines, which meant, working deep in the Libyan Desert.

Wavell supported the proposal. Bagnold felt the most appropriate men for the task would be 'colonials' and that the Australians from the desert and bush areas would be best suited. It seems that the Australian commanders were not keen though for Australian soldiers to serve under British command.[21] Bagnold then approached the New Zealanders. Initially two officers and eighty-five other ranks volunteered, but later in the War more soldiers were added, including men from Rhodesia and Britain. At one point about 300 men were in the specialised unit, about half of them New Zealanders, and the other half from other nations.

The unit began operations in September 1940 and continued throughout the course of the Egypt and Libyan Campaign. They were based in different locations, especially Kufra and Siwa Oasis. On most occasions they operated alone, but on a number of other occasions they acted as guides and supports for raids by commandos and SAS, and they were a constant problem for both the Italian and later the German high command.

Churchill's concerns for Egypt and Malta

Although Churchill's prime consideration was the safety of Britain during the prolonged and severe German blitz, he nevertheless held grave concern for the maintenance of the Middle East, so much so that on 10 July 1940 he set-up a special Ministerial Committee to advise him on Middle East affairs. One of the first recommendations of this Committee was the despatch as soon as possible of more tanks to Egypt.[22]

Churchill understood that one of Mussolini's key objectives would be the capture of Egypt, and for this reason he did all he could to bring as many troops as possible to defend Egypt. One of his strong desires was for bringing the Commonwealth soldiers garrisoning Palestine forward to Egypt, and to equip the Jewish people for defence in Palestine, who he stated 'with proper weapons would have made a good fight against all comers.'[23]

He also understood the strategic importance of Malta. If Malta fell to the Italians, Britain

20 HaCohen, D. *Time to Tell*, (New York, 1985), p. 112cf ; Lossin,Y. ibid, p. 299.

21 Long Range Desert Group website, www.lrdg.hegewisch.net, which utilised the book by John Gordon, *The Other Desert War*.

22 Churchill, W. *Finest Hour*, p. 423-4. Wavell was summoned to Britain and met with Churchill on 8 August 1940.

23 Churchill, W. *Finest Hour*, p. 422.

would lose control of the sea routes throughout the central Mediterranean. The retention of garrison Malta would henceforth be a major Allied concern.

Closely associated with the retention of Malta were the naval operations in the Mediterranean. Once France collapsed and Italy became an adversary the dynamics in the Mediterranean completely changed. Although Britain still maintained a naval presence at Gibraltar and at Alexandria in Egypt, free access through the central Mediterranean was now no longer an option. Britain would need to contend with the quite powerful Italian Fleet which included six battleships and over 100 submarines. The Italians also boasted quite a large and strong air force, which because of their bases both in Italy and Libya, was able to strike far inside British held territory.

While escorting a convoy from Malta to Alexandria in early July 1940 Admiral Cunningham of the Eastern Mediterranean Fleet encountered and defeated an Italian naval force. This encouraged Churchill to ensure the Allied naval presence remained strong in the Mediterranean, especially as already in July 1940 he feared the impending presence of the Germans in the Mediterranean.[24]

Churchill desperately wanted to get fifty tanks and their crews to Egypt as quick as possible, but the Admiralty was reluctant to send any slower moving merchant ships with such a valuable cargo through the Mediterranean, preferring them to go via the slower but safer route via the Cape.

Yet, Malta was supplied with much needed material between 30 August and 5 September in what was known as Operation *Hats* when British ships approached both from Gibraltar and Alexandria. In the wake of this success, Churchill strongly encouraged Cunningham 'to strike at the Italians' because, as he reiterated, 'as time passes the Germans will more than likely try to lay strong hands upon the Italian war machine, and then the picture will be very different.'[25]

Churchill, rightly as it would prove, saw the value in destabilising the Italian war machine before Germany entered onto the scene. In addition he saw the need to stabilise and shore up the defences at Malta before such a German involvement occurred. What was sorely needed for the garrison at Malta were AA guns and aircraft – both of which were also sorely needed in Britain during the same period. Thanks to Admiral Somerville of the Western Mediterranean Fleet based at Gibraltar sufficient of each had arrived in Malta before the end of 1940.

24 Prime Minister to the First Sea Lord, 15 July 1940, in Churchill, W. *Finest Hour*, p. 443.

25 *Prime Minister to General Ismay*, for transference to Admiral Cunningham, 8 September 1940, in Churchill, W. *Finest Hour*, pp. 451-2.

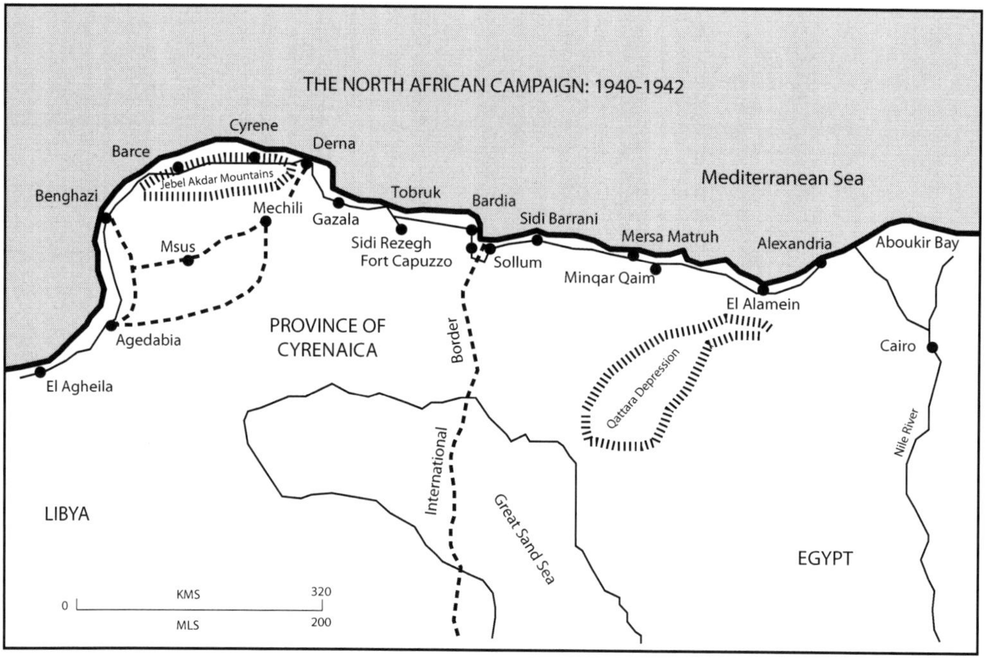

THE NORTH AFRICAN CAMPAIGN: 1940-1942
Cyrene
Barce
Derna
Jebel Akdar Mountains
Benghazi
Tobruk
Bardia
Mediterranean Sea
Mechili
Gazala
Sidi Barrani
Msus
Sidi Rezegh
Fort Capuzzo
Sollum
Mersa Matruh
Alexandria
Aboukir Bay
Minqar Qaim
El Alamein
Agedabia
PROVINCE OF
CYRENAICA
International
Border
Qattara Depression
Cairo
El Agheila
Nile River
LIBYA
Great Sand Sea
EGYPT
0
KMS
320
MLS
200

Chapter 5

Italy invades British Somaliland, Egypt and Greece

Italy strikes in east Africa

One matter which gravely concerned Churchill was the presence of a large Allied force in East Africa, especially in Kenya, awaiting an anticipated Italian attack south from Abyssinia. Churchill wanted many of these men transferred as soon as possible northward to face the more imminent Italian attack in Egypt. There were some 25,000 Allied troops in this region, including Indian troops and part of the 1st South African Division.

Before this could happen, though, Italian forces invaded British Somaliland on 3 August 1940. They advanced quickly and captured a major British position, forcing the commander, General Godwin Austin to order a general withdrawal. This defeat caused general jubilation in Italy and concern in London and Egypt. As a result Churchill ordered the despatch from Britain of four heavy bombing squadrons to the Middle East.

Mussolini had struck his major blow for an expanded Italian Empire in the East.

Italy's invasion of Egypt

On 16 August 1940 Churchill issued a firm and comprehensive directive to the Secretary of State for War and the CIGS[1] concerning various troop movements and realignments in view of the impending attack in Egypt. This directive made it abundantly clear that Churchill saw the defence of Egypt as of paramount importance.[2] The Italians, however, seemed somewhat oblivious to the weakness of the Allied position in Egypt in the middle of 1940.

Although there was a gradual build-up of Italian forces in Libya, the Italian commander in the field Marshal Graziani was still reluctant to attack.[3] In a Memorandum sent by the German ambassador in Rome on 19 August 1940, Count Ciano stated that the hold-up was not due so much to the oppressive summer heat, but to Marshal Graziani needing to develop his plan of action.[4]

When Mussolini then heard in early September that Graziani was still procrastinating, the Duce informed him that if he never attacked 'on Monday he would be replaced.' Ciano recorded that 'Never … has a military operation been undertaken so much against the will

1 Chief Imperial General Staff.

2 Churchill to Secretary of State for War and CIGS, 16 August 1940, in Churchill, W. *Finest Hour*, pp. 428-432.

3 Ciano recorded as much in his diary on 8 August 1940. Ciano, Diaries, p. 281, cited in Churchill, W. *Finest Hour*, p. 469.

4 *Memorandum by the Ambassador in Rome*, Rome, 19 August 1940, Document No. 367, ibid, Vol. X, p. 513.

of the commanders.'[5]

On 13 September 1940 Marshal Graziani sent his troops comprised of six infantry divisions and eight tank battalions streaming into Egypt from Libya. All that was facing him was a significantly smaller British force at Sollum, which then made a slow and orderly withdrawal back to Sidi Barrani, a withdrawal which took four days. Although there were few experienced Allied troops in the region eastward of Sidi Barrani, Marshal Graziani decided to halt there on 16 September and consolidate. His consolidation lasted three months.

Interestingly, despite this clear violation of their sovereignty, the Egyptian Government did not declare war on Italy nor offer its army in any way to help the British to defend Egypt,[6] and this considering the negative attitude which most Egyptians had towards the Italians. If Egypt had done so, there was a strong likelihood there would have been serious ramifications in the future primarily due to the close relationship between Italy and Germany, and the desire of many in Egypt not to be opposed in any way to Germany.

Simultaneous to the Italian incursion Italian planes based in Libya and even in southern Italy, also began bombing civilian targets in Tel Aviv and the large oil refineries near Haifa. Young Alex Carmel, a recent Jewish emigrant from Germany, vividly remembered those raids, and then being sent away from Haifa by his parents to a kibbutz for safety.[7] The danger to the British administration in Palestine was now palpable. The danger to the Jewish community in Palestine also now increased, especially as Italy was allied to Germany.

At this stage of the war, however, there was no coordinated Axis battle plan. The Germans were occupied north of the Alps and the Italians were doing their own thing in the Mediterranean region. One complaint from the Germans was that they had no idea of Mussolini's battle strategy. That Mussolini thought he could manage it all by himself without German involvement is evidenced by his refusal of an offer by Hitler for some German armoured units. This proved to be a very costly refusal.[8]

While Graziani settled down at Sidi Barrani, Mussolini became progressively impatient. He had every right to be impatient, for each day that he waited provided Wavell and O'Connor with the opportunity of bringing their raw colonial recruits, especially the Australians and New Zealanders, up to battle preparedness, and for the much awaited armour to arrive via the Cape.

5 Churchill, W. *Finest Hour*, p. 469.

6 Kirk, G. ibid, pp. 193-98.

7 Interview with the late Alex Carmel, on *The Battle for Zion* documentary, Daystar Ministry, UK.

8 Admiral Raeder informed Hitler on 26 September 1940 that he doubted the ability of the Italians to capture the Suez Canal, and suggested even then some form of German involvement. Hitler subsequently sent General Von Thoma to Libya to ascertain the true picture there. Upon his assessment, when Hitler and Mussolini met at the Brenner Pass on 4 October 1940 Hitler offered Mussolini 'the participation of one armoured division in the Western Desert,' Mussolini declined the offer. See Kirk, G. ibid, p. 106.

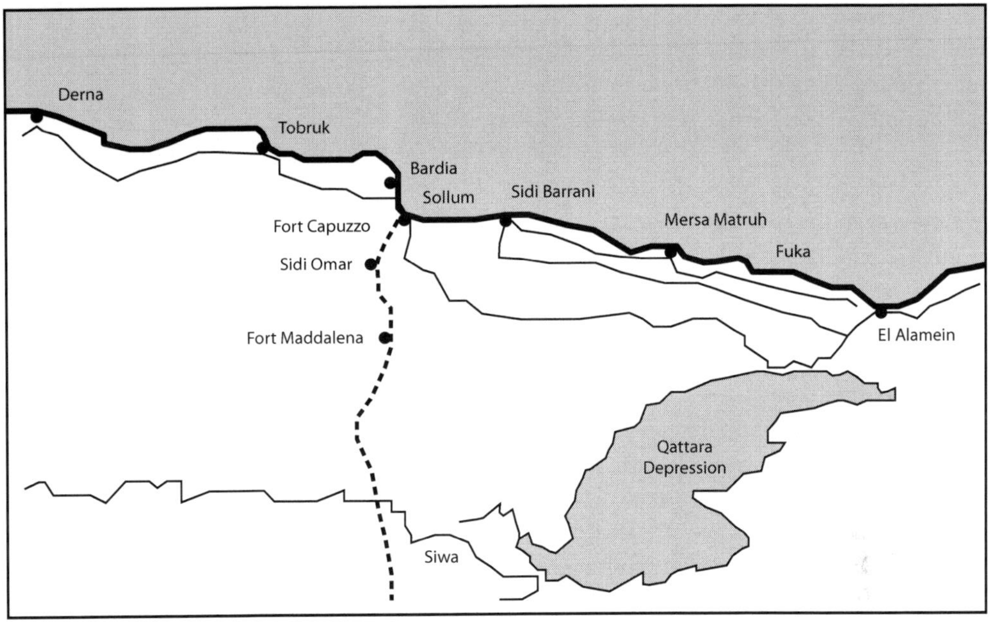

Mussolini invades Greece

While Graziani procrastinated at Sidi Barrani, Mussolini's lust for a grand Italian empire took another twist when on 28 October 1940 he invaded Greece.[9] Churchill explains that the Greeks then 'invoked the guarantee given by Mr. Chamberlain on April 13, 1939, of which, Churchill stated 'we were bound to honour.' Then, following advice from the War Cabinet, and from his own convictions, King George 'replied to the King of the Hellenes: "Your cause is our cause; we shall be fighting against a common foe."' Churchill gave a similar pledge to General Metaxas.[10]

The overall British position is evidenced in a message Churchill shortly after sent to Foreign Secretary Anthony Eden who was then in Cairo, when he stated:

> Greek situation must be held to dominate others now. We are well aware of our slender resources. Aid to Greece must be attentively studied lest whole Turkish position is lost through proof that England never tries to keep her guarantees.[11]

This new development presented Churchill with some fresh strategic problems. If Britain did not honour its agreements with the smaller nations, then other neutral nations, such

9 On that day the Italian Minister in Athens presented the Greek Prime Minister, General Metaxas, an ultimatum to permit an Italian take-over. Simultaneously Italian troops invaded the Greek mainland. Understandably the Greeks refused to accept the Italian ultimatum.

10 Churchill, W. *Finest Hour*, p. 533.

11 Churchill to Eden, 2 November, 1940, in Churchill, W. *Finest Hour*, p. 536.

as Turkey could be swayed to join with the Axis powers. It was imperative from the British perspective that Turkey enter the war on the Allied side. Additionally, if the Italians managed to defeat the Greeks then they would be in a better strategic position to attack British possessions in the Eastern Mediterranean.

Even at this early stage Churchill dreaded a potential German presence in that region, and it was with this consideration in mind that upon agreeing to come to Greece's aid, Britain asked for and received an airfield on the Greek mainland, and obtained permission to utilise Suda Bay on Crete as a naval base.

The arrival of other Commonwealth forces

Following the defeat of France and Italy's entrance into the War, the Australian Government recognized the dangers to the Suez Canal and the link to Britain. They sanctioned the raising of two more divisions for service in the Middle East, the 7th and 9th, and one more division, the 8th for home defense in case Japan entered the war. The 8th Division would defend Australia from Malaya.

Another division ready to depart for the Middle East was the 2nd South African Division, which included Ron Turrel. Turrel wrote about the period prior to his departure:

> My immediate superior was Sergeant-Major "Mo" Oblovitz from Cape Town, and I couldn't have had a better man in that position. He was one of a fair number of Jews who had gravitated to our unit, but he alone felt it to be necessary to change his name – just in case he fell into enemy hands, as, in fact he was going to do in the not so far distant future.[12]

Mo Oblovitz became Mo Raphael!

During the impasse in fighting, while Mussolini was being defeated by the Greeks and in the process incurring the serious dissatisfaction of Adolf Hitler, and while Wavell gathered his strength, most of the 7th and 9th Australian Divisions arrived in the Middle East.

The 7th Australian Division encamped in Palestine in November 1940. Amongst the thousands of new volunteers were Roden Cutler from New South Wales, and Lindsay Bear from Victoria.

Among the thousands of volunteers in the 9th Division was a young South Australian named Thomas Derrick, part of the 2/48th Battalion. Another was Frank Beech of the 2/7th Field Regiment from Western Australia.

Derrick and his mates disembarked at Kantara and headed east. Derrick's diary entry for this day was very succinct, 'Disembarked at Kantara. Entrained there and went 180 miles inland to camping ground. Detrained 2400 hours.'[13] The men of these two divisions now followed the same routine as the men of the 6th Division before them.

12 Turrel, R. ibid, p. 174.
13 Farquhar, M. *Derrick V.C.* (Adelaide, 1982), p. 37.

Sinking of the *Patria*

During these tense months Jewish authorities were trying to smuggle as many Jewish people as possible out of Europe and bring them to Palestine. Colonial Secretary Lord Lloyd had decreed that all such illegal Jewish immigrants were to be deported to the island of Mauritius.

An ironical part of this episode is that the Nazi regime established a special Committee for Sending Jews Overseas, headed up by SS Lieutenant, Adolf Eichmann. The purpose of this Committee was to send some Jewish refugees by boat to Palestine, and by thus doing so embarrass the British authorities there. When the three ships, carrying some 3,600 Jews arrived off Palestine they were indeed apprehended by the British Navy. Most of the occupants were then placed aboard another ship, the *Patria*, which was due to sail with them to Mauritius.

The *Haganah*, however, planned to bomb the ship while it was in Haifa harbour, thereby delaying its departure. Unfortunately the explosives were too strong and the ship sank on 25 November 1940, killing some 267 of those on board. It was a tragedy.

General Wavell informed Churchill, that regardless, the survivors would still be sent to Mauritius, for if they were permitted to remain in Palestine, he stated:

> … it will be spread all over Arab world that Jews have again successfully challenged decision of British Government and that policy of White Paper is being reversed. This will gravely increase prospect of widespread disorders in Palestine.[14]

Churchill was aghast at such a suggestion and overruled it.

The survivors remained in Palestine, while future intercepted 'illegal' Jewish immigrants would be sent to Mauritius, where they mostly remained behind barbed wire for the duration of the war.

14 Wavell to Churchill, telegram of 30 November 1940: Premier papers, 4/51/2, quoted in Gilbert, M. *Churchill and the Jews*, p. 179.

CHAPTER 6
WAVELL'S CAMPAIGN

Italian Navy attacked at Taranto

Admiral Cunningham now had the luxury of having Allied ships based at Gibraltar, Malta, Crete and Alexandria. If he was ever going to neutralise the strong Italian Fleet it had to be now. Accordingly on 11 November 1940 he ordered an attack upon much of the Italian Fleet anchored at Taranto in southern Italy. Amidst the carnage following this assault three of Italy's supreme battleships were damaged, and would be out of operation for at least six months.

This result was a tremendous boon for the British and a tremendous morale loss for the Italians. It was one of three significant blows the Italians were about to encounter. The second of these was in Greece, where by the end of November Mussolini's forces had been heavily defeated and forced back even into neighbouring Albania. Such a defeat finally forced Mussolini to accept a German *Luftwaffe* presence in Italy.[1]

Wavell assaults Sidi Barrani

While the Italians consolidated their position at Sidi Barrani, Wavell waited behind his thinly manned line at Mersa Matruh. Wavell, together with the commander of the Army of the Nile, General Maitland Wilson, however, were not merely waiting for an Italian assault. They were preparing to go onto the offensive.

Wavell and Wilson were determined to keep their plan secret – even from Churchill – lest it become known by the Italians. Churchill for his part was determined to send as much aid to Greece as possible, but Wavell could not oblige without jeopardizing his planned assault. Eden informed Churchill on 1 November:

> We cannot from Middle East forces send sufficient air or land reinforcements to have any decisive influence upon course of fighting in Greece. To send such forces from here, or to divert reinforcements now on their way or approved, would imperil our whole position in the Middle East *and jeopardise plans for an offensive operation now being laid in more than one theatre....*[2]

Wavell, Wilson and Eden also realized that if they were able to inflict a heavy impact upon the Italians in Libya then this would naturally impact the Italian position in Greece – these

1 Ambassador Mackensen to Foreign Ministry, Rome, 11 December, 1940, Document No. 494, ibid, Vol. XI, pp. 844-45.

2 Eden to Churchill, 1 November, 1940, in Churchill, W. *Finest Hour*, p. 537. Italics Churchill's.

plans being formulated before the Greeks defeated the Italians.

The British build-up at Mersa Matruh, according to a German Memorandum became known to the Italian intelligence service, who informed Graziani on 6 December, but he failed to undertake adequate precautions.[3]

Then suddenly on 9 December 1940 the British and Indian forces under the command of General O'Connor attacked the Italians at Sidi Barrani and the following day Italian forces closer to Mersa Matruh were also assaulted. By the evening on 10 December 1940 Sidi Barrani had been captured. During those first few days of fighting some seven thousand Italians were captured.

The British-led force then drove the Italians back past Sollum, over the imposing Halfaya Pass separating Egypt from Libya, and by 15 December 1940 the remainder of the Italian Tenth Army was at Bardia in Cyrenaica, one of the provinces of Libya.[4]

The ousting of the Italians was greeted with considerable enthusiasm in Egypt as the Egyptians preferred a British presence there to an Italian one.

Axis reactions

News of these initial defeats reached Mussolini on 10 December, and according to Ciano, Mussolini was not overly perturbed. When news reached him from Marshal Graziani, however, on 13 December and then again two days later, whereby Graziani stated the possibility of withdrawing to Tripoli, Mussolini became very concerned.[5]

The German Ambassador in Rome, Von Mackensen, reported on 20 December 1940:

> The Duce has given orders that Bardia, which is already encircled, keep fighting to the last, and that the same be done later at Tobruk and Derna, in order to retard the English advance. Since no corresponding combat contingents can be opposed to the superior English armored and motorized forces, he requests that a large armored force, one to two divisions, be sent to Libya for the defense of its western half.[6]

Mussolini's request for German armoured reinforcements revealed the extent of his concern, and also now placed the German High Command into a new and different situation: the possibility of an Italian defeat in North Africa, and how to effectively work in conjunction with the Italian armed forces in 'their' sphere of operations.

3 Report from German General at Italian Armed Forces to High Command of Wehrmacht, 2 January 1941, Rome, Document No. 597, ibid, Vol. XI, p. 1005.

4 Until this point some 38,000 Italians had surrendered, while British and Indian losses were 133 killed, 387 wounded and 8 missing. Churchill, W. *Finest Hour*, p. 614.

5 Churchill, W. *Finest Hour*, pp. 618-9, citing Ciano diary. See also Ambassador Mackensen to German Foreign Ministry, 15 December, 1940, Rome, Document No. 520, ibid, Vol XI, p. 878.

6 Mackensen and Rintelen to German Foreign Ministry, 20 December, 1941, Rome, Document No. 541, ibid, Vol. XI, p. 917.

The Battle for Bardia

At this point the Indian Division was transferred to fight the Italians in Eritrea, and was replaced by the 6th Australian Division, who prepared for Australia's first major action of the War.

One of those preparing for his battle was Signaller Arthur Leggett, who recalled:

> I moved into the Battle of Bardia carrying a field telephone exchange, a Lucas lamp and stand, a telescope and stand, two signalling flags, a quantity of cable, a satchel c/w message pad and pencil as well as my rifle and ammunition. I looked like a mass of signalling gear, with a tin hat on top, moving across the face of the desert and I reckon the Italians could have hit me with an anti-tank shell and it would have bounced off.[7]

Another getting ready for his first combat action was Bob Holt of the 2/3rd Battalion, who wrote:

We were allocated our positions outside Bardia and endeavoured to dig slit trenches but it was just not possible, for six inches to a foot down we struck solid rock. We dug long trenches we could lie full length in. It was hot as billyho through the day, but as cold as charity during the night.[8]

Later he also recorded:

> ... we had sewn a patch of white cloth, so that our own troops following in the dark would recognize us. I understand the device was first used by Australians at Lone Pine on Gallipoli in 1915.[9]

The 7th British Armoured Division had cut off all possible retreat routes for the Italians, so this would be a do or die battle for the Italians holed up inside Bardia.

The battle for Bardia began on 3 January 1941, when some 16,000 Australians as well as some British forces of the 16th British Infantry Brigade, moved towards their objective. The town was surrounded by a thirty kilometre fortified encirclement, manned by an Italian garrison of some 40,000 men.

The intense fighting continued for two solid days, and ended on 5 January. The men, mostly of the 6th Australian Division, had won a resounding victory, of which Holt wrote:

> We saw a lot of fighting in the next three days but we were more highly trained than we knew and out of the 700 men in the battalion at Bardia we lost 5 officers and

7 Leggett, A. *Don't Cry For Me*, p. 122.
8 Holt, B. ibid, p. 35.
9 Holt, B. ibid, p. 40.

61 casualties. "T'was a glorious victory", but I suppose you could have got into an argument about that from the relatives of the 61 casualties. The division put 40,000 of Musso's men into the cage … [10]

In all the 6th Australian Division lost 130 men killed and 326 wounded in this its first battle of the Second World War. Most of the surviving Italians were captured.[11] Other Italians were now holed up in the next major town, Tobruk. These too were hindered from escaping as the 7th British Armoured Corps sealed off all escape routes.

Meanwhile Thomas Derrick and the other men of the recently arrived 7th and 9th Australian Divisions were envious of their brothers in the 6th Division and Derrick recorded in his diary on 6 January 1941, 'Heard 6th Divy had taken Port Bardia. Hope she's right and would like to be giving a hand.'[12]

The Battle for Tobruk

The next objective for the Western Desert Force (later the Eighth Army) was another key port named Tobruk. The main attacking force to assault Tobruk would again be the 6th Australian Division. Signaller Arthur Leggett recalls of the time after the capture of Bardia:

We didn't hang around Bardia. The next day we were on our way to Tobruk eighty miles along the road towards Benghazi.

Tobruk, from our point of view, was similar to Bardia. It was a town snuggling around a harbour below a 300 foot high escarpment. It was fortified by an anti-tank ditch, supplemented by barbed wire and an occasional booby trap, stretching around the town's perimeter and along the top of the escarpment.

The British Armoured Division had already made a sweep from Bardia and was now astride the road leading to Derna on the other side of Tobruk.[13]

Bob Holt reflects upon the move from Bardia:

… we drove the hundred miles to Tobruk in captured transport in comparative comfort though we finished as dry as chips and covered in inches of dust. We immediately proceeded to dig our slit trenches and found the same set of rules as at Bardia – solid rock about a foot down.[14]

As at Bardia an artillery barrage preceded the actual attack. This began in the early hours of

10 Holt, B. ibid, p. 41.

11 According to Churchill 45,000 Italians surrendered. Churchill, W. *Finest Hour*, p. 614.

12 Farquhar, M. *Derrick V.C*, Adelaide, 1982, p. 37.

13 Leggett, A. ibid, p. 124.

14 Holt, B. ibid, p. 53.

21 January 1941. Two days later this crucial port was in Australian hands. The casualties were less than at Bardia, with 49 killed and 306 wounded, while Italian casualties were considerably higher, and included another 27,000 Italian prisoners.[15]

Tobruk was a key town as it could become the forward port, replacing Alexandria, in the thrust towards Benghazi and Tripoli beyond. The reason why Wavell had to press on and not be content just with thwarting the Italian thrust into Egypt was the need to push the Italian forces as far as possible from the Egyptian frontier before any Italian reinforcements arrived.

While some of the Allied troops, including Leggett, then headed towards Derna and Benghazi beyond, those who had been mostly involved in the capture of Tobruk remained behind in the port town. Bob Holt was one of them, and he was soon to discover what the Italians had left behind:

> We moved to the waterfront and made ourselves lean-to's ... Someone fixed up an Italian truck for a few days and we helped ourselves to loads of Vichy water, wine and tins of tuna fish which we dumped alongside our Humpies. The truck was eventually taken from us but by this time we had all the necessities for good living, including a four-gallon aluminium water tin of arak ... The drink is treated with respect by the indigenous people, but not always so by the Australians.[16]

Jewish soldiers from Palestine at Tobruk

Numerous auxiliary troops now crammed into Tobruk. One of these was the 'Jewish Transport Corps' from Palestine. Although ultimately the British did permit 27,000 Palestinian Jewish volunteers, few were permitted into combat roles, so most had to be content with auxiliary units such as transport.

Moses Mosenson was in the 'Jewish Transport Corps' and like Holt, now rested up in Tobruk. One of the first tasks that Mosenson and the Jewish soldiers had there was cleaning up the Jewish synagogue that had been desecrated.

They then happened upon a shelter, where, he later wrote to his wife:

> Some Australians were gathered...as well as some enemy prisoners and English and Scottish boys. When...the Australians noticed the Star of David that I was wearing on my helmet, they welcomed me noisily, drew out their bottles of liquor and we drank together to Palestine and to Australia.[17]

News of the Allied victory in Libya was heavily reported back in the Hebrew and English press in Palestine. The Jewish-owned *Palestine Post* wrote proudly on 27 January 1941:

15 Private John Crombie, died in this action. In 1992 while in Egypt for the 50th anniversary of the battle of El Alamein, I visited his grave at Sollum on the Libyan border.
16 Holt, B. ibid, p. 57.
17 Mosenson, M. *Letters from the Desert,* p. 26.

'Palestinian troops were among those who first entered Bardia and Tobruk, fighting with the Australians...'[18]

The push to Benghazi – and beyond.

The Allied push into Libya continued unabated and men mostly from the 6th Australian Division travelled along the coastal route, the *Via Balboa*, from Derna via Barce towards Benghazi, which they entered on 6 February 1941. Benghazi, the principal town in Cyrenaica, was captured.

General O'Connor sent the 7th British Armoured Division through the central route, from Mechilli then on a south-west route to Msus. This area they captured on 5 February. From Msus they went to the west to cut off the route leading out of Benghazi, and they captured Beda Fomm on 7 February.

With the capture of the strategic positions of Soluch, south of Benghazi and Beda Fomm, the remainder of the Italian army was captured. Leggett wrote of this accomplishment, 'The 7th Armoured Division had made one of the most spectacular cross-country dashes in modern history and cut off the Italians south of Benghazi'.[19] Leggett soon afterwards found himself detailed to take care of the thousands of Italian prisoners which were captured by the enterprising dash of the British armoured division.

While the 6th Australian Division consolidated its positions along the coast down to Benghazi, the 7th British Armoured Division continued onto Agedabia, Mersa Brega and El Agheila. This later position was on the southern edge of the Gulf of Sirte and was effectively the border between the two main Libyan provinces of Cyrenaica and Tripolitania.

The entire Cyrenaica campaign came at a cost of 476 Allied killed, 1225 wounded and 43 missing.[20] In comparison, the entire Italian 10th Army was lost, with some 130,000 captured.

The Jewish community in Benghazi

There was quite a large Jewish community in Benghazi, which under the Italian administration had been mostly left unmolested, despite some anti-Semitic directives in the late 1930's. Shortly after its capture by the Allied force, the *Vaad Leumi*, the National Council of the Jewish people in Palestine, sent the following message to the Jewish communities in Libya:

> It was with unbounded joy that we heard the good news that, by the will of God, the forces of Great Britain had entered the gates of your land and entered your cities victoriously...
>
> Among the victorious British forces are many young Jews, especially in the Palestine units, who will no doubt welcome the opportunity of meeting their Jewish brethren in

18 *The Palestine Post.* 27 January 1941, p. 4. Palestinian invariably referred to Jewish soldiers from Palestine.
19 Leggett, A. ibid, p. 133.
20 Montgomery, B; Deighton, L; Pitt, B, *Alamein and the Desert War*, (London, 1976) p. 14.

your towns. We would ask you to proffer them your friendship.

We once more congratulate you on securing your salvation and liberation through the action of the British Army, and trust that the ties between us will never be severed.[21]

Oddly enough, this was the actual time when Jewish salvation and liberty was being celebrated. It was the time of *Purim*, when the Jewish people recall their salvation from the cruel regime in Persia. This occasion is one of much merriment, and it seems that some Australian soldiers roamed the streets of Benghazi and stumbled across one Jewish household which was celebrating this festival of deliverance. They were invited in by the Ben Dusa family to join the festivities.

Later Moses Mosenson was invited by the same Jewish family to enjoy a Shabbat meal with them. Unfortunately the same Australian soldiers, obviously in search of some gaiety, also turned up. Mosenson attempted to get these obstinate soldiers to leave, but they refused, and even refused to believe that Mosenson was actually a Jewish soldier from Palestine.

In response one of the soldiers stated, 'Listen boy all of us were in Palestine and we like Jews. But a little while ago they had a big celebration here. They sang and drank and invited us too. We want to join you tonight.'

Well they had a good sense of direction that was for sure, as they had been to a big celebration at the Ben Dusa house before. Unfortunately the Shabbat meal was not the same kind of occasion. 'Finally,' Mosenson continued, 'I persuaded them to leave and we continued singing our Sabbath hymns.'[22]

Meanwhile as Cyrenaica was being captured men of the New Zealand Division in Egypt and the other Australian Divisions in camps back in Palestine were getting restless. Derrick recorded, 'Seen in the local rag the fall of Derna. Doesn't look like us getting a go at the ding.'

Shortly after he wrote again after the fall of Benghazi: 'When will we get a move? Been wondering if we are going to help at all.'[23] Derrick's desire to be involved would soon be fulfilled.

21 Quoted in *The Palestine Post,* 19 February 1941, p. 3.
22 Mosenson, M. *Letters from the Desert,* p. 42.
23 Farquhar, M. ibid, p. 41.

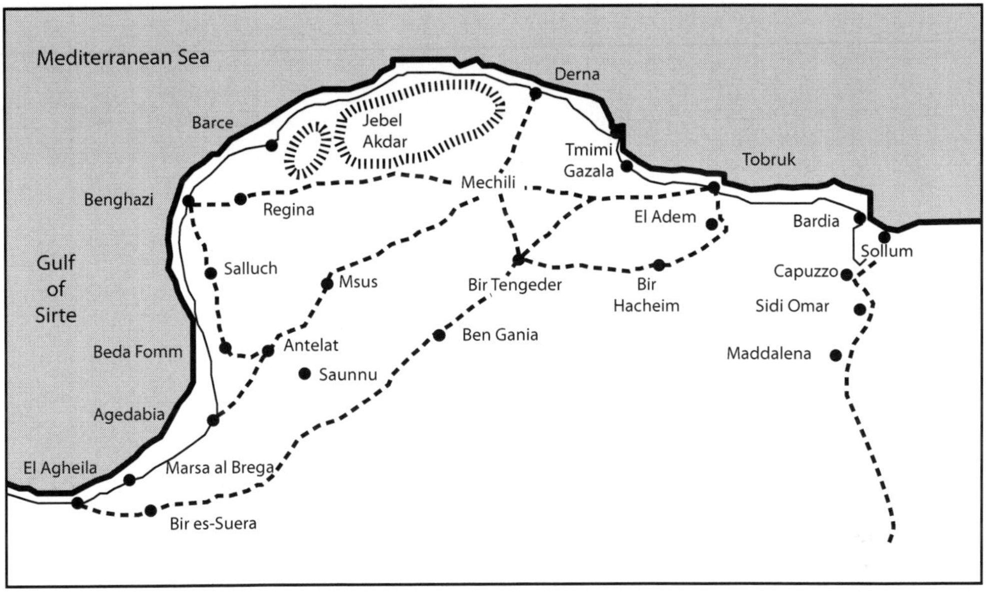

Mediterranean Sea
Derna
Barce
Jebel
Akdar
Tmimi
Gazala
Tobruk
Benghazi
Mechili
Regina
El Adem
Bardia
Sollum
Gulf
of
Sirte
Salluch
Msus
Bir Tengeder
Bir
Hacheim
Capuzzo
Sidi Omar
Ben Gania
Beda Fomm
Antelat
Maddalena
Saunnu
Agedabia
El Agheila
Marsa al Brega
Bir es-Suera

CHAPTER 7

IRAQI AND ARAB NATIONALIST CONTACT WITH NAZI GERMANY

The Mufti in Baghdad and Iraqi approaches to Germany

While in Baghdad, Haj Amin had been granted considerable autonomy and freedom of movement, as well as being financially well rewarded for his presence. He was strongly encouraged by the pro-German group (especially the 'Golden Square') to agitate for an active German involvement in Iraq, as well as continuing with his anti-Jewish propaganda.

The entrance of Italy into the War caused considerable concern for many Arab nationalists in the region. Germany had determined that the Middle East and Eastern Mediterranean region was the Italian sphere of interest, but the Arab nationalists were very sceptical of Italian aspirations and ambitions. They did not want to see British and French imperialism ousted from the region only to see Italy usurp that position. Such sentiments are evidenced by the words of the Iraqi Minister of Justice Naji Shawkat who met with the German Ambassador to Turkey, Von Papen, in Istanbul, on 6 July 1940:

> As the Arab national movement had fought Anglo-French imperialism, so it would have to oppose Italian imperialism. It was therefore to the interest of the Axis Powers for Germany to use her influence with Italy, in order to support a solution that would be compatible with the interests of the Arab movement.[1]

Many Iraqis and Arab nationalists wanted Germany to take a leading role, and they wanted Germany to fully support and endorse their aspirations. In exchange for such German support and endorsement the Arab nationalists would support the Axis powers. The Iraqi Minister informed Von Papen that Germany 'would undoubtedly receive the support of the Iraq Army against England when the time came.'[2]

The Mufti, representing the Arab nationalist movement, also contacted Von Papen, with a letter introducing his private secretary whom Haj Amin was sending to the Axis capitals to express the sentiments of the Arab nationalist movement and many Iraqi politicians.

After having congratulated the Germans on their successes, Haj Amin stated:

> Palestine, which has for the past 4 years been fighting the democracies and international Jewry, is ready at any time to assume an active role and redouble her efforts both at home and in the other Arab countries. The Arab people, slandered, maltreated, and deceived

1 The Ambassador in Turkey to the Foreign Minister, 6 July 1940, Document No. 125, ibid, Vol. 9, p. 142.
2 The Ambassador in Turkey to the Foreign Minister, 6 July 1940, Document No. 125, ibid, Vol. 9, p. 142.

by our common enemies, confidently expect that the result of your final victory will be their independence and complete liberation, as well as the creation of their unity, when they will be linked to your country by a treaty of friendship and collaboration.[3]

Herein lay the seeds of a future relationship between the Arab nationalist movement, and its undisputed spokesman Haj Amin el-Husseini, and the Nazi German Government. Haj Amin was seeking 'a treaty of friendship and collaboration.' He was now sending his private secretary to Berlin and Rome 'in order to initiate the preliminary negotiations with a view to a close and direct collaboration between the Arab countries and the Axis.'[4] Shortly later the Mufti's secretary met with Von Papen in Ankara, and presented the Mufti's requests to this senior German diplomat.[5]

The German Government, however, was initially somewhat reticent to take the Arab nationalist movement under its protection, as it did not want to jeopardize its relationship with its ally, Italy.[6] Germany's reticence became evident with the despatch of a Top Secret Circular to its embassies and legations on 20 August 1940. The Circular stated:

> Germany pursues no political interests in the Mediterranean area, whose southern and eastern part is formed by the Arab world. Germany will therefore let Italy take the lead in the political reorganization of the Arab area. This consequently rules out any German claim to political leadership, or the sharing of leadership with Italy in the Arab territories, which consist of the Arabian peninsula, Egypt, Palestine, Transjordan, Syria-Lebanon, and Iraq.[7]

The Circular went on to state, however, that this did not mean that Germany was not interested or was not to be involved, but that all matters needed to be settled 'in concert with Italy.' It was imperative, though, that these instructions not be divulged with others, especially 'Arab personalities.' Concerning such Arab personalities, the Circular stated, 'It was desirable on every occasion to stress to them the common German and Arab interest in England's defeat, and assure them of Germany's full sympathy in their people's fight for liberation.'[8]

3 *The Ambassador in Turkey to the Foreign Minister*, 6 July 1940, Document No. 125, ibid, Vol. IX, p. 144.
4 *The Grand Mufti to the Ambassador in Turkey*, Baghdad, 22 July 1940, Document No. 209, ibid, Vol. X, p. 275.
5 *The Ambassador in Turkey to the Foreign Minister*, Therapia, 6 August 1940, Document No. 289, ibid, Vol. X, pp. 415-6. Von Papen also stated that these complex questions would be further discussed in Rome and Berlin. The secretary also stated that with diplomatic relations restored with Germany the Iraqi Government would depose the pro-British Foreign Minister Nuri Said.
6 The official viewpoint of the Reich is summed up in a Memorandum that Herr Woerman sent on 21 July 1940 whereby he points out that the '... Area of the Mediterranean and Near East (the Arab world) was under the jurisdiction of the Italians.' See Memorandum by the Director of the Political Department, Berlin 21 July 1940, Document No. 200, ibid, Vol. X, p. 261.
7 *Circular of the Foreign Ministry*, Berlin, 20 August, 1940, Document No. 370, ibid, Vol. X, p. 515.
8 *Circular of the Foreign Ministry*, Berlin, 20 August, 1940, Document No. 370, ibid, Vol. X, p. 516.

The Arab nationalist request to Germany

The Mufti's secretary Osman Haddad, met with Fritz Grobba of the Ministry of Foreign Affairs in Berlin on 26 August 1940. Haddad delivered a personal message from the Mufti, reiterating the dissatisfaction of many in Iraq concerning the decision by Foreign Minister Nuri as-Said to sever diplomatic relations with Germany. At that time, the secretary stated, Iraq was threatened by the presence of the French Army of the Orient and British troops stationed in the country.

Haddad also mentioned that a 'committee for collaboration among the Arab countries has been formed in Iraq under the chairmanship of the Grand Mufti' which included a number of notable Arab men. This Committee, Haddad stated, 'had decided some months ago that it should seek to establish contact with Germany.'[9] Since that initial decision, the situation in the Middle East had changed, primarily due to the defeat of France. This defeat meant there was no longer a threat from the Army of the Orient, and that many of the British troops and aircraft formerly based in Iraq had been transferred to Egypt. The Iraq Army itself had now also grown numerically and in equipment.

As a consequence of the above mentioned points, Iraq had now felt emboldened to refuse the transfer of British and Indian troops through their country, from India and from other regions of the Indian Ocean.[10]

The 'Arab Committee' as alluded to by Haddad, then put forward a proposal to be submitted to both the Italian and German Governments, in which they stated their desire for both the Axis Governments to declare, in writing, their accord with:

a) the expressed wish of the Iraq Government to restore diplomatic relations with Germany…
b) the willingness of the Iraq Government to accord to Germany and Italy a preferred position with respect to the exploitation of Iraq mineral resources …
c) the willingness of the Iraq Government to offer its good offices to enable Germany and Italy to achieve a like understanding with the other Arab countries, especially Syria, Palestine, Transjordan, and Saudi Arabia.[11]

Once agreed upon in principle, Haddad stated, the 'Arab Committee' wanted negotiations to begin, in Ankara, and then a secret agreement to be made between the three governments. Once this was done, then they would orchestrate a 'general uprising in Transjordan and Palestine' where 'Up to 10,000 men and the required number of officers will be made

9 *Memorandum by an Official of the Foreign Ministry*, Berlin, 27 August, 1940, Document No. 403, ibid, Vol. X, p. 556. This Committee including a number of men from the Iraqi Cabinet and Army, as well as representatives from Syria and Saudi Arabia, and the Mufti being the representative of the Arabs of Palestine.

10 Some of these troops were from British Somaliland where the Italians had defeated them. It was felt safer to take them to Egypt via Iraq rather than the Red Sea as this was then deemed unsafe. Britain complained that Iraq's refusal was a violation of the Anglo-Iraq Treaty of Alliance, but the Iraqis countered this.

11 *Memorandum by an Official of the Foreign Ministry*, Berlin, 27 August, 1940, ibid, p. 558.

available.' Weaponry would need to be supplied by the Italians from the stockpile of the French Army of the Orient from Syria, 'which are to be surrendered to Italy in accordance with the French-Italian armistice agreement.' Finances would also be required for such an uprising, the majority of which they were expecting Germany and Italy to provide.

To ensure the Axis Powers realized there was something definitely tangible for them, the 'Arab Committee' also wrote:

> There are still 30,000 to 40,000 English troops in Palestine, which the Arabs believe they can handle.[12]
>
> Tying down these troops in Palestine and preventing the shipment of Anglo-Indian troops from India, Bahrain, or Aden to Egypt will substantially relieve Italy's military situation in the eastern Mediterranean.[13]

This proposal from the 'Arab Committee' was tantamount to treason as it was a clear violation of the existing Anglo-Iraq Treaty. On 27 August 1940 the German Foreign Ministry drafted the following response to these overtures from the 'Arab Committee' in Iraq:

> I. The German and Italian Governments recognize the full independence of the Arab countries which are already independent or under French mandate (Syria and Lebanon) or under British mandate and protectorate (Transjordan, Palestine ...)
>
> II. Germany and Italy recognize the right of the Arab countries to shape their national unity in accordance with their wishes...
>
> III. Germany and Italy recognize the right of the Arab countries to solve the question of the Jewish elements in Palestine and the other Arab countries in a manner that conforms to the national and ethnic interests of the Arabs, and to the solution of the Jewish question in the countries of Germany and Italy.
>
> IV. Germany and Italy have no imperialistic designs with respect to Egypt and Sudan...
>
> V. Germany and Italy have no greater wish than to see each Arab nation enjoying abundant prosperity and taking its historical and natural place in the sun...[14]

The 'Arab Committee' was operating without the full backing of the Iraq Government, but its power base was considerable, as evidenced by a further more in-depth Memorandum sent by Haj Amin in September 1940, which he stated had the agreement of 'the Iraq

12 Most of those troops at that time were not in fact English (read British), but were Australian, with some New Zealand and Polish.

13 *Memorandum by an Official of the Foreign Ministry*, Berlin, 27 August, 1940, ibid, p. 559.

14 *Memorandum by an Official of the Foreign Ministry*, Berlin, 27 August, 1940, Document No. 403, ibid, Vol. X, p. 560. There were several clauses later added. See Footnotes 4 and 5.

Government (except for Nuri as-Said), the Saudi Arabian Government, and leading statesmen of Syria…'[15] The Memorandum was basically a call for the Axis Powers to recognize, amongst many issues:

a) The independence of the Arab countries, including Syria, Palestine with Transjordan, Egypt, the Sudan, as well as the border regions of the Arabian Peninsula, which are under an English Protectorate, including Aden as an integral part of Yemen.

Among the many clauses within this Memorandum, two are of particular interest:

1.d) Right of the Arab countries to solve the Jewish question in the national and racial interest on the German-Italian model.

5) Organize against England a large scale rebellion in Palestine-Transjordan, with its base in Syria, with captured French equipment and financial support from the Axis Powers up to half of the required amount, that is, up to some 20,000 pounds sterling, in gold.[16]

This Memorandum confirmed the previous communiques and was regarded as an official request to the German Government. The State Secretary, Weizsacker wrote, 'The Reich Government takes a positive stand on this matter … but it would only proceed in agreement with Italy.'[17] The request was then duly referred to the German Embassy in Rome in order to be discussed with the Italians.

Several days later, on 12 September 1940, the Iraq Minister of Justice, Naji Shawkat, also requested that the Reich Government 'associate itself in written form with the written declaration of the Italian Government regarding the independence of the Arab states of Iraq, Transjordan, Palestine and Syria.' Only with this statement, the Minister stated, could they 'foment immediately new disorders in Palestine.' Secretary Weizsacher was again very positive concerning this potential new ally against the Allied position in the Middle East.[18]

Official German support

Foreign Minister Ribbentrop agreed on 24 September 1940 in principle to the request by the Mufti of Jerusalem,[19] and the Foreign Ministry thereupon worked on an oral statement of agreement, which would be broadcast in Arabic on the radio. The proposed statement was conveyed to Haj Amin's secretary, and said:

Germany's desire has always been that the Arab countries should rid themselves of

15 State Secretary to Ambassador von Mackensen, 9 September 1940, Document No 35, telegram No 1232, ibid, p. 44.

16 State Secretary to Ambassador von Mackensen, 9 September 1940, ibid, p. 45.

17 State Secretary to Ambassador von Mackensen, 9 September, 1940, ibid, p. 45.

18 State secretary to Embassy in Italy, 12 September 1940, document No 51, telegram No 1253, ibid, p. 65-6.

19 Reference was made to this decision, but the original document was not located.

English and French rule, enjoy greater autonomy than heretofore, and achieve complete independence. The Arab countries may therefore count on Germany's full sympathy in their efforts to attain this goal.[20]

The Iraqi Government was also awaiting the outcome of these discussions, as it desired to re-establish diplomatic ties with Germany.[21] Interestingly, though, this overture to Germany did not necessitate an automatic relationship with the Nazi power, as they had also considered the possibility of the Soviet Union being their senior partner. The Mufti's private secretary stated the following to the German Foreign Ministry:

> Examining the possibility of making use of the present world situation to achieve complete independence of the Arab countries, the Arab leaders had also studied the question whether a collaboration with Soviet Russia would be advisable. They had rejected this idea, however, as Soviet Russia's striving toward a warm water port, constituted a threat to the Arab countries, and as the Communist system was unacceptable to Mohammedans. They [the Arab leaders] had decided, therefore, to try a rapprochement with the Axis Powers. If, however, they saw their independence threatened by Italy, they might possibly consider alignment with Soviet Russia as the lesser evil, since they would presumably enjoy greater independence as a Soviet Republic than under Italian rule.[22]

It appears that the Iraqis and other Arab nationalists were looking for the highest bidder in their quest to oust the British and the French from the region, and it appeared that they preferred Nazi Germany above all the other possible candidates.

Once tacit German support had been gained the Mufti turned his attention to the Italians. Through the influence of the Germans, the Italian Government agreed to host the Mufti's private secretary. Also, Von Mackensen informed the Foreign Ministry on 2 October 1940, that, 'The Italian Government will inform the Iraq Minister President through its Minister in Baghdad that the Reich Government agreed to Iraq's resumption of diplomatic relations …'[23]

Although Italy was willing to offer support to the Arab nationalist movement, she was not as yet willing to accept what the Mufti sought, 'a federation of the Arab countries.'

20 Memorandum by the Director of the Political Department, 28 September 1940, Document No 127, ibid, p. 220. The text of this statement was later changed to, "Germany has always followed with interest the struggle of the Arab countries to attain their independence. In their striving toward this goal, the Arab countries will be able in the future also to count upon the full sympathy of Germany." See Weizsacher to German Embassy in Italy, Document No 133, telegram 1367, 30 September 1940, ibid, p. 228.

21 It was obvious in this correspondence that the Italian Minister in Baghdad had given the Iraqis a false indication of Italian support and sympathy for the Arab independence movement. The Italians did, however, later concur with such sentiments.

22 Memorandum by an Official of the Foreign Ministry, Document No 134, 30 September 1940, ibid, pp. 228-9.

23 Ambassador Mackensen to Foreign Ministry, Document No 143, telegram No 1785, 2 October 1940, ibid, pp. 238-39.

The Germans thereupon decided not to endorse this request by Haj Amin in deference to their erstwhile ally.[24]

German position concerning the Arab world

Notwithstanding their reluctance to offer written support of this 'federation of the Arab countries' Germany was willing to offer tacit support for the Arab struggle. On 23 October 1940 the following statement was read in Arabic on the German radio:

> Germany, which has always been animated by sentiments of friendship for the Arabs and cherishes the wish that they may prosper and be happy and assume a place among the peoples of the earth in accordance with their historic and natural importance, has always watched with interest the struggle of the Arab countries to achieve their independence. In their efforts to attain this goal the Arab countries can count upon Germany's full sympathy also in the future. In making this statement, Germany, finds herself in full accord with her Italian ally.[25]

This was the first official step, and although it fell short of what the Arab nationalist leaders were seeking, it was at least a beginning in this attempt by Haj Amin and others to establish a firm political relationship between them and Nazi Germany.

Haj Amin's *Memorandum* on behalf of the Arab nationalist movement provoked the German Foreign Ministry into action. They put together their own Memorandum (entitled a 'Brief') concerning *German Policy in Arabia* for a Conference on 9 December 1940. In this 'Brief' they stated that 'Germany saw in Arab nationalism her natural ally, while Italy finds the latter irksome…'

As Germany had given Italy the political lead in the Arab Middle East though, Germany needed to be wise in her position, and hence the reason why there was merely 'an *oral* statement to the effect that we *were watching with interest the struggle of the Arabs for independence and would continue to sympathize with their efforts to achieve freedom*.'[26]

The German 'Brief' also stated that there was general unrest in Syria and Iraq. Concerning Iraq, the Memo stated that the German oral statement of support was insufficient in order to assist Iraq make a stand against the British initiatives there. The British, it was stated, were aware of rapprochement between Iraq and the Axis, and were willing to step in and stop it.

In the wake of the recent Italian military defeats Italian prestige in the East had suffered, which resulted in an increase in British prestige. This situation, unless checked, would not auger well for Germany in the future.

24 Weizsacher to Embassy in Italy, Document No. 160, telegram No 1401, 6 October 1940, ibid, Vol. XI, p. 269.
25 This same text later appeared in German newspapers and was transmitted from Ambassador von Papen in Ankara to the Iraq Minister Gaylani on 2 January 1941. See Von Papen to Foreign Ministry, 2 January 1941, Document No. 596, telegram A5683, ibid, Vol. XI, p. 1005.
26 *Brief for the Conference in the Office of the State Secretary on December 9, 1940*, Document No. 481, ibid, Vol. XI, p. 826.

The 'Brief' made some interesting observations concerning Egypt, stating:

> The older officials and rich families are for the most part pro-English, the younger officials and officers of the insignificant Egyptian Army probably pro-German. The lower classes are not interested in politics. The goal of Egyptian policy is to keep the country out of the war and preserve its outward independence.[27]

The conclusion of this 'Brief' was very significant when considering present and future German attitudes:

> We have no reason at all to be sentimental about these people who are basically anti-European and torn by religious, family, and tribal differences. But the Arabs, as inhabitants of the land-bridge and routes leading to southern and eastern Asia as well as East Africa, and as the foremost representatives of Islam in the world are a tremendously important power factor. Germany must not jeopardize her great prestige here if she does not wish to suffer most severe reverses for a long time to come.[28]

The 'Brief' again highlighted the possible alignment of Arab nations to the British *if* Germany did not now take more of a leading role on behalf of the Axis Powers. If Germany were to do this, they had to do so without upsetting the Italians. Hence among the six proposals then put forward for furthering German involvement with the Arab nations, there were several which included joint German-Italian representation, such as the sending of a German Armistice delegation to Vichy controlled Syria to join the Italian delegation there. Such a delegation would actually provide the opportunity of numerous leading Germans to be actively present 'legally' in Syria.

One of the proposals for future German involvement, proposal 6, was very ominous for the welfare of the Jewish people in Iraq, and indeed the Middle East:

> In general, the Arab world could be promised a solution of the Jewish question that it would find tolerable. As a result of this and the suggestion of the possibility of creating a Greater Syrian state, very great difficulties would probably arise for the English in Palestine.[29]

It was already clear what Hitler saw as the 'solution of the Jewish question', and what Haj Amin's policy was for a 'solution of the Jewish question'. The danger now was of the possibility of there being unison of both entities on how to deal with the Jewish problem in Palestine.

27 *Brief*, ibid, p. 828.
28 *Brief*, ibid, p. 828.
29 *Brief*, ibid, p. 829.

Positive responses to Germany's statement

The German oral statement of support which had been aired on the radio engendered immediate responses throughout the Arab world. In a *Memorandum by the Head of Political Division VII* of the German Foreign Ministry on 11 December 1940, it was written that the statement, 'has met with a vigorous response in the entire Arab world.'[30]

Following recommendations from certain Arab circles the same statement of support was then published in the German press on 5 December 1940. These Arab circles also suggested that the same statement of support now be specifically given to the Iraqi Government in writing, to strengthen the hand of Prime Minister Rashid Ali al-Gaylani as he attempted to steer the government into a firm pro-Axis position. It was imperative that the Iraqi Government be assured of German support as the British ambassador in Baghdad was now threatening the Iraqi government that they were becoming too pro-Axis.

As far as Iraq was concerned, as sympathetic as the government may have been to the German position, they would not make any significant political changes unless there was a definite German show of support. The British had forces on either side, in Palestine and Egypt and in India, and the Iraqi Army was not at that point a match for these British forces. In view of these considerations the German Foreign Ministry now proposed that the German Reich officially provide such tangible expressions of support.[31]

The British-led campaign in Libya

Political alignments had much to do with the prevailing military situation. The Italian setbacks in 1940 had seriously dented the prestige of the Axis. From the beginning of 1941 this dynamic increased, for with each Allied victory over Italy in Libya, Axis prestige further diminished in the Arab world. Many Arab leaders may have detested the British (and the French) but at that stage there was no viable Axis alternative. Such attitudes were expressed in a Memorandum by the Director of the Political Department on 3 January 1941, in which Woermann stated, 'The English offensive in Egypt naturally had a certain influence on sentiment in Iraq.'[32]

What was at stake here was of tremendous importance for the balance of power throughout the Middle East. If Germany would openly support Iraq and even become militarily involved in that strategically located land, then the entire region over night could become anti-British. Such a situation would not benefit any people groups regarded as being pro-British, particularly the Jewish people.

Interestingly, on 2 January 1941, Ambassador von Papen in Turkey delivered the statement of German intent to the Iraqi Prime Minister al-Gaylani.[33] With this statement

30 *Memorandum by the Head of Political Division VII*, 11 December 1940, Document No. 496, ibid, Vol. XI, p. 846.

31 *Memorandum*, ibid, p. 847.

32 Memorandum by the Director of the Political Department, 3 January 1941, Document No. 601, ibid, Vol. XI, p. 1013.

33 Ambassador von Papen in Ankara to the Iraq Minister Kamil Gaylani on 2 January 1941. See Von Papen to Foreign Ministry, 2 January 1941, Document No. 596, telegram A5683, ibid, Vol. XI, p. 1005. This was the same text which had previously appeared in German newspapers.

Gaylani could now begin to manoeuvre towards a political realignment in Iraq.

German Armistice Commission

The possibility of German infiltration into Syria was different to Iraq. Syria was controlled by the Vichy Government which although, neutral, was at least in a diplomatic relationship with Germany. The Germans desired to send a delegation to Syria in order to determine the true situation there. The only possible way would be to send a delegation of the German Armistice Commission. Following an initial rebuttal, the French authorities authorised Herr Hentig to lead a group of the German Armistice Commission to Syria, although the French maintained that the timing 'was inopportune.'[34] The assignment given to Hentig was:

a) To report on the political and military situation in Syria and, so far as possible, the neighbouring areas. Does England constitute a serious threat to Syria by way of Palestine? Are the resources of France adequate for defense? What progress is being made by the de Gaulle movement? What are the methods with which English propaganda is operating and what success does it have?
b) To gather relevant data for our policy toward the Arab states.
c) To observe Germany's own interests of an economic and cultural nature and to report on them.[35]

The German Armistice Commission offered the Germans a legitimate opportunity of sending a delegation to the Middle East, but Hentig was instructed that he was not to do anything to harm German-Vichy French relationships.[36] Unfortunately the presence of Germans in the area did trigger off anti-French sentiment, and many people were killed as a result.

The Mufti's letter to Hitler

As a result of the positive German announcements (on the radio and in the newspapers) Haj Amin wrote a very detailed letter directly to Hitler on 20 January 1941, part of which said:

> …By a geographical coincidence, the Arab people find themselves at the center of the land and sea crossroads, which form, according to the English, the principal hub of "Imperial British communications." For this reason, no means were spared to create perpetual obstacles hampering the freedom and development of the Arab people…[37]

34 State Secretary Weizsacher to Herr Hentig at German Embassy in Turkey, 8 January 1941, Document No. 626, telegram No 15, ibid, Vol. XI, p. 1053.
35 State Secretary Weizsacher to Herr Hentig at German Embassy, 8 January, 1941, ibid, p. 1054.
36 Unfortunately Herr Hentig's subsequent visit triggered off numerous disturbances which left some 100 people dead. See Memorandum by Minister Hahn, 30 July 1941, Document No. 165, ibid, Vol. XIII, pp. 252-53.
37 The Grand Mufti to Adolf Hitler, Baghdad, January 20, 1941, Document No. 680, ibid, Vol. XI, p. 1152.

Haj Amin then launched into a detailed analysis of the perfidy of British and French imperialism in Iraq, Syria, Egypt and Arabia. He retained most of his venom however for the situation of Palestine, part of which is recorded below:

> Now ... there comes Palestine. Her cause, Your excellency, is well known to you because she, too, has had to suffer from the perfidy of the English. It is a case of creating an obstacle to the unity and independence of the Arab countries by pitting them directly against the Jews of the entire world, dangerous enemies, whose secret arms are money, corruption, and intrigues, in addition, moreover, to the bayonets of the British. For 20 years now we have been face to face with these various forces. Armed with an invincible faith in their cause, the Arabs of Palestine, have fought with the most rudimentary means. The question of Palestine, moreover, has united all the Arab countries in a common hatred for the English and the Jews. If a common enemy is the prelude to the formation of national unity, one may say that the Palestine problem has hastened this unity. From the international point of view, the Jews of the entire world have given their allegiance to England in the hope that, if she is victorious, she will be able to make their dreams come true in Palestine and even in the neighboring Arab countries. If the Arabs are aided in defeating the Zionist aims, the Jews, and especially those in the United States, will be so demoralised at seeing the object of their dream fade into nothingness that they will lose their enthusiasm for aiding Great Britain and will retreat before the catastrophe.[38]

It would almost seem that the Mufti was quoting from sections of *Mein Kampf*! After then analysing the situation in the various countries, Haj Amin then collated his presentation and expressed that:

> The warmest sympathy of the Arab peoples for Germany and the Axis is now and henceforth an established fact. No propaganda can change this truth. Freed from certain material impediments, the Arab peoples are everywhere prepared to act, as is proper, against the common enemy and to take their stand with enthusiasm on the side of the Axis to do their part in the well-deserved defeat of the Anglo-Jewish coalition.
>
> Arab nationalism owes to Your Excellency a debt of gratitude and of recognition for having again and again brought up in ringing speeches the question of Palestine. I am anxious here to reiterate my thanks to Your Excellency and to assure Your excellency of the sentiments of friendship, of sympathy, and of admiration which the Arab people pledges to Your Excellency, great Fuhrer, and to the courageous German people.[39]

Haj Amin then mentioned that he was sending again his private secretary to Rome and Berlin 'in order to initiate in the name of the strongest and largest Arab organization and

38 The Grand Mufti to Adolf Hitler, Baghdad, January 20, 1941, Document No. 680, ibid, Vol. XI, pp. 1153-54.
39 The Grand Mufti to Adolf Hitler, Baghdad, 20 January, 1941, Document No. 680, ibid, Vol. XI, pp. 1154.

in my own name the negotiations necessary for sincere and loyal cooperation in all fields.'[40]

Shortly later the Mufti's private secretary was in Ankara en-route initially from Rome, and informed the German Embassy that Nuri as-Said, the pro-British Iraqi Foreign Minister had resigned, thereby opening the way for a pro-Axis Government. This news however was not to be broadcast for fear of a British reaction. 'The Iraq Government' Von Papen wrote 'is now prepared to cooperate with us in every way.' Von Papen also recorded that the secretary expressed the opinion that arms would best be sent to Iraq via Russia and Iran.[41]

The time had possibly come for a serious German investment into Iraq. A serious German investment in Iraq though would naturally cause much concern for the large and vibrant Jewish community which lived there and elsewhere. The combination of Nazi ideology with the ideology of people such as Haj Amin would not benefit the Jewish people in Iraq.

Any potential German involvement in Iraq took a step backwards when following pressure from Emir Abdul-Illah, al-Gaylani resigned his position as prime minister on 31 January 1941, and a pro-British Government came into power. Such a government was good – so long as the British-led forces continued to win victories in Libya.

40 The Grand Mufti to Adolf Hitler, Baghdad, 20 January, 1941, Document No. 680, ibid, Vol. XI, pp. 1154-55.
41 Von Papen to Foreign Ministry, 28 January 1941, Document No. 722, telegram No. 78, ibid, Vol. XI, p. 1215.

Chapter 8

Germany re-enters the Middle East

Germany considers supporting her ally

The Jewish community of Iraq was fortunate that at this very same time Germany was considering investing in another part of the Middle East. In a Memorandum from the German Embassy in Rome on 30 December 1940, it was revealed by Herr Bismarck that the defeats in Libya had seriously influenced Italian attitudes towards German involvement in the Mediterranean. Bismarck stated:

> From a number of statements of Italian political and military personages that have come to me, I gather that under the impact of Italy's failures, there is a growing conviction of the need for a closer military collaboration between Italy and Germany.[1]

Bismarck concluded his Memorandum by clearly stating, 'I have reached the conviction that strong German influence on the Italian conduct of the war is absolutely necessary.'[2] Other senior ranking Germans too were reaching the same conclusion. On that same day the German Ambassador in Rome discussed this issue with the heads of the various German military departments in Italy, and they 'had decided to urge the Reich Foreign Minister that on the German side they exert influence on the Italian conduct of the war and on the military situation in the Mediterranean.'[3]

A top secret report by General von Rintelen, the Wehrmacht General attached to the Italian Armed Forces, issued on 2 January 1941 was quite scathing in its analysis of the reasons for the Italian defeat, stating that as a consequence:

> The failure hitherto of the Italian armed forces in almost all areas has produced great *disappointment and a crisis of confidence*, not only among the soldiers, but among the people as a whole. The supreme military and political leader, the Duce, is being reproached for having given the Army tasks without providing it with the necessary means for carrying them out.[4]

The report admitted that such criticism was valid, and cited, amongst other matters,

1 *Memorandum* by Bismarck, 30 December 1940, Rome, Document No. 583, ibid, Vol. XI, p. 984.

2 *Memorandum* by Bismarck, 30 December 1940, Rome, Document No. 583, ibid, Vol. XI, p. 987.

3 *Memorandum* by Bismarck, 30 December 1940, Rome, Document No. 583, ibid, Vol. XI, Footnote 7, p. 987, citing the draft entry in the War Diary of the Wehrmacht Operations Staff (Dec 1, 1940 – Mar. 24, 1941), and the entry for 28 January 1941.

4 Report from German General at Italian Armed Forces to High Command of Wehrmacht, 2 January 1941, Rome, Document No. 597, ibid, Vol. XI, p. 1008.

Mussolini's previous refusal to accept a German tank division. As a consequence of this latest military set-back, the report stated 'one can now often hear it said by Italians, including officers, although not as yet by responsible authorities, that they *wished there were exercise of German influence* and a German supreme war command.' They had, however, now asked for some German assistance, and, the report continues, that if this request is granted, 'we must demand a voice in the conduct of the operations, so that the arms assistance we give is also used in the right way for the achievement of the war aim.'[5]

Ribbentrop broached the matter with Hitler on 9 January 1941, but Hitler 'declined to undertake anything which might offend the Duce and thereby lead to the loss of the most valuable binding element of the Axis, namely the mutual trust of the Chiefs of State…'[6]

Hitler's change of opinion

Several days later, however, Hitler's attitude had changed and in his Fuhrer's Directive No. 22 on 11 January 1941, he stated that a 'blocking unit' would be fitted out and sent for the defense of Tripolitania, 'particularly against the English armored divisions.' This unit would need to be sent immediately following the sending of an Italian armored division and motorized division, slotted to begin after 20 February. There would also be the dispatch of X Air Corps to Sicily to combat 'English naval forces and the English sea connection between the Western and Eastern Mediterranean.'[7] In addition, German forces would also be sent to assist the Italians in Albania and to fight against the Greeks.

These moves were ominous for the soldiers directly facing this German military juggernaut, the soldiers of Greece, Britain, Australia, New Zealand, India, South Africa and the various groups who had managed to escape from Nazi occupied Europe to continue the fight. More particularly though these moves were ominous for the welfare of the Jewish people living in the regions where these German forces were to potentially fight - the Jewish people in Greece, Libya, Egypt and Palestine.

Hitler also stated in this directive that the OKW (German Higher Command) would determine with the Italian Armed Forces an appropriate chain of command for the future conduct of the war, in view of the potential presence of German forces alongside Italian forces. The separation of areas of operations by the Germans and Italians was about to end.

This directive was confirmed soon afterwards when Hitler met with Mussolini on 20 January 1941.[8] In this meeting Hitler stated the importance of Libya being held, as it possibly would 'be needed as a point of departure for clearing up the Morocco question.'[9]

5 Report from German General at Italian Armed Forces to High Command of Wehrmacht, ibid, p. 1009.

6 *Memorandum* by Bismarck, 30 December 1940, Rome, Document No. 583, ibid, Vol. XI, Footnote 7, p. 987, citing the draft entry in the War Diary of the Wehrmacht Operations Staff (Dec 1, 1940 – Mar. 24, 1941), and the entry for 28 January 1941.

7 Fuhrers Directive No. 22, 11 January, 1941, Document No. 642, ibid, Vol. XI, p. 1074.

8 This meeting took place at Fuschi, and also present were Foreign Ministers Ribbentrop and Count Ciano, Field Marshal Keitel, General Jodl, General von Rintelen, General Guzzoni and General Marras.

9 Record of the Conversation between the Fuhrer and the Duce, 21 January 1941, Fuschi, Document No. 679, ibid,

From a German perspective, the loss of Libya would potentially threaten the French position in North Africa, and consequently create fresh internal problems in France. It was imperative therefore that Italy not lose the war in Libya.

Immediately after the conclusion of the meeting between Hitler and Mussolini, Hitler presented a fresh Directive on 21 January 1941, which stated, 'The discussions of the Fuhrer and the Duce … have led to the conclusion that the promptest possible dispatch of the designated formation to Tripoli (Operation *Sonnenblume*) is greatly desired.'[10] In addition the Directive stated that the designated formation for Operation *Sonnenblume* was to begin as early as 15 February 1941.

These deliberations were made before the capture of Tobruk by Wavell's forces. The capture of Tobruk and subsequent conquest of Cyrenaica by Wavell's forces caused Hitler to write to Mussolini on 5 February 1941 that in view of the current reverses it would only make sense to send German forces to Libya 'if it is capable of being *really successful*, that is, *if it is able to bring about a turn of fate.*'

In view of the loss of almost all of Cyrenaica, Hitler summated, it was no longer viable to send just a blocking unit, it was now necessary to send an entire German armored division, for, he continued 'the further advance of the English cannot be prevented by the purely defensive holding of a position.' To counter this, he proposed, '*The defense itself must be carried on offensively! An armored unit must be thrown against the British armored forces which can meet them at any time and shoot them up or destroy them in a battle of movement.*'

Two interconnected actions were necessary, Hitler postulated, if Libya was not to be lost, one being the presence of the strong armoured force, and the other being a 'combined operation of naval and air forces against British transport and supply ships and the naval force escorting them.'[11] On top of the list of priorities for disturbing the British in the Mediterranean was the complete destruction of Malta.

Hitler informed Mussolini that if he accepted this offer of German involvement then the man he intended sending to head up the German armoured division was General Erwin Rommel. 'General Rommel', Hitler stated 'is the most daring general of armored forces whom we possess in the German Army.'[12] Rommel was informed of his new commission by Field Marshal von Brauchitsch[13] – even before Mussolini had given his final agreement to the German plan. That very afternoon Rommel met with Hitler.

The criteria for German involvement in Libya were basically worked out in Berlin on 6 February, and were: Tripoli must be held, not by establishing a defence barrier around the city, but by establishing a frontier some 200 kilometres further east; Germany would only

Vol. XI, p. 1145. 'So long as there was a lingering question over the situation in Morocco, Germany could not take any serious step against the French Government. All she could do was to threaten the French cabinet through the Paris press. At Vichy the reins were in the hands of the reaction and the Church. Both were foes of Germany.'

10 *Directive of the High Command of the Wehrmacht,* 21 January, 1941, Document No. 683, ibid, Vol. XI, p. 1158.

11 Hitler to Mussolini, 5 February, 1941, Document No. 17, ibid, Vol. XII, pp. 26-28.

12 Hitler to Mussolini, 5 February, 1941, Document No. 17, ibid, Vol. XII, p. 29.

13 Rommel, E. *The Rommel Papers*, edited by B.L. Liddell-Hart, (De Capo Press, New York, 1953), p. 98.

send a blocking force if this strategic plan was adopted; the *Wehrmacht* High Command desired that the Italian mobile units would also be under the command of General Rommel. The Memo summarizing these points then concluded, 'If Italy does not agree to these proposals the High Command of the Wehrmacht will not send one man to North Africa, and if any small German units are already committed there it will withdraw them in a suitable manner.'[14]

Mussolini accepts the German offer

Much hinged now upon whether Mussolini would be willing to forego his own ambitions and ego and accept the German offer. If he accepted it, he would relinquish Italian control of the running of the war in the Mediterranean.

General Rintelen presented Hitler's letter to Mussolini on 9 February 1941 and thereupon reported that Mussolini 'announced to me his agreement to the German conception regarding the conduct of battle for the defence of Tripolitania.' Rintelen did have to negotiate further with the Italian dictator about certain minor points but the general outline was accepted.[15]

A mobile group was then formed which was to be for offensive purposes, and the 'Italian High Command agreed to placing all the mobile units under the command of the German General (Rommel).'[16] This decision was of great importance for the conduct of the North African campaign over the following eighteen months.[17] The mobile group, or force, would henceforth be known as the Panzer Army Africa, of which the German component was known as the *Afrika Korps.*

Rommel met with the Italian Chief of Staff, General Guzzoni in Rome on 11 February 1941 whereupon the German plan to defend Tripolitania from the Gulf of Sirte was approved. Rommel was to be commander of the mobile forces, under the overall command of General Graziani.

While in Sicily en-route to Tripoli Rommel heard than the British-led forces had captured Benghazi. This news made him realize that at this rate the British forces would be in Tripoli before he had a chance to get his Panzer division assembled. He took the initiative and ordered the immediate bombing of Benghazi and the British supply lines by the *Luftwaffe.* This request was initially refused. Incensed, Rommel immediately contacted Hitler's HQ – and permission was promptly given. Then, Rommel states, 'A few hours

14 Memorandum by Ambassador Ritter, 6 February, 1941, Berlin, Document No. 24, ibid, Vol. XII, p. 45.

15 Rintelen to General Staff of the Army, Attaché Department, 9 February, 1941, Document No. 35, ibid, Vol. XII, p. 62.

16 Rintelen to General Staff of the Army, Attaché Department, 9 February, 1941, Document No. 129, ibid, Vol. XII, p. 63, Footnote 3.

17 OKW directive 19 February 19, 1941 (M179/M005708), quoted in Mussolini to Hitler, 22 February, 1941, Document No. 76, ibid, Vol. XII, p. 137, footnote 8. Mussolini's official acceptance to Hitler came by way of a letter on 22 February 1941, in which he provided an overview of the huge problems facing Italy at that time. In his acceptance letter, he also made mention of a second German armored division, a directive which Hitler sanctioned on 19 February.

later the first German bombers took off on their mission to cripple the British supply traffic to Benghazi.'[18]

Even before he had arrived in Libya, Rommel's direct and uncompromising approach was evident to all.

Rommel arrives in Tripoli

Rommel arrived in Libya on 12 February 1941 whereupon he was informed that General Graziani had resigned, and had been replaced by General Gariboldi, who now commanded the Fifth Italian Army. When Rommel explained the plan to hold the British up at Sirte he found Gariboldi 'very dubious about it all.'[19] This attitude confirmed in Rommel's mind that he needed to take more direct command over the front.

He made a reconnaissance flight to the region of Sirte that afternoon, and fully appreciated the weakness of the front line. As it would take time to move more troops forward, he asked the *Luftwaffe* to step in and bomb the British positions in and around El Agheila. These bombings had the desired effect and stalled British movements forward.

Meanwhile an available Italian division began moving forward, and then on 14 February the first German units arrived in Tripoli. That evening some 6,000 tons of equipment was unloaded, and the following day the first contingent of the *Afrika Korps* lined up for inspection in Tripoli. Rommel noted, 'They radiated complete assurance of victory , and the change of atmosphere did not pass unnoticed in Tripoli.'[20] These men shortly afterwards began the long trip eastwards to the Bay of Sirte.

Rommel took over command of the front line on 16 February, and with the arrival of German troops, he began to reconnoiter and scout the region, seeking out the British held positions. He reported that on 24 February 1941, 'the first clash occurred between British and German troops in Africa.'[21]

From this point Rommel felt more secure to establish his position in the region of Sirte, taking and consolidating an area known as Mugtaa. Although an insignificant location, Rommel was able to establish a strong defensive line with mines inland from the coast to a salt marsh, where, if the Allied force (now commanded by General Neame) wanted to move westwards they would have easily been pinned down by Rommel's meager forces. He wrote, "Our operations against Mugtaa resulted in a British withdrawal eastward and we now supposed their main body to be lying round Agedabia and along the coast to Derna."[22]

Little did he realize it at that time, but the Allied position in and around El Agheila and Agedabia was not as strong as he had anticipated. This weakness was due in part to the seasoned 7th British Armoured Division being returned to Egypt for rest and being

18 Rommel, E. *The Rommel Papers*, p. 100.
19 Rommel, E. *The Rommel Papers*, p. 101.
20 Rommel, E. *The Rommel Papers*, p. 102.
21 Rommel, E. *The Rommel Papers*, p. 103.
22 Rommel, E. *The Rommel Papers*, p. 104.

replaced by only part of the 2nd British Armoured Division. In addition other troops, including the by now experienced 6th Australian Division was also withdrawn, not for rest, but for redeployment.

These German movements were now picked up by the British intelligence and the Chief of Staff became concerned and they let their concerns be known to Cairo. On 2 March 1941 Wavell sent a reply which indicated that the British could hold their position, especially at El Agheila.[23] The British intelligence at this point was unaware that the commander of the new German formations arriving in Tripoli was General Erwin Rommel. During this lull in fighting, Rommel flew to Germany and met with Hitler on 19 March 1941.

While in Germany he was informed by Field Marshal von Brauchitsch that there would not be many German reinforcements going to Libya, and that he was expected to limit his operations as far as Benghazi. Such operations, however, were not to be initiated until May when all the troops and equipment was expected to be in Libya. Rommel's objections that it would be necessary to take all of Cyrenaica, fell on deaf ears.[24]

Towards political re-involvement

While deliberations were taking place concerning the active involvement of Germany's military in the affairs of the Mediterranean, similar developments were taking place within the political sphere. As the potential military involvement of Germany in the affairs of the Middle East were ominous for the Jewish people living in that region, so too were there ominous signs if Germany became politically involved in the region.

Although Hitler had entrusted this entire region to Italy, with the decision to become militarily involved there was a significant change of attitude within the political sphere as well. The attitudes of many Germans are summarized in the following excerpts from a Memorandum presented by the Chief of the High Command of the *Wehrmacht* on 5 February 1941:

> The German decision to give the Italians freedom of action also with respect to their political action in the Mediterranean area to all appearances needs to be re-examined as regards the Arab countries. The Italians have no interest in independent Arab countries, since they themselves want to play the chief role there later on. Valuable connections with Arabia have during the last few months been broken off or have deteriorated.[25]

After analysing the British plans for the region, the German Memorandum then provided its own ideas for the future German political involvement in the Middle East:

23 Wavell to Chiefs of Staff, 2 March 1941, in Churchill, W. *The Grand Alliance*, p. 198.

24 Rommel, E. *The Rommel Papers*, p. 106.

25 Memorandum by order of Herr Burkner, Chief of the High Command of the Wehrmacht, 5 February, 1941, Berlin, Document No. 18, ibid, Vol. XII, p. 31.

1. In our opinion the time has come to direct the future political activity in the Middle East from Germany and to take quick and vigorous action in this matter.
2. This includes our recognition of the independence of Arabia as a war aim of the Axis. We are in a favourable position in so far as we need not promise the Arabs a merely "tolerable" solution of the Jewish question in Palestine but can with a good conscience make the Arabs any concession in this field.
3. Whether we are to envisage any political structures in the Middle East and, if so, which ones, or whether we must already take an open stand on this issue which can be answered only by specialists.[26]

The Memorandum went on to outline aspects of re-establishing political contact with Ibn Saud and Saudi Arabia. For the purpose of our topic, however, the important factors were the statements of the growing desire to be politically active in Arab affairs, and the mention of a '"tolerable" 'solution of the Jewish question in Palestine'.

Such a rapprochement between Germany and the Arab Middle East had been part of Haj Amin's strategy now for quite some time.

In February 1941 Foreign Minister Ribbentrop instructed the Director of the Political Department of the Foreign Ministry, Herr Woermann, 'to submit a proposal for the further handling of the Arab question, especially as to how this problem is to be dealt with in view of our aim of defeating England.'[27]

Herein lies the crux of this new development. Germany's goal was to defeat Britain. Until early 1941 this goal, as far as the Mediterranean and Middle East was concerned, had been entrusted to Italy. But now, due to the Italian military failures, Germany was now taking on this responsibility in conjunction with Italy. Germany therefore now had to look at all possibilities for defeating Britain. There were the military options, which included the despatching of German air and land forces to the region, and there was also the issue of fostering allies who could be enlisted to fight against the British forces in the region. The Arab nationalist movement was one such potential ally.

Woermann directed Ribbentrop's question on to the German Embassy in Paris, which, because of the Vichy connection had to be very sensitive concerning any German statements concerning Arab nationalist ambitions. He informed them:

> For this proposal it is of importance whether we are to comply with the Arab wish that we issue a new declaration on the future of the Arab countries in the sense of an over-all Arab solution. In this respect we are to some extent hampered by considerations for Italy...
>
> I should appreciate a statement as soon as possible on whether in your opinion account should be taken of French-Syrian relations in issuing declarations regarding a Greater

26 Memorandum by order of Herr Burkner, Chief of the High Command of the Wehrmacht, ibid, pp. 31-32.
27 Woermann to the Embassy in Paris, 25 February, 1941, Berlin, Document No. 83, ibid, Vol. XII, p. 156.

Arab empire.[28]

The German Ambassador, Abetz, replied on 28 February, that public knowledge of any 'secret German promises to Arab states concerning help in the establishment of a Great Arab Empire would undoubtedly give a decisive impetus to the very strong de Gaullist movement in Syria and be considered by the French Government as contrary to the Armistice Agreement, under which France is committed to maintain French authority in the colonies and mandated territories.' He advised much caution at the present, and advocated the formation of a federation which would include the mandated territories of Syria, Palestine and Transjordan.[29]

For the time being Germany stalled from any further movement into the political affairs of the Middle East for fear of French reactions. The last thing the Germans wanted at this point was any major internal uprising in France or the French colonies, which would require further expenditure of manpower. Germany had plans at the moment which encompassed all of its available military manpower.

28 Woermann to the Embassy in Paris, 25 February, 1941, Berlin, Document No. 83, ibid, Vol. XII, p. 157. Later, on 26 February Woermann wrote again, asking if he thought there would be French objections to stating to Arab representatives: "Germany and Italy declare that they have no objection to Syria and Lebanon obtaining complete independence." See footnote No. 2.

29 Abetz to Woermann, 28 February, 1941, Paris, Document No. 103, ibid, Vol. XII, p. 189.

CHAPTER 9
GREECE BECKONS

Concern for Greece

In view of their victories against the Italians, the Greeks were now faced with an imminent German attack, and because of this the British Government felt it needed to send in troops to aid their Ally. The Greek Government though was not interested in only a token force. For the Greeks, combatting the Italians was one thing, combatting the Germans was another thing altogether. The Greek Government now had to take stock of the bigger picture: if they were to be committed to the Allied cause and not buckle to German aggression, they needed to be assured of substantial Allied support. The position is expressed by Churchill in his communique to Wavell on 12 February 1941:

> Our thoughts must be for our ally Greece, who is actually fighting so well. If Greece is trampled down or forced to make a separate peace with Italy, yielding also air and naval strategic points against us to Germany, effect on Turkey will be bad. But if Greece, with British aid, can hold up for some months German advance, chances of Turkish intervention will be favoured. Therefore, it would seem that we should try to get in a position to offer Greeks the transfer to Greece of the fighting portion of the army which has hitherto defended Egypt, and make every plan for sending and reinforcing it to the limit with men and material.[1]

Churchill further expressed to Wavell that he was unsure if Greece would accept this offer, and that he was not aware of what plans the Greeks had for defending their northern borders from a possible German attack from Bulgaria and Yugoslavia. If the Greeks were not receptive, then Churchill wanted to try and maintain the use of Crete for the British naval force, and to be certain of the Greek islands for the air-force.

One is able to see here the overall geo-political situation: how to ensure Greece never fell to the Axis, meaning German control. If Greece fell, then there would be more pressure upon Turkey to also come under Axis influence. With an Axis influence over Greece and Turkey then pressure could more easily be exerted upon the Suez Canal and British territories such as Palestine.

The issues at stake here were large, and so Churchill despatched Foreign Minister Anthony Eden and the CIGS General Dill to Cairo, to meet first with Wavell, and then to continue onto Greece and Turkey. In Cairo the three leaders agreed that it was important to help Greece as best as they could to thwart the anticipated German move southwards.

1 Churchill to Wavell, 12 February 1941, *The Grand Alliance*, p. 65.

However, they also realised that without supporting air power it would be difficult to secure a line at Thessalonica (Saloniki).

No-one was under the illusion that this was a simple undertaking. Eden informed Churchill that it was a 'gamble to send forces to the mainland of Europe to fight Germans at this time' but that 'though campaign is a daring venture, we are not without hope that it might succeed to the extent of halting the Germans before they overrun Greece.' The alternative of not assisting, as Eden expressed, was, 'If we fail to help the Greeks there is no hope of action by Yugoslavia, and the future of Turkey may easily be compromised.'[2]

When the British leaders arrived in Athens they were informed by Prime Minister Korysis, that regardless of any help that the British would offer, they, the Greeks, were determined to fight to protect their land from the Germans.[3] The Greek leaders including General Papagos then worked on the finer details. Much of the plan depended upon whether Yugoslavia joined in opposing the Germans. If they did, then the Allies could defend Thessalonica; if not then they could not defend Thessalonica. The defence of Thessalonica was supremely important, not for the sake of Greece, but for the sake of the approximate 56,000 Jewish people who lived there.

The British Cabinet were unanimous in support. A vote to help there may well have been, but from where would the soldiers come? The only available pool of troops were the 1st British Armoured Division the 6th Australian Division, the 2nd New Zealand Division and numerous auxiliary forces. The Australian Prime Minister Robert Menzies was also present in London, and he said he would first need to contact Australia. The New Zealand Government would also need to be informed and their permission gained. Prime Minister Fraser was supportive, but anxious.[4]

This is not the place to explain all the intricacies of how Australian and New Zealand soldiers became involved in such an operation.[5] But there were political intrigues and miscommunications abounding in this episode; between the British Government and the Australian Government, particularly concerning Menzies; between the British High Command in the Middle East and particularly concerning General Blamey; between Blamey and both Menzies and the Australian Government. Ultimately both General Blamey and the New Zealand commander General Freyberg were opposed to sending the small Anzac force to Greece, deeming it as militarily unfeasible. Churchill, though, was adamant that a strong blow could be made against Germany from the soft underbelly of Europe.

2 Eden to Churchill, 21 February 1941, *The Grand Alliance*, p. 72.

3 Summary of decision by Greek Cabinet, as summarized by Eden to Churchill, 22 February 1941, in Churchill, W. *The Grand Alliance*, pp. 73-4.

4 Sandford, K. ibid, pp. 52-53.

5 For more detailed information about the Greek Campaign I refer you to Hill, Maria. *Diggers and Greeks*; Churchill, W. *The Grand Alliance;* Crombie, K, *Anzacs, Empires and Israel's Restoration*, chapter 23.

Hitler's change of policy concerning Greece

Hitler was displeased with Mussolini's invasion of Greece in 1940. Now he had no choice but to ensure the soft underbelly of Europe was not exposed to any potential Allied offensive. Writing to Mussolini on 28 February 1941 Hitler mentioned that he was sending troops into Bulgaria on 2 March. 'The advance to the Greek border,' he stated 'will take place in the course of the next few weeks. I hope that with this there will be a noticeable relief along the Albanian border.'[6] In addition, he implored upon Mussolini to retain the Italian controlled islands in the Dodecanese, stating:

> It would very greatly facilitate the conduct of the air war in the eastern Mediterranean if these islands could be held. A more secure build-up of Rhodes would probably definitely block the Suez Canal for England.[7]

Now committed to assisting the Italians in the Mediterranean, Hitler was covering every possible base for ensuring the defeat of Britain in that region. The situation in Greece was both militarily and geo-politically quite complex. This is exemplified by a communique from the German Embassy in Rome to the Foreign Ministry on 1 March 1941, in which they stated how the Italian High Command desired to defeat the Greeks in Albania for the sake of the prestige of the Italian Army. This could only happen, so the Italians intimated, if the Greeks withdrew men from the Albanian front.[8] The Greeks would only be induced to withdraw if the Germans entered the fray.

Anzac and British forces depart for Greece

The Allied deployment to Greece began in early March 1941. In addition to the British, New Zealand and Australian forces and the auxiliary troops, including over a thousand Jewish men from Palestine, seven squadrons of RAF were also despatched to Greece.

The 6th Australian Division was pulled out of their forward positions in Cyrenaica, and were to be replaced primarily by the 9th Australian Division, and also by some of the 7th Australian Division. The 7th Australian Division was mostly reserved for a later embarkation for Greece. Holt recalls when the two convoys passed each other in the North African desert:

> … we passed convoys carrying battalions of the Seventh and Ninth Divisions and we chiaked one another unmercifully… we exchanged the usual ribald remarks and we certainly gave them the business … "We've won the war and you … are just arriving" … "You're travelling the wrong way – the war is this way."[9]

6 Hitler to Mussolini, 28 February, 1941, Document No. 110, ibid, Vol. XII, p. 197.
7 Hitler to Mussolini, 28 February, 1941, Document No. 110, ibid, Vol. XII, p. 198.
8 German Embassy to Foreign Ministry, 1 March, 1941, Rome, Document No. 111, ibid, Vol. XII, p. 199.
9 Holt, B. ibid, pp. 76-77.

Little did these men realize that soon the war would be both this way and that. In other words the Allied soldiers would soon be fighting in both Greece and North Africa.

The first troops to arrive in Greece were the New Zealanders. One New Zealander, J. Westbrook, wrote of their reception there:

… the people gave us a marvelous reception, cheering and clapping throughout the short journey to the camp. Most of us went AWOL that night into the city and we were literally besieged. Everyone was wanting to take us out, shout us drinks.[10]

The New Zealanders moved to the north of the country to the area around Katerinei on the east coast. Upham's platoon of the 20th battalion was based near Riakia, where they spent seventeen days 'digging in, erecting wire, settling their defensive lay-out in anticipation of the German attack.'[11]

When the 6th Australian Division arrived on 19 March the combined Anzac troops were then officially named the *Anzac Corps*. The 1st Armoured Brigade moved north, followed by the New Zealanders. By the end of March the Australians joined their British and New Zealand mates and together with the Greek soldiers, made every effort to stabilise this line of defence.

After a few days in the camp at Daphne, Bob Holt and his mates were travelling to the north of the country. He wrote following their arrival:

> We got off the trucks and marched into the mountains. We eventually reached our positions and dug ourselves in at a forward defence location overlooking a small white village in Yugoslavia. It was bitterly cold and to say the least of it we were uncomfortable. Fetching, carrying, digging and trying to load Bren gun magazines in the dark and freezing weather was no joke.[12]

The key to the defence of Greece was the northern border and Greece's second largest city Thessalonica (or Saloniki) with a population of some 300,000 people. One line of defence named the Metaxas Line was north of Thessalonica and ran from the Aegean Sea to the Bulgarian border. Another line, the Aliakhmon Line was south of Thessalonica running from the Aegean Sea to the Yugoslav border near the Monastir Gap. (see p.105)

Fate of the large Jewish community in Thessalonica in the balance

If either of these two lines were broken, Thessalonica would fall. If Thessalonica fell the fate of the 56,000 Jewish people living there would be sealed.[13] If Greece fell the fate

10 King, M. *New Zealanders at War,* p. 171.
11 Sandford, K. ibid, p. 53.
12 Holt, B. ibid, p. 93.
13 Population details from, Savich, C. *The Holocaust in Greece, 1941-1944,* www.balkanalysis.com/2005/11/30/the-holocaust-in-greece-1941-1944-part-2/

of all the Jewish communities living there would be sealed. Under German control the Jewish communities in Greece would be destined for the same fate as Jewish people in other areas of German conquered Europe.

While the Greek Jewish community had immediate concerns, the Jewish people in Palestine were also concerned. German victory in Greece would bring the Nazis one step closer to Palestine. In addition over a thousand Jewish personnel from Palestine were serving in the Greek campaign, attached to the RAF, as well as bomb-clearers, and 'diggers' with the Royal Engineers, the Service Corps and the Pioneer Corps.

With stability, apparently, in Libya all eyes were now trained on Greece.[14]

German movements

The situation in the Balkans grew progressively tenser during March. While Britain sent troops to Greece to honour its commitment, the German Government began expressing its position that it needed to support its ally, Italy, and that the onus was upon the Greeks to come to terms with Germany. The German position is evidenced in a Memorandum put together by Weizsacher following a meeting with the Greek Ambassador, Alexander Rizo-Rangabe, in Berlin on 18 March 1941, in which he stated to the Greek diplomat:

> Two things were certain: Greece was at war with our ally and she had drawn units of the British armed forces into her country. But it was intolerable for us to have the English on the Continent.[15]

It was now becoming increasingly difficult for the Greek Government. Although most Greeks did not desire an armed conflict, the only possibility of evading such a conflict would be to adhere to the Axis demands. One of these demands included the eviction of British personnel from Greek soil. If the Greeks complied with these demands, then the Italians would maintain a foremost position in Greece. For most Greeks this situation was intolerable. But if they did not comply with this German position, then Germany would move its troops into Greece from Bulgaria. In this situation the Greeks 'would fight to the last man.'[16] It really was a no-win situation.

The first military victory in the battle for Greece was won by the Royal Navy, when it severely hammered the Italian Fleet in what became known as the Battle of Matapan on 28 March 1941. Admiral Cunningham's initiative in attacking the Italians at night proved successful and provided the Allied force with security in transporting further men and supplies to Greece.

Unfortunately this would prove to be the first, and the last Allied victory in the Greek Campaign.

14 In 1996 I spent two weeks retracing the footsteps of the Anzac Corps, from Thessalonica, to the Yugoslav border, south to Athens, the Pelepponese Peninsular, including the key port of Kalamata and to Crete, and visiting most of the key battle sites.

15 Memoradum of Weizsacher, 18 March, 1941, Berlin, Document No. 180, ibid, Vol. XII, p. 316.

16 Ambassador Erbach to Foreign Ministry, 12 March, 1941, Athens, Document No. 155, ibid, Vol. XII, p. 279.

Renewed calls for Jewish Division

In the midst of these delicate geo-political dynamics Chaim Weizmann never gave up on his desire for a fully-fledged Jewish Division serving under the British Army. The Jewish battalions from Palestine were a good start, but what he and others were pressing for was a full Division of 12,000 men with its distinct flag and insignia. In 1917 Jabotinsky and others fought for the same concept, but this had then been denied to them and the 'Jewish Legion' when finally agreed to, had to become part of the Royal Fusiliers.

Weizmann and Churchill had discussed this before he became prime minister. The matter came up again in early 1941. When it was presented to Wavell, he responded in similar fashion to how he did on previous occasions, that this would upset the Arab world.[17]

Wavell's opposition did not impress Churchill (nor the Jewish leadership), who understood much better the real dynamics of what was taking place in the Middle East. Yet because at this point Wavell was heavily involved in preparing for the despatch of the BEF to Greece, Churchill did not press him on the matter.

Later, however, when German forces became involved, Churchill did return to the matter. Churchill and others in the Government were aware that there was a chance that Turkey could either enter the war, or permit the passage of German troops through their territory. If this occurred then the Axis forces could threaten British territories from the north as well as from North Africa. Churchill wrote to the new Colonial Secretary, Lord Cranbourne on 10 May 1941, 'I have always been most strongly in favour of making sure that the Jews have proper means of self-defence for their colonies in Palestine. The more that you can get done in this line, the safer we shall be.'[18]

For now, the question of most importance for the Jewish people was, 'How safe would their community be in Greece?'

17 Gilbert, M. ibid, p. 181.

18 Churchill to Viscount Cranbourne, 10 May 1941; Churchill papers, 20/36, quoted in Gilbert, M. *Churchill and the Jews*, p. 183.

CHAPTER 10
ROMMEL CAPTURES CYRENAICA ...

New Allied movements into Cyrenaica

While Rommel prepared for this 'minor' thrust, the 7th and 9th Australian Divisions continued to make their way westwards, filling the void left by the 6th Division. As the 7th Division was earmarked for ultimate transfer to Greece, they mostly remained at Mersa Matruh, half way to the Libyan border.

From atop the Halfaya Pass 'Diver' Derrick wrote on 17 March 1941:

> Have never seen so much destruction ... passed through Capuzzo and again we see ruins and hundreds more "ding" tanks, lorries, shells, LMG's, AkAks, heavy guns and crashed planes, some of which were destroyed on the ground.[1]

General Neale oversaw the movement of these new troops into their positions. Not only were these new troops mostly raw, much of their essential equipment had been given to the British Expeditionary Force for Greece. In addition, the British command, especially Wavell, was basically oblivious of the degree of German involvement. They were also ignorant at this stage that the new commander of the forward Axis troops was the most distinguished Panzer commander in the German Army.

Such deficiencies in their intelligence were soon to have a disastrous effect. Wavell reported on 20 March that he was anticipating a limited German attack, and that if the forward positions were overrun there was no position that they could hold until Benghazi.[2]

Rommel's thrust for the Suez Canal

Upon his return from Germany Rommel oversaw the strike against the British line at El Agheila on 24 March 1941.[3] His Panzer Army Africa, and especially the *Afrika Korps* quickly overwhelmed the weakly defended British position there, and the garrison withdrew to the Marsa el Brega defile further east.

This victory, militarily small as it was, nevertheless enabled Rommel to sense that the British forces facing him were not as strong as he had anticipated. He now began to regroup in readiness for a thrust forward.

As he waited for the arrival of the remainder of his German Panzers and troops,

1 Farquhar, M. ibid, p. 48.

2 Churchill, W. *The Grand Alliance*, p. 202. In a telegram to Wavell on 26 March Churchill alludes to 1st and 2nd South African Divisions being transferred to the North Africa sphere.

3 This date is according to Rommel. Churchill states 31 March. See Churchill, W. *The Grand Alliance*, p. 203.

Rommel observed the British consolidating their new line. He was then faced with the decision of waiting for his troops and equipment, and thereby permitting the British to establish a strong defensive line, or attacking while their line was still weak. He chose to attack, which he did on 1 April.

Although initially being stalled by the British armoured force, late on 1 April the 5th German Light Division, broke through and took the strategic Mersa el Brega position. German reconnaissance determined that the British were steadily falling back, so Rommel, contrary to his orders, chose to attack Agedabia. While the Panzer Army Africa was making its thrust into Cyrenaica, the Allied garrison force was oblivious to what was happening. At Derna on the other side of the Jebel Akhdar Mountain range, Thomas Derrick and his mates of the 2/48th Battalion were nonchalantly playing a game of cricket. Although he top scored with twelve runs, Derrick wrote, 'I'm no Bradman.'[4]

The speed of the Axis movement surprised the British command. Wavell informed Churchill on 2 April that he may even have to withdraw from Benghazi. To this Churchill responded immediately, '… any serious withdrawal from Benghazi would appear most melancholy' and added 'I cannot understand how the enemy can have developed any force at the end of this long, waterless coast road, and I cannot feel that there is at this moment a persistent weight behind his attack in Cyrenaica.'[5]

The Axis forces not only moved along the *Via Balboa* towards Benghazi, but also through two central routes which converged at Mechili. From Mechilli routes branched out to Benghazi to the west, Derna to the north and Tobruk to the east.

Wavell, though, finally ordered the evacuation of Benghazi on 4 April. This withdrawal included leaving Benghazi poste-haste before the quick moving Axis troops arrived. The Allied soldiers referred to this period as the 'Benghazi Handicap' as they tried desperately to evade the closing noose of Rommel's forces. The withdrawal allowed Rommel to write to his wife:

> We've already reached our first objective, which we weren't supposed to get until the middle of May. The British are falling over each other to get away. Our casualties small. Booty can't yet be estimated. You will understand that I can't sleep for happiness.[6]

Rommel might have been sleepless from happiness, but for the thousands of Allied soldiers, especially men of the 9th Australian Division, they went sleepless for another reason. Absolute speed was now of the essence for both sides: for Rommel to cut off the retreating Allied troops, and for the Allied troops to evade the encircling Axis force. The following day Rommel was able to write to his wife that he had just received congratulations

4 *Diary of Thomas Derrick*, in Farquhar, M. ibid, p. 52.

5 Churchill to Wavell, 2 April, 1941, in Churchill, W. *The Grand Alliance*, p. 204.

6 Rommel, E. *The Rommel Papers*, ibid, p. 111.

from Hitler, who sanctioned his ongoing operations.[7]

Some of the Axis forces moved along the north coastal route while some went through the interior towards Derna, and more importantly towards Tobruk, the key port on the coast. With Tobruk in his hands, Rommel could then mount his decisive assault upon Egypt – and the Suez Canal beyond.

The key position to be captured from the Axis perspective, and to be held from the Allied perspective, was Mechilli. Wavell sent armoured units, mostly from the 3rd Armoured Brigade to Mechilli in order to protect the withdrawal of any Allied soldiers coming through the interior route from Benghazi. Most of the Australian troops were withdrawing along the coastal route. Derrrick recorded on 7 April, 'Awakened 0130 hours, all the company out of Derna by 0230, taken by truck to Tobruk and lost rest of coy. Dug in and slept in terrible dust storm. Everyone has been evacuated from Derna and valuable items blown up. Jerry attacking at Barce about 100 miles from Derna, and seems to be making the pace a cracker.'[8]

Rommel was in the vanguard of the German force which aimed for Mechilli and he relentlessly travelled in both his plane and vehicle trying to rally all of his available forces for the attack upon this strategic position. The relentless energy he invested is evidenced in a letter he wrote to his wife, dated 8 April, but in which he stated, 'I've no idea whether the date is right. We've been attacking for days in the endless desert and have lost all idea of space or time.'[9]

Mechilli was attacked and captured by the Axis on 8 April as well as Derna to the north, whereupon Rommel was able to gloat, there 'were 800 prisoners, including to my great joy, almost the entire British staff. Among them were General P. Neame, C-in-C. British Troops in Egypt and Transjordan, and General O'Connor, the man who had so roughly handled the Italian Army.'[10] All of the Allied troops, mostly 9th Australian Division were now retreating as best they could towards Tobruk.

Withdrawal to Tobruk

The loss of Benghazi had wider ramifications. If it was seen that British forces were again defeated by the Germans, those watching the events, such as in Greece and Turkey, might very easily change their position. It was absolutely imperative now that the Allied troops stand and make a concerted fight against the German-led force.

Following the capture of Mechilli the object of both forces was now Tobruk, which now became the all-important strategic location. Churchill wrote in a Memo to Wavell on 7 April 1941:

7 Rommel, E. *The Rommel Papers*, ibid, p. 112.
8 *Diary of Thomas Derrick*, in Farquar, M, ibid, p. 59.
9 Rommel, E. *The Rommel Papers*, ibid, p. 116.
10 Rommel. E. *The Rommel Papers*, ibid, p. 118.

You should surely be able to hold Tobruk … at least until or unless the enemy brings up strong artillery forces. It seems difficult to believe that he can do this for some weeks … Tobruk, therefore, seems to be a place to be held to the death without thought of retirement.'[11]

Until this point much of the 7th Australian Division was in reserve at Mersa Matruh awaiting deployment to Greece. This incisive German attack prompted Wavell to delay their transfer to Greece, and to retain them as a strategic reserve in Egypt, and one regiment proceeded west to link up with the 9th Australian Division. They ended up in Tobruk.

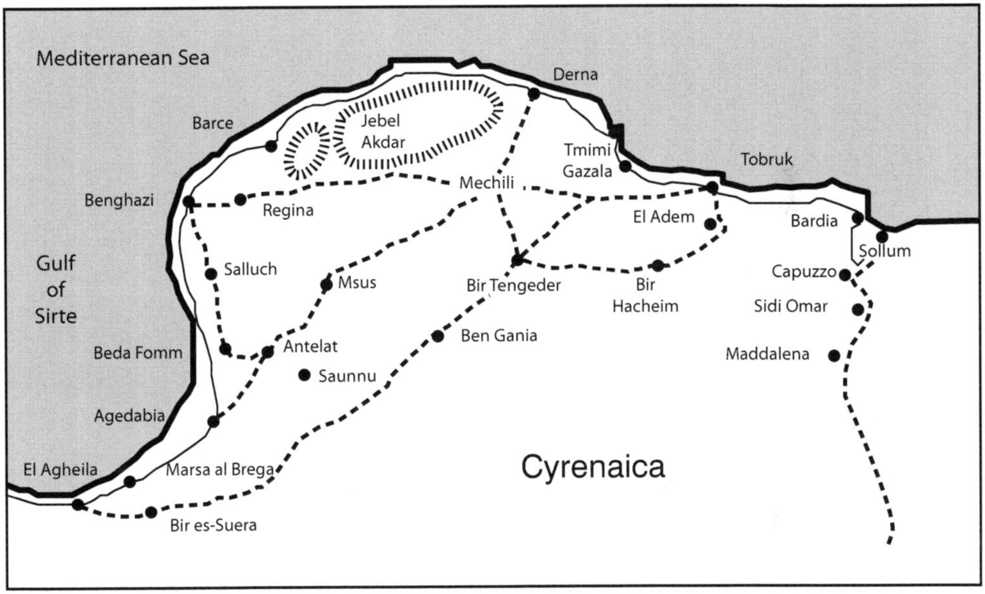

11 Churchill to Wavell, 7 April 1941. In Churchill, W. *The Grand Alliance,* p. 207.

CHAPTER 11
... EXCEPT TOBRUK

Destination Tobruk

This regiment of the 7th Australian Division reached Tobruk on 8 April, whereupon Wavell, who had flown there from Cairo, instructed the divisional commander General John Lavarack:

> Your main task will be to hold the enemy's advance at Tobruk, in order to give time for the assembly of reinforcements, especially of armoured troops, for the defence of Egypt.[1]

The defense of Egypt, and thus of the Suez Canal, was now to be Tobruk, at least 500 miles (800 kms) to the west. Tobruk was now the focus of Rommel's move eastwards. He wrote, "It was now of the utmost importance to appear in strength before Tobruk and get our attack started as early as possible, for we wanted our blow to fall before the enemy had recovered his morale after our advance through Cyrenaica, and had been able to organise his defence of Tobruk."[2]

By 9 April remnants of the 9th Australian Division which had managed to outrun Rommel's fast moving forces, also entered Tobruk. Ultimately overall command of the Tobruk garrison was entrusted to the commander of the 9th Australian Division, General Leslie Morshead.

Another to reach Tobruk that day was Moses Mosenson. It was the evening of the major Jewish festival of Passover, when Jewish people recall the deliverance from the tyranny of Pharaoh in Egypt.

Two days later, on 11 April, Good Friday, the Germans mounted a major assault, which was repulsed - much to Rommel's annoyance. Mosenson wrote to his wife:

> It is hard for us living in caves and hiding in rocks, with hellish noises raining down from above, to write now. I will write you at length if things get a little more comfortable.[3]

It would be some time before life became 'comfortable' for Mosenson, and the remainder of the garrison force at Tobruk, which was a composite force comprised of British and mostly Australian troops.

1 Badman, P. *North Africa 1940-1942. The Desert War.* (Sydney, 1988), p. 91.
2 Rommel, E. *The Rommel Papers*, ibid, p. 121.
3 Mosenson, M. *Letters from the Desert,* p. 50.

The Jewish soldiers in particular were far from annoyed however by being holed up in Tobruk. They knew the likely consequences if Tobruk was quickly overrun. Virtually nothing was stopping Rommel's forces from quickly enveloping the weakened Allied forces and moving on into Egypt, over the Suez Canal – and into Palestine.

One aspect of the campaign thus far did disturb Mosenson though. He wrote to his wife expressing how Jewish soldiers made every attempt to extricate Jewish civilians from the towns they evacuated in Cyrenaica, particularly Benghazi. The majority, however, could not be evacuated – and were now under German control.[4]

Following Wavell's return to Cairo he informed Churchill of the desperate situation, and hinted at a possible withdrawal even from Tobruk.[5] In response Churchill and the Chiefs–of-Staff drafted a message informing Wavell in very clear terms to stay in Tobruk, concluding, 'We are convinced you should fight it out at Tobruk.'[6] This they never sent as they then heard afresh from Wavell that he had every intention of remaining steadfast at Tobruk.

The following days were crucial as Rommel recommenced his attack. All of his main formations had now arrived and encircled the port town. He was so optimistic that he wrote to his wife on 14 April, 'To-day may well see the end of the Battle of Tobruk. The British were very stubborn and had a great deal of artillery. However, we'll bring it off.'[7]

Churchill wrote an eleven point Directive on 14 April 1941 concerning operations in North Africa. In this Directive he emphasized the importance of Tobruk being held, and that it was imperative that both the Mediterranean Fleet and Royal Air Force hassle the Axis supply lines, both the convoys going from Italy to Tripoli, and along the *Via Balboa* as they brought supplies to their forward lines. As much as Rommel was determined to take Tobruk, Churchill was determined to hold it. The eyes of the world were now focused on Tobruk and the events in North Africa.

King Farouk's message to Hitler

The entrance of Rommel and German forces into the North African campaign created new dynamics in the region for even King Farouk of Egypt now expected Rommel to 'bring it off.' On 14 April 1941 the Egyptian Ambassador in Tehran, Zulfikar Pasha (father-in-law to King Farouk) met with the German Ambassador, Herr Ethel. Farouk wanted a message conveyed to Hitler. Ettel's telegram to the Foreign Ministry in Berlin stated:

> Pressure by England on the King to declare war on the Axis Powers was constantly growing … In his refusal the King was relying on a 90 percent majority of the Egyptian people who did not want war and whose sympathies were with Germany.[8]

4 Mosenson, M. *Letters from the Desert*, p. 50.

5 Wavell to Churchill, 9 April 1941, in Churchill, W. *The Grand Alliance*, p. 208.

6 Churchill and Chiefs of Staff to Wavell, 10 April 1941, in Churchill, W. *The Grand Alliance*, p. 208.

7 Rommel, E. *The Rommel Papers*, ibid, p. 124.

8 Ambassador Ettel to Foreign Ministry, 15 April 1941, Document No. 350, telegram No. 226, ibid, Vol. XII, p. 558.

The Ambassador stated that the 45,000 strong Egyptian Army was loyal to the King but was in no position to oppose the numerically stronger British forces. King Farouk had instructed Ambassador Pasha to state the following, 'He was filled with strong admiration for the Fuhrer and respect for German people, whose victory over England he desired most sincerely. He was one with his people in the wish to see victorious German troops in Egypt as soon as possible as liberators from the unbearably brutal English yoke.'[9]

The Egyptian Ambassador also candidly stated that when the Italians were defeated the Egyptians were exuberant, seeing the Italians as imperial masters, but they were excited that the Germans were coming closer, whom they did not see as oppressors.

Ribbentrop spoke to Hitler about King Farouk's message, and Ribbentrop in turn relayed the Fuhrer's response to the King, via his Ambassador in Tehran, on 30 April 1941. In this communique Ribbentrop wanted the King to fully appreciate that 'Germany's fight was not directed at Egypt or the other Arab countries of the Near East, but only against the common foe of Germany and the Arab countries: England.'[10]

Ribbentrop then continued:

> It was the immovable purpose of the Axis Powers to eliminate for the entire future the fatal influence which England had exerted in the past in Europe as well as in the Near East, and in its place to bring about a new order of things which would be based upon the principle of respect for the rightful interests of all nations. As far as Egypt in particular was concerned, the Fuhrer had already stated earlier that Germany had no territorial aspirations of any sort in regard to the Arab countries, but rather – and in this he was also in agreement with the Duce – desired the independence of Egypt and the entire Arab world.[11]

Ribbentrop also stated that Hitler was willing to have closer cooperation with the King, and invited him to send an appropriate representative for discussions. The Egyptian Ambassador then informed the German Reich that at this stage it was impossible to send such a delegate as the British authorities in Cairo would quickly learn of such a move, and that in the meantime all deliberations between the two parties could be channelled through him, who 'had been provided with the necessary full powers by the King.'[12]

Despite the lack of direct communication, this dialogue now presented further evidence to the Reich Government that pending a decisive military victory in the Middle East they

9 Ambassador Ettel to Foreign Ministry, 15 April 1941, ibid, p. 559.

10 Ribbentrop to the German Legation in Iran, 30 April 1941, Document No. 427, telegram No. 197, ibid, Vol.XII, p. 680.

11 Ribbentrop to the German Legation in Iran, 30 April 1941, ibid, p. 680.

12 Ambassador Ettel to Foreign Ministry, 4 May 1941, Document No. 448, telegram No. 331, ibid, Vol. XII, p. 701. In another communique on 4 May 1941, the Director of the Political Department of the Foreign Ministry, Herr Woermann, instructed the German delegation in Bern, Switzerland, that the offer of the Egyptian *Charge d'Affaires* there, Assal Bey, to convey Germany's answer personally to King Farouk, 'not be taken up for the time being.' See Memorandum by the Director of the Political Department, 4 May 1941, Document No. 452, ibid, pp. 710-11.

could anticipate local support, especially in Egypt.

Tobruk holds out

The possibility of a German-Arab alliance though was being held up at the gates of Tobruk. Rommel wrote again to his wife on 25 April 1941, 'Things are still very warm in front of Tobruk ... The Battle for Egypt and the canal is now on in earnest and our tough opponent is fighting back with all he's got.'[13]

The garrisoned force at Tobruk was indeed fighting with everything they had. The stakes were high, a matter not lost on the Jewish community in Palestine. The *Palestine Post* wrote on 28 April 1941:

> While Tobruk holds out – and with the Royal Navy in control it is easily reinforceable from the sea – the attacking army is in no position to contrite its forces against the defence of Egypt proper.[14]

Tobruk now became a household word in every Jewish home in Palestine. Indeed it became a household name throughout the world, and especially in Australia. Survival in North Africa and the Middle East very much depended upon the defenders in this tiny port town in Libya.

Moses Mosenson wrote to his small daughter back on Kibbutz Na'an:

We are fighting the Germans; if we did not fight them here, far from home, we would have to fight them at home.[15]

Winston Churchill wrote to General Morshead, commander of the garrison at Tobruk:

> To General Morshead from Prime Minister England. The whole empire is watching your steadfast and spirited defence of this important outpost of Egypt with gratitude and admiration.[16]

The defence of Tobruk was entrusted to ordinary men, many of whom produced extraordinary exploits. The German propagandist 'Lord Haw-Haw' gave these men the derogatory entitlement of 'Rats'. The defenders turned this supposed slur into a term of great honour, and they henceforth wore with pride the title 'Rats of Tobruk'.

Most, but not all of those 'Rats of Tobruk' were Australians. Rommel on one occasion observed some Australian 'Rats' being marched off as prisoners, and stated that they were

13 Rommel, E. *The Rommel Papers*, ibid, p. 131.

14 *Palestine Post,* 28 April 1941, p. 4.

15 Mosenson, M. *Letters from the Desert,* p. 52.

16 Quoted in Badman, P. *North Africa 1940-1942: The Desert War,* p. 100.

'immensely big and powerful men, who without question represented an elite formation of the British Empire, a fact that was also evident in battle.'[17]

Another of those 'Rats' was a young man named John 'Jack' Edmondson. Edmondson won Australia's first Victoria Cross of World War Two during these early crucial days of fighting at Tobruk. His bravery was an example to all of the garrison troops.

Apart from such heroism and the general fortitude of the garrison force, however, everyone realized that what they had witnessed and experienced during the previous week had been nothing short of a humiliating military defeat. The last thing they now needed was another devastating military defeat. Tobruk could not fall. In Tobruk Moses Mosenson wrote to his wife in late May:

> It is months now since we have taken our clothes off when going to sleep, and nobody minds in the least. We get used to everything. We get used to eating everything full of sand and dust and joke about it.[18]

Later he wrote of a rare swim in the Mediterranean:

> At the beach we met some young Australians who had come to rest from the front lines. We played in the water like little boys. The atmosphere was charged with joy and high spirits. We forgot about everything. For once our bodies and heads were clean of sand. I dipped my clothes in water too, scrubbed them and laid them to dry on the rocks. But suddenly, the paradise was destroyed. Over our heads the cursed planes circled. We found shelter among the clefts of the rocks along the bay. How helpless soldiers look when they are naked, without steel helmets and with ammunition belts – like forlorn children.
>
> When the immediate danger was past, we jumped into the water again and dove down into it...and again we enjoyed ourselves. The Australians are good playmates...

And after meeting some old friends among these Australian soldiers, he commented quite gleefully 'The bond of comradeship has remained undiminished.'[19] If Tobruk was to withstand the continuous German assaults, it needed to have resolute soldiers who were dedicated to the goal of holding on.

German defence line established at Gazala and attack on Sollum

In their thrust in April the Axis forces had continued on to the border town of Sollum, and captured it. In addition, as he anticipated a British counter-attack Rommel established a solid defence line at Gazala west of Tobruk in May 1941. General Wavell was in fact planning a counter-offensive, and wanted to attack before the anticipated arrival of the

17 Rommel, E. *The Rommel Papers*, ibid, p. 132.
18 Mosenson, M. *Letters from the Desert*, p. 64.
19 Mosenson, M. *Letters from the Desert*, pp. 64-65.

15th Panzer Division.

General William Gott attacked the region of Sollum on 15 May 1941 with the 7th Armoured Brigade and 22nd Guards Brigade and despite gaining some positions, Gott decided to withdraw and several days later the positions of the two sides were similar to how they were before the attack. Thereafter Rommel received his new Panzer division, while Wavell received a shipment of new Matilda and cruiser tanks.[20]

Then Rommel attacked the British positions at Halfaya on 27 May 1941 and succeeded in capturing them. Thereafter he set about consolidating the defensive position in the region of Sollum-Halfaya and Bardia.

There were several major problems facing the Germans at this point. Tobruk was one. While Tobruk held out, Rommel could not press ahead. Another was the Italian Army. There was a possiblity for more German troops to come to the theatre, but the Italians objected, as that would have placed the Germans in a stronger position than them.[21]

Despite these and other obvious problems such as mis-understandings with his superiors back in Berlin, and the heat, Rommel and his forces continued to consolidate their position, in expectation of a renewed Allied attack to relieve the Tobruk garrison. General Wavell and his subordinates meanwhile laboured over the best plan for such an assault. After their tanks arrived, the plan firmed up.

Arrival of 1st and 2nd South African Divisions

Meanwhile more infantry was also arriving in Egypt. The vanguard of the 1st South African Division arrived at Suez on 3 May 1941, with the remainder of the division arriving later. Initially they were stationed at Mersa Matruh on defensive duties, consolidating the defence line. Their commander, General Brink, however, was dissatisfied about this, as he wanted his troops trained and ready for offensive operations.

On 10 June 1941 the 2nd South African Division departed from Durban. Warrant Officer Ron Turrel was one of them. The first evening out one of Turrel's mates, Jimmy Stewart got out his radio and finally picked up the German language radio station which beamed out a programme entitled "From the enemy to the enemy" from Germany. Turrel records:

> After some pleasantries, the voice of the announcer grated out – "This afternoon the Second South African Division sailed from Durban in the Ile de France, Mauretania, and Nieuw Amsterdam, heading for Suez in Egypt. We hope they will have a pleasant trip while it lasts, and that they won't find the water too cold, or the sharks too numerous." Jimmy switched off the set, and a silence fell upon the lot of us .... Suddenly we all felt terribly vulnerable.[22]

Some days later the three large passenger liners were due to arrive at Suez, and Turrel

20 These tanks had come via a convoy through the Mediterranean, a risk which Churchill was willing to take.

21 Rommel, E. *The Rommel Papers*, p. 139.

22 Turrel, R. *It's Only Me*, p. 188.

recalled that 'The ship's officers had made it clear that they wanted to unload passengers and goods just as quickly as they could, to get out of harbour before nightfall. Jerry night bombers had already made a couple of unwelcome visits to the port, and the size of these three ships would make them very tempting targets indeed.'[23] After disembarking and traversing through Cairo, Turrel next found himself at the Mena Camp near the Pyramids.

After savouring the legacy of the Pharaohs the South Africans were on the road again, and their camp was near Alexandria. This city impressed Turrel, who stated that it was 'a military target of no mean importance, with its naval dockyard, huge repair depots, and many other army installations.'[24]

The Axis forces also saw Alexandria as a strategic target, for that very same night the air raid sirens sounded, lights were put out, the Ack-Ack guns fired, and, he states 'We sat and watched the spectacle, fascinated.' Some time later the onlookers saw a German plane go up in flames and tumble to the ground, causing Turrel to reflect, 'No doubt about it, we were getting closer to the war.'[25]

They may have been experiencing war for the first time, but such was not the case for Alexandria. During 7-8 June 1941 two massive *Luftwaffe* raids on Alexandria resulted in considerable damage to the military installations, but also killed some 650 people.[26] The raid might have been a spectacle for these men, but for the people of Alexandria it was a reminder that the war really was at their doorstep. So long as Tobruk held out, though, the reality of war would be limited to air raids.

23 Turrel, R. ibid, p. 189.
24 Turrel, R. ibid, p. 195.
25 Turrel, R. ibid. p. 196.
26 Kirk, G. ibid, pp. 200-01. Kirk also relates how the Egyptian Government was severely criticized as a result of these raids and they also asked the British authorities to remove all military installations from Alexandria and Cairo. The British replied that this was just not possible.

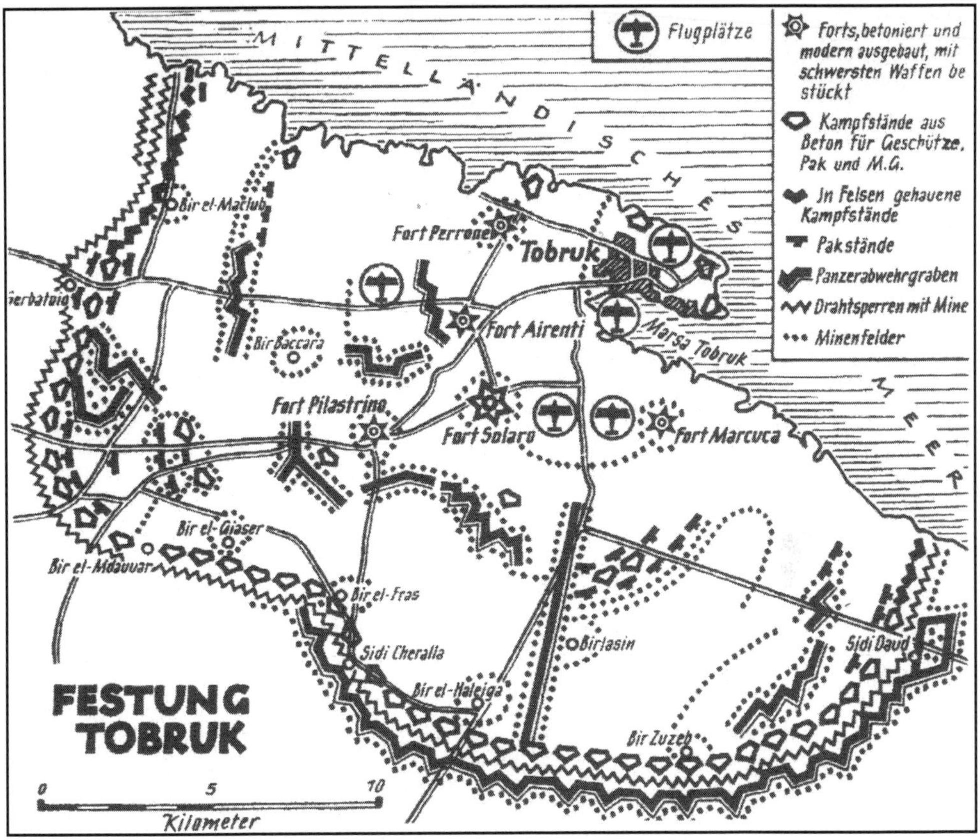

German plan of Tobruk (Map from Strategic Design Project)

CHAPTER 12
DEFEAT IN GREECE

Germany invades Greece and Yugoslavia

On 6 April the Greek Foreign Minister in Athens and the Greek Legation in Berlin were handed a Memo which stated that the Greek Government by:

> ...permitting strong English forces to enter its country has itself brought about a situation toward which Germany can no longer remain inactive. The Reich Government has therefore now ordered its troops to expel the British forces from Greek soil. Any resistance offered to the Wehrmacht will be ruthlessly crushed. In the note it is emphasized that the German troops do not come as enemies of the Greek people ... rather the blow which Germany is compelled to strike on Greek territory is aimed at England.[1]

On the same day some 200,000 German troops invaded Greece and Yugoslavia. While one German army headed for Belgrade, the 12th Army commanded by General List invaded Serbia and Greece through Bulgaria. The German Army was well-equipped with support from Panzer tanks and the *Luftwaffe*. Within days the Yugoslav Army began to disintegrate under the immense pressure exerted by the powerful German forces.

The *Luftwaffe* heavily bombed strategic positions, and particularly the port of Piraeu, where that evening the ship *Clan Fraser*, which was full of supplies and TNT was blown up, destroying much of the harbour in the process. It was a severe blow for the Allied cause.

The Aliakhmon and Metaxas Lines broken

The three Greek Divisions and other forces of the Greek Macedonian Army manning the Metaxas Line faced a formidable German assault. They were no match for the *Wehrmacht* and within days began to disintegrate, allowing German troops to capture Thessalonica (Saloniki) on 9 April.

Then as Yugoslav resistance weakened against the overwhelming German assault, German troops headed south towards the Monastir Gap separating Yugoslavia and Greece. Along both lines the German Air-force was far superior to the Allied Air-force, and their superiority was evident on the ground.

German and Allied troops were engaged in battle on the Aliakhmon Line from 10 April. Holt and the men of the 6th Australian Division were now joined by some New Zealanders

1 Ribbentrop to German Legation in Athens, 5 April, 1941, Berlin, Document No. 274, ibid, Vol. XII, p. 464.

including Charles Upham and the men of his 20th Battalion in the region of Servia, south of the Monastir Gap. Upham's first brush with combat was being strafed on the road by a German fighter plane. When the shock of this introduction was over, the noise of more engines became apparent, and Upham looking up, suddenly yelled, 'Duck, quick … they're Heinkels!' Thereupon his platoon was inundated with bombs from the *Luftwaffe* bomber.[2]

Shortly later another fighter (probably a Messerschmidt) came roaring in and Upham grabbed a Bren gun and attempted to bring it down, cursing that he had missed.[3] Westbrook, recalled of a similar incident:

> … we suffered the worst machine gunning we have ever had. Twelve Messerschmidt 110's appeared very suddenly and strafed us for about half an hour and I think that that was the most scared I'd ever been. Lying face down in an outfield, the only thing that I could do to pass the time away was to try and drown the ants with the perspiration that was streaming off my nose.[4]

While New Zealand, Australian, British and Greek soldiers fought their hardest they were no match for the German juggernaut. The entire Allied force then had to withdraw south by 14 April.[5] It was a harrowing time. 'We travelled through the mountain', Holt wrote, 'and over the narrow winding roads. The trucks were bumper to bumper. Hold-ups were common as the truck drivers were very tired and very often went to sleep at the wheel.'[6]

On one occasion German forces overwhelmed a unit of the Jewish Pioneers who were clearing the roads. The Reuters correspondent wrote of this action, that, 'A squad of Australians came to their assistance and together the two units retreated, firing until their ammunition was exhausted. Only a few escaped.'[7]

Such a story was repeated on numerous occasions. The Allied soldiers had to keep moving as the Germans were always right up against them. Arthur Leggett recalled that on one occasion the look-out spotted dive bombers and yelled at the men to get out of the truck. He wrote of what followed:

> The truck thumps to halt. We burst out of the back and take to the countryside, putting as much distance between ourselves and the roadway as the available time allows before burrowing into the earth and making ourselves as small as possible.
>
> A Stuka attack is a nerve-wracking, morale-destroying experience.[8]

2 Sandford, K, ibid, p. 55.
3 Sandford, K. ibid, p. 56.
4 King, M. *New Zealanders at War*, p. 171.
5 The surrender of Yugoslavia on 17 April further exacerbated the desperate situation of the Greeks.
6 Holt, B. ibid, p. 96.
7 *The Palestine Post,* 11 May 1941, p. 3.
8 Leggett, A. *Don't Cry For Me*, p. 141.

The Allied forces were no match for the Germans who had overwhelming superiority of arms. Their constant bombing of targets such as Athens and Piraeus Harbour caused considerable concern for the Greek Government.

Yugoslavia surrenders followed by Greece

Yugoslavia surrendered on 17 April. This placed an extra huge burden on the Greek Government, as well as the Allied high command. At this time Rommel's advance into Cyrenaica created considerable concern, as a potential assault upon Egypt and the Suez Canal was now a distinct possibility. Churchill on 18 April informed General Wilson that any potential evacuation from Greece took second priority over securing victory (or at least thwarting the German-led movement) in Libya.[9]

As the Allied troops withdrew south it was decided to make a stand at the famous location of Thermopylae. The Allied troops began arriving there on 20 April. After running communication wires out to the various positions, Leggett waited like the rest of the Allied soldiers, and reflected, 'Tired men waited for a superior enemy to commence the battle.'[10]

Once the Germans arrived the battle began in earnest. There were some encouraging early signs, as Leggett notes, 'Our troops were giving the Germans a rough time but we had no mortars and our artillery lines were in danger of encirclement. We were in a rather precarious position.'[11] The New Zealanders held a position near Kriekouki Pass, and while there, Upham was so sick with dysentery that he could hardly walk. Unperturbed, he located a donkey and thereupon rode around and inspected his positions.

The precarious position at Thermopylae was made even worse when the Greek forces facing the Germans on the western side of the line capitulated, thereby exposing Thermopylae to German encirclement. There was no choice but to withdraw and continue to move further south to the next position near Brallos.

The situation thereafter became so desperate for the BEF and for the Greek Army that on 21 April the Greek Government informed General Wilson that it was for the best of the country if the BEF and remnants of the Greek Army withdraw as quickly as possible. Three days later on 24 April 1941, the Greeks surrendered to the Germans.

The evacuations began on that same day, some from beaches on the mainland, others from locations on the Pelponesse Peninsula. Arthur Leggett joined some 3,500 other men and scrambled aboard the *SS Thurland Castle* at one of the beach pick-ups, and quickly headed off escorted by *HMS Coventry*. It didn't take long before they were spotted by German aircraft which, Leggett stated, '...came in a determined manner, machine gunning the decks and dropping bombs meant to blow us to hell but landing close by in the ocean.'[12]

9 Chiefs of Staff to Commander-in-Chief, 18 April 1941, in Churchill, W. *The Grand Alliance*, p. 227.
10 Leggett, A. ibid, p. 143.
11 Leggett, A. ibid, p. 143.
12 Leggett, A. ibid, p. 149.

The attacks persevered and miraculously the ship on which Leggett was travelling arrived at Suda Bay in Crete.

Those who didn't manage to get extricated from the beaches on the mainland then had to make the long trip to Kalamata at the southernmost tip of the Peloponesse Peninsular. Without air covering these forces would need to arrive at their destinations before the German aircraft and paratroopers arrived first. It was a rush against time.

The Royal Navy ultimately extricated most of the troops from the various ports. Constant harassment by German aircraft forced the Navy to retire on 29 April, leaving behind a staggering 10,500 stranded troops, mostly at Kalamata.[13]

Although some Allied soldiers did manage to escape into the hills most of these men then spent the following years of the war in German POW camps. The majority of the Allied troops which were evacuated were taken to Crete, and there they hurriedly prepared for an impending German invasion.

The Holocaust reaches Greece

The capture of Thessalonica on 9 April marked the beginning of the darkest period ever for the large and vibrant Jewish community of this ancient city. The editor of the *Palestine Post* stated on 24 April 1941:

> The Nazi juggernaut has driven over another corner of Europe, and in the wake of the mechanized battalions and serried divisions a mob of Gestapo jackals are already at their hideous work. As usual, it is the Jewish communities of the occupied territories which are singled out as the first victims. In all the occupied Balkan countries anti-Jewish legislation on the approved Nazi model is being introduced … No military success, no gloating conquest, can quench the Nazi hatred of the Jew.[14]

On 17 May 1941 Hitler issued a new Directive concerning German military operations in the Greek and Crete region, and apart from providing military and political information relating to the demarcation between German and Italian jurisdiction in occupied Greece, he made an important statement which would seriously affect the approximate 56,000 strong Jewish community in Thessalonica (Saloniki). He stated:

1) In the *area around Saloniki* the Wehrmacht alone has the authority for all military measures. The OKH (Commander in Chief of the German troops in the Balkans) shall submit recommendations regarding the exact demarcation of that area.[15]

13 The approximate casualties for this ill-fated campaign were: Britain, 256 killed, 132 wounded and 6,708 captured; Australia, 320 killed, 494 wounded and 2,030 captured; New Zealand, 291 killed, 599 wounded and 1,614 captured.
14 *Palestine Post,* 24 April 1941, p. 4.
15 *Fuhrer's Directive,* 17 May 1941, Directive No. 29, ibid, Vol. XII, p. 846.

There could only be one reason why he singled out the area around Saloniki for special German treatment. Shortly after the conquest the Jewish people began to be moved into a designated area of the city, basically a ghetto. Associated with the forced move into the ghetto the Nazis thereafter began placing humiliating restrictions upon the Jewish people. Initially the Jewish Affairs Commission began confiscating Jewish libraries and archives and moving these materials to Germany. Various forms of persecution then increased.

Then beginning on 15 March 1943 the Nazis began to place the Jewish people onto trains destined, so they were informed, for labour camps in Poland. Many Church leaders in Greece opposed this deportation. The most outspoken was the Archbishop of Greece, Damaskenos.

All such protests, however, made no difference, and each day trains carrying some 2,000 Jewish people were sent to locations in Poland, mostly to Auschwitz-Birkenau and some to Treblinka. At these camps some of the inmates were kept for slave labour, while the majority were earmarked for death, mostly by gassing, their bodies being immediately cremated.[16]

Of the 46,091 Jewish people who were deported from Thessalonica, only some 1,950 survived – less than 5%. In all, before the German invasion there were between 60-70,000 Jewish people living in Greece. Apart from Thessalonica about 3,000 lived in Athens, while the remainder were spread in small communities all over the mainland and on many of the islands.

The Germans, thereafter, began systematically locating Jewish people wherever they lived, and either sent them to Auschwitz, or killed them where they were. From that initial number of 60-70,000 (even up to 76,000) some 54,000 were murdered - about 70% of the entire Jewish population of Greece. A figure of between 8-10,000 Jewish people survived, primarily due to the unwillingness of the Greek people to surrender them to the Nazis.[17]

The fate of the Jewish people in Greece was a clear example of what would befall the Jewish people in any country which was overrun by the German Army. Inevitably behind, or even associated with the *Wehrmacht* were the SS and those dedicated to implementing to the fullest the Nazi programme of murdering Jewish people.

The official policy behind the systematic murder (or genocide) of the Jewish people will be covered in chapter 20.

16 See Chapter 20 which deals with the decision to implement the final genocide of the Jewish people.

17 Population details from Savich, C. *The Holocaust in Greece, 1941-1944*, in www.balkanalysis.com/2005/11/30/the-holocaust-in-greece-1941-1944/part2. Also Jewish Virtual Library, Shira Schoenberg, www.jewishvirtuallibrary.org/jsource/vjw/greece.html#World%20War%2011. See also, United States Holocaust Museum, onhttp://www.ushman.org/museum/exhibit/online/greece/greece.pdf. Several sources were accessed to gather this information and there were some variations in the numbers.

YUGOSLAVIA
BULGARIA
Monastir Gap
The Metaxas Line
Edessa
Thessaloniki
(Saloniki)
TURKEY
ALBANIA
Vevi
Veria Pass
The
Aliakmon
Line
Kozani
Servia
Gallipoli
Mt Olympus
Lemnos
Tempe Gorge
GREECE
Larisa
Aegean Sea
Lamia
Thermopylae
The Thermopylae Line
Brallos
Patras
Athens
Corinth
Piraeus
Rafina
Rafti
PELOPONNESE
Navplion
Kalamata
Bay of Navarino
Monemvasia
BRITISH AND ANZAC EVACUATION
Mediterranean Sea
Suda Bay
Maleme
CRETE
Sfakia

CHAPTER 13
THE IRAQ CRISIS

Britain's concerns for Iraq

There was a brief period of political quiet in Iraq following the initial Italian set-back in Libya, but following the German victories in Libya and Greece in March 1941, the mood changed again. The British position in the Eastern Mediterranean was suddenly very vulnerable. Axis forces were on the move everywhere, with the potential for further anti-British and anti-Allied movements in other Middle Eastern locations.

The pro-German group in Iraq continued to grow in influence, and Rashid Ali al-Gaylani and other members of the 'Golden Square' planned to assassinate the regent, Emir Abdul-Illah.[1] When he became aware of this plot, Abdul-Illah fled the country on 31 March. Rashid Ali al-Gaylani then orchestrated a *coup d'etat* on 1 April and seized power on 3 April 1941 by overthrowing the former pro-British government. The signs were now ominous for Britain. If Iraq became a fully-fledged ally of Nazi Germany, and if Germany conquered Greece, then Vichy-controlled Syria could easily be taken over by Nazi Germany. Britain's interests in the region would be encircled.

Churchill, on 8 April, asked the Secretary of State for India Lord Linlithgow to send some spare troops to the strategic port of Basra. Linlithgow and General Auchinleck, the Commander-in-Chief in India, complied. Following the first arrival of these troops on 18 April, Rashid Ali, in violation of the Anglo-Iraq Treaty of 1930, then forbade any further troop arrivals in Iraq. Rashid Ali was waiting for German aid, and was endeavouring to ensure the British did not build up a strong force in Iraq before any German aid arrived.

Meanwhile the anti-British sentiment increased, forcing Britain to order the evacuation of all its subjects, especially from Baghdad, to the strategic Habbaniya air force base to the west of Baghdad. After 230 civilians were airlifted there on 29 April 1941, the air force base housed about 2,200 fighting men and 9,000 civilians.[2] When the Iraqi forces then surrounded the base with some 9,000 troops, it became impossible for any more people to enter. All remaining British and Allied personnel were then housed in the British Embassy and United States legation in Baghdad.[3]

Tensions now rose daily, in and around Habbaniya, in Baghdad, and amongst the 100,000 strong Jewish community of Iraq, especially those living in Baghdad. The British were now in the most critical time of the war concerning its interests in the Middle East. A crisis for the British also meant a crisis for the Jewish people.

1 Abdul-Illah was regent for his four year old nephew, Faisal II.

2 Churchill, W. *The Grand Alliance*, p. 255.

3 Kirk, G. *The Middle East in the War*, p. 70.

Ribbentrop's Brief of Iraq to Hitler

The German interest in Iraq continued to grow, and on 27 April 1941 Foreign Minister Ribbentrop put together a 'Brief for the Fuhrer'. In this 'Brief' Ribbentrop reiterated that the Iraqi Government and Army were decidedly anti-British. As a result of recent British forces landing in Iraq, the Iraqi Government had requested material assistance from Germany, and the German Reich was in the process of preparing some 500-600 tons of military equipment to be sent to Iraq.

There were several different ways in which this military equipment could arrive in Iraq, via Syria, using an Italian intermediary, or by a direct airlift by the *Luftwaffe*. Ribbentrop concluded his 'Brief' by stating, 'The Iraq Government should by no means be induced to enter into an open fight against England until it is certain that Iraq is strong enough with the aid of the Axis to hold her own against the English.'[4]

The Battle for Iraq begins

The impending arrival of more British reinforcements at Basra forced Rashid Ali to attack Habbaniya base sooner than he wanted, as he would have preferred to wait until the German reinforcements and aid had arrived. That battle began on 2 May 1941.

It would take time before any British reinforcements could arrive at Basra and then get to Habbaniya in time. Churchill then requested Wavell to put together a relief force from Palestine. Wavell was already distraught with the set-backs in Cyrenaica and Greece and having to now prepare Crete for an anticipated German airborne assault, and had few troops to spare. Churchill and the Chiefs of Staff then reiterated the official position to Wavell:

> A commitment in Iraq was inevitable. We had to establish a base at Basra, and control that port to safeguard Persian oil in case of need.
>
> A line of communication to Turkey through Iraq has also assumed greater importance owing to German air superiority in the Aegean Sea … The security of Egypt remains paramount. But it is essential to do all in our power to save Habbaniya and to control the pipeline to the Mediterranean.[5]

Wavell still procrastinated, which elicited another, even firmer directive from Churchill on 6 May. The consequences of procrastination could be very serious. If the Iraqis managed to capture Habbaniya they could consolidate their position in central and northern Iraq, which would then in turn provide extra time to await the anticipated German support.

If Iraq was reconstituted as a fully-fledged Axis ally, it could easily have engineered anti-Allied activities throughout the region, as well as providing the Axis forces with easier

4 Memorandum by the Foreign Minister, 27 April 1941, Document No. 415, 'Brief for the Fuhrer, ibid, Vol. XII, pp. 655-6.

5 Churchill, W. *The Grand Alliance*, p. 257.

access to fuel sources, and establish them close to the Suez Canal, and closer to India. In addition, although it may not have factored much in Wavell's planning, there was also the matter of the welfare and safety of the approximately 100,000 Jewish people who lived in Iraq.

The stakes were high, as Churchill knew, and wrote accordingly to Wavell on 9 May 1941, '...what matters is action; namely swift advance of the mobile column to establish effective contact between Baghdad and Palestine. Every day counts, for the Germans may not be long.'[6]

Wavell now began to pull together this composite force, but it would not arrive at Habbaniya until 12 May. Named *Habforce* (short for Habbaniya force), this composite group included elements of the 1st Cavalry Division, the 1st Battalion Essex Regiment, 60th Field Regiment RA, and some other smaller units including the Arab Legion from Transjordan. It also included some Jewish men from Palestine, primarily men associated with the *Irgun* who were demolition experts.[7] This group was led by David Raziel and seconded by Yaacov Meridor, later a leading Israeli politician. Overall command was under General John Clark, and was comprised of a flying column named *Kingcol,* and the main group.

While they were assembling and moving out the small force within Habbaniya went out on forays and combined with an attack by a few Wellington bombers, the Iraqi force there began to weaken in resolve. It was now a race against time, and the issue was which side would receive aid and reinforcements first, the British from Palestine or the Iraqi's from Germany.

German-Vichy-Iraqi collaboration

Meanwhile the Iraqi's sent out a fresh request to the Germans. The Germans now realized that if such support was going to arrive quickly, then it would need to be trans-shipped via Vichy-controlled Syria, and would need to include material from the French Army stockpile under the control of the Italian Armistice (or Control) Commission.

General Dentz, head of the Vichy government in Syria asked for clarification from the Vichy Government concerning any dealings with the Germans at this point. On 4 May the Vichy Minister of War wrote to him:

> It is not impossible that you may shortly be faced with a German attempt to give assistance to Iraq. If formations of German aircraft should seek to land on your airfields or should fly over your territory, it would be expedient to consider that France is not in the position of a neutral Power with respect to Germany. It is not possible to treat the armed forces of Germany as hostile, but you would naturally oppose with force any intervention by

6 Churchill to Wavell, 9 May 1941, in Churchill, W. *The Grand Alliance*, p. 261.

7 The *Irgun* was associated with the Revisionist Zionist movement established by Zev Jabotinsky and was often opposed to the Central Zionist movement led by David ben Gurion and Chaim Weizmann..

the British forces in case they should seek to intervene in any manner whatever.[8]

The Germans then approached the Vichy government in France for permission to use this material, and negotiations took place in Paris between 6-7 May, and included Admiral Darlan, Marshal Petain's deputy in the Vichy Government. An agreement was finally struck, which stated in brief:

a) The stocks of French arms under Italian control in Syria would be made available for transport to Iraq;
b) Assistance would be given in the forwarding of arms shipments of other origins that arrive in Syria by land or sea for Iraq;
c) Permission was given for German planes destined for Iraq to make intermediate landings and take on gasoline in Syria;
d) Permission was granted for other specific arms to be given to the Iraqi Army;
e) An airfield in Syria was to be made available especially for intermediate landing of German planes.[9]

The Germans stated at the conclusion of the negotiations, 'These French concessions go considerably beyond what could have been expected on the German side.'[10] These French concessions, however, came as a result of numerous important concessions they received from the Germans, which included a promise to negotiate on, a) a reduction in the war indemnity, b) a reduction in the area of France occupied by German troops, and c) a large release of French POW's.[11] France stood to gain considerably from this agreement.

A senior German diplomat, Rudolph Rahn was immediately despatched to Syria in order 'to prepare for the purchase of French arms for the equipment of the Iraq Army.'[12] A French diplomat, Jacques Guerard, accompanied him, who would 'transmit to General Dentz an instruction from Darlan that all the measures desired by Guerard with regards to arms deliveries and transports by German planes to Iraq are to be taken at once.'[13] German Minister Grobba was also flying directly to Iraq at the same time.

German-Vichy-Iraq alliance

Rahn was commissioned to accomplish a very complicated task. He had to overcome

8 Vichy Minister of War to Dentz, 4 May 1941, quoted in George Kirk, ibid, pp. 92-93, who sourced it from London, G. *Dentz*, (Lyons, 1945), p. 247.

9 Record of meeting between Admiral Darlan, Finance Minister Bouthillier, Ambassador Abetz, General Vogl, and minister Hemmen, on 6-7 May 1941, Document No. 475, ibid, Vol. XII, p. 740.

10 Record of meeting between Admiral Darlan etc, ibid, p. 741.

11 *Memorandum by Minister Rahn,* Westfalen 30 July 1941, Document No. 165, ibid, Vol. XIII, p. 237; George Kirk, *The Middle East in the War*, p. 93.

12 *Memorandum by Minister Rahn,* Westfalen 30 July 1941, Document No. 165, ibid, Vol. XIII, p. 237. Several Germans from the French Embassy also accompanied Rahn, including Eital Mollhausen.

13 Memorandum by the Director of the Political Department (Woermann), 8 May 1941, Document No. 476, ibid, Vol. XII, p. 742.

possible 'de Gaullists' and pro-British opposition in Syria, ascertain the best method of transferring the arms to Iraq, and to hide the true nature of his mission from the British espionage ring. As Syria was ostensibly neutral, any noticeable German presence in Syria would provide the British with a 'justifiable' cause to invade Syria.

Rahn's delegation landed initially in Aleppo where he determined that the best method of shipment was by railway, partly on the Baghdad Railway, part of which ran through Turkish territory. Turkish permission would thereby be needed.

General Dentz, the Vichy commander in Syria was somewhat apprehensive, citing that the visit of Minister von Hentig in January 1941 had triggered off anti-French demonstrations and cost some 100 lives.[14] Rahn emphasised that his visit was to further French-German relations. At this point Dentz agreed to offer whatever assistance he could to facilitate the transhipment of arms to Iraq, so long as it did not jeopardize their fighting strength.

Dentz pointed out to Rahn, however, 'that the Army of the Levant was exposed to strong Anglo-de Gaullist propaganda, and that, in the event of a British attack on Syria, he could not vouch for its reliability.'[15] For this reason Dentz insisted that the profile of Rahn's German delegation be kept as low as possible. In other words there could be absolutely no outward sign that German officers or representatives were in Syria.

Another potential obstacle was convincing the Italian Control Commission and its commander General de Giorgis, to release the weapons needed, and to have the planes which were impounded flown to various airfields spread throughout Syria. This Rahn managed to accomplish.

By 10 May Rahn had managed to elicit the agreement and cooperation of all the parties involved, and permission was granted for the first shipment of arms to Iraq. Shortly later twenty-seven fully loaded wagons were ready in Aleppo to be entrained to Iraq. Despite numerous obstacles and complications the first train bearing arms for the Iraqi Army arrived in Iraq on 13 May 1941, Rahn having to employ a touch of deception to force the Turks to agree to this initial transhipment. Further trainloads arrived thereafter until the Turks objected, and the British destroyed the rail bridge.

The first German bombers landed in Damascus on 10 May,[16] and despite Rahn's requests for them not to arrive there (where they could easily be spotted by British surveillance aircraft) they continued to do so. Finally when a British reconnaissance plane did appear over the airfield in Damascus, 'the High Commissioner placed the entire country in a state of defence and concentrated troops on the Palestinian border.'[17] These were the first of between 106-120 German planes which flew to Iraq via Syria until 6 June 1941.[18]

The planes arriving in Syria then transported equipment to Iraqi bases in the north at Mosul on 13 May. The arrival of German planes in the north at Mosul now made it

14 *Memorandum by Minister Rahn,* Westfalen 30 July 1941, ibid, p. 239, and footnote No. 4.

15 *Memorandum by Minister Rahn,* Westfalen 30 July 1941, ibid, p. 239.

16 Other sources, including Kirk, state 12 May 1941.

17 *Memorandum by Minister Rahn,* Westfalen 30 July 1941, Document No. 165, ibid, Vol. XIII, p. 243.

18 Dentz states there were 120 planes and the Free French state there were 106. See Kirk, ibid, p. 94 and footnote 1.

imperative that the Allied reinforcements get to Habbaniya quickly, link up with the British force there and quickly capture Baghdad – before the German forces in the north could move south.

The Iraq situation presented an opportunity for both Germany and France to enter into fresh negotiations concerning their relationship. Further meetings were held in which Marshal Petain was also involved, and on 14 May 1941 Darlan informed Dentz in Syria, that:

> Franco-German conversations ended. The Government, under the presidency of the Marshal, have adopted the principle of collaboration with Germany. This collaboration does not imply a declaration of war against Britain, but the orders to resist with force any British attack are confirmed.[19]

While pressure was now on for the Allied relief column to arrive in Iraq, and after the RAF bombed the airfields of Palmyra, Rayaq and Mezze in Syria on 14-15 May which the German planes were using for the transhipment of arms to Iraq,[20]pressure mounted in Germany to increase their presence in Iraq. In a Memorandum on 16 May 1941 the head of the Political Department of the Foreign Ministry stated, 'After first viewing an operation in Iraq with scepticism, the Wehrmacht, and in particular the Luftwaffe have now realized the importance of such a venture, even if in the long run it should not be crowned by complete success.'[21]

This same Memorandum also highlighted that due to Turkish opposition to the transhipment of arms, 'The main weight of the effort is with the Luftwaffe.'[22] A tangible result from Air Marshal Goring's new interest in the venture was the establishment of a quite sizeable air flotilla, named 'Air Commander Iraq', and also the decision to send an army delegation headed by General Helmut Felmy. When a German liaison officer, Captain Darjes, returned from a fact-finding mission to Iraq, he was summoned to a meeting with Hitler. The German interest in the Iraq venture was now increasing; but would the aid and help arrive too late to be of any effective good?

Timely arrival of *Habforce* and Hitler's direct endorsement

The advanced troops of *Habforce* arrived at Habbaniya on 18 May and the following day they joined the British forces from Habbaniya, which had broken out, and were at Falluja some 25 miles from Baghdad. Soon after arrival a German Messerschmidt bombed the vehicle in which Raziel was travelling and killed him. The RAF meanwhile bombed many

19 London, G. *Dentz*, p. 249, as quoted in George Kirk, ibid, p. 94.

20 Kirk, G. ibid, p. 94.

21 Memorandum of Political Department, 16 May 1941, Document No. 528, ibid, Vol. XII, p. 833. Apparently much of this enthusiasm resulted from a personal letter from Ribbentrop to Goring, the original of which had not been found.

22 Memorandum of Political Department, 16 May 1941, Document No. 528, ibid, Vol. XII, p. 833.

of the German planes at Mosul, thereby hindering the expected German movement southwards.

The British-led offensive was now vying with the impending higher level German involvement in Iraq. The extent to which the Germans were now committing themselves is evidenced in a Directive from Hitler, on 23 May 1941, which reveals his active interest in the campaign. Part of this directive states:

> 1. The *Arab liberation movement* in the Middle East is our natural ally against England. In this connection the rising in Iraq has special importance. It strengthens beyond the boundaries of Iraq the forces hostile to England in the Middle East, disturbs English communications, and ties down English troops and shipping space at the expense of other theatres of war.
>   I have therefore decided to advance developments in the Middle East by giving *assistance to Iraq.*[23]

Although the defeat of the British in Iraq was of importance, Hitler made it clear though that the ultimate defeat of 'the English' between the Mediterranean and the Persian Gulf, would only be decided after *Barbarossa.*[24] Nevertheless the support Hitler was prepared to offer the Iraqis was quite substantial. This support would be, as stated by Hitler:

a) To advise and assist the Iraq Armed Forces;
b) To establish military liaison, where possible, with forces hostile to England also outside of Iraq;
c) To gain experiences and data for the German Wehrmacht in this area.[25]

The Iraq mission was to be commanded by General Felmy, who was to oversee the multifarious activities to be carried out through this operation. The military and political developments then intensified towards the end of May 1941, with the Vichy French military command 'weeding' out officers suspected of not being committed to the present Vichy-German collaborationist relationship; the Germans shipping some 5-6,000 Syrian mercenaries over to Iraq (for a price); as well as the defection of numerous Vichy French soldiers over to the Free French stationed in Palestine, as well as other activities.[26]

News of these developments in Syria exacerbated the already stretched British High Command, and prompted General Wavell to bring two brigades of the 7th Australian Division out of Egypt and back to Palestine, and form a potential invasion force comprised also of the Free French and units of the 1st Cavalry Division. There they were placed under the command of General Maitland Wilson, to form the nucleus of a force to invade

23 *Fuhrer's Directive*, 23 May 1941, Directive No. 30, Document No. 543, ibid, Vol. XII, p. 862.
24 *Fuhrer's Directive*, 23 May 1941, ibid, p. 862. Operation *Barbarossa* was the impending invasion of the Soviet Union.
25 *Fuhrer's Directive*, 23 May 1941, Directive No. 30, Document No. 543, ibid, Vol. XII, p. 862.
26 Kirk, G. ibid, p. 95.

Syria if there were clear signs of a German presence there. This redeployment further weakened the defences of Egypt.[27]

Investment of Baghdad and massacre of Jewish people

The combined force of *Habforce* and the troops from Habbaniya defeated the Iraqi forces at Falluja on 29 May, and then headed towards Baghdad. The force arrived on the outskirts of Baghdad on 30 May, causing Rashid Ali al-Gaylani and the Mufti of Jerusalem to flee to Iran.

The British forces, however, did not enter Baghdad immediately, preferring the pro-British regent Abdul-Illah and the new Iraqi government to handle the situation. This decision, however, had disastrous consequences for the Jewish community. Due to damaging pro-Nazi and anti-Jewish propaganda, Arab mobs rampaged into the Jewish suburbs, in a modern day *pogrom*. One who survived this massacre was Nazima Muallem-Cohen, who wrote:

> "All night we heard shots and screams. Towards morning it was quiet. My father went to the synagogue in the morning. He did not pray. When he returned, he told mother what had happened: they burned Jewish houses. They raped girls, plundered Jewish homes, burned a synagogue. And then, just as father was telling us this, they broke into our house … with shouts and clubs, and my father took us up the stairs to the roof. We began to go up … Suddenly mother heard a gunshot. She turned around and saw my father killed … A policeman came and mother started to cry … and she said to him: 'They killed my husband…' And he said to her: 'What death would you like to die?' And he hit her in the head with the butt of his rifle …"[28]

During 1-2 June 1941 at least 180 innocent Jewish people were massacred, and hundreds more were seriously maimed. The damage to Jewish property was exceedingly high, and smaller outbreaks of violence occurred elsewhere in the country. This blatant and callous massacre provoked the Zionist movement into action in Iraq. Thereafter thousands of young Jewish Iraqis prepared themselves for self-defence and even for ultimate immigration to Palestine.

End of the Iraq Crisis and Churchill's assessment

Despite the re-taking of Baghdad, the German delegation continued to press for German and French collaboration in fighting the British forces who had now landed in Mosul. This situation was potentially dangerous for all three parties involved, but the French finally prevailed upon the Germans to withdraw their presence from Syria on 4 June 1941, thereby ending the ill-fated German-Iraq venture.

27 Wavell, A. *Despatch*, iv, paras 90-91, in Kirk, G, ibid, p.96.
28 Lossin,Y. ibid, p. 303.

Ironically the situation in Iraq could have turned out quite differently had it not been for the consequences of an Allied defeat – at Crete. That battle had caused so many German casualties, that the reinforcements intended for Iraq never arrived as intended. Winston Churchill later addressed the House of Commons:

> … Rashid Ali appealed constantly to the Germans to make good their promises, but only 30-40 German aeroplanes arrived from Syria … But meanwhile there was an explanation for this failure of the Germans. The German parachute and air-borne corps, which no doubt was to have operated in Iraq and would have been assisted on its journey across Syria by the Vichy French, had been largely exterminated in the battle of Crete … This specialist corps was so badly mauled in the ferocious fighting that, although they forced us to evacuate Crete, they were themselves in no condition for further operations.[29]

There was after all some consolation from the military debacle that was Crete.

Although the Nazi threat from Iraq had now been forestalled, there was no guarantee of long-term peace in this strategic region. Hitler at this very time was preparing for his greatest military venture, the invasion of the Soviet Union. If everything would go as planned the Germans could still enter into the Eastern Mediterranean region – via the Caucasus. To get to the Caucasus, however, would entail capturing the key city of Stalingrad. The military danger to the Middle East from the north and east was by no means over.

The Mufti's movements

The British-led victory in Iraq caused the Mufti to seek a new haven, and he and Rashid Ali al-Gaylani quickly fled to Iran. The Director of the Political Department of the Foreign Ministry, Herr Woermann, wrote a Memorandum on 6 June 1941 stating that the Mufti and al-Gaylani were planning to visit Berlin and then later to settle in Syria. Woermann stated:

> Gaylani and the Grand Mufti are of value for us and for the Arab movement only if they are in a position to participate actively. This will hardly be possible from Syria at the present time. Moreover, the situation in Syria is so uncertain that they would run unnecessary risks there. Therefore the journey to Syria should be postponed.[30]

Woermann suggested that Gaylani and Haj Amin 'come to Berlin for a short sojourn.'[31] While the Mufti was free, and based in the very centre of the Nazi regime, there was still further danger for the Jewish people in the Middle East.

29 Speech of Winston Churchill in House of Commons, 9 September 1941. Quoted in Pearlman, M. *The Mufti of Jerusalem*, (London 1947), pp. 38-39.

30 *Memorandum by the Director of the Political Department*, 6 June 1941, Document No. 599, ibid, Vol. XII, p. 972.

31 *Memorandum by the Director of the Political Department*, 6 June 1941, ibid, p. 972.

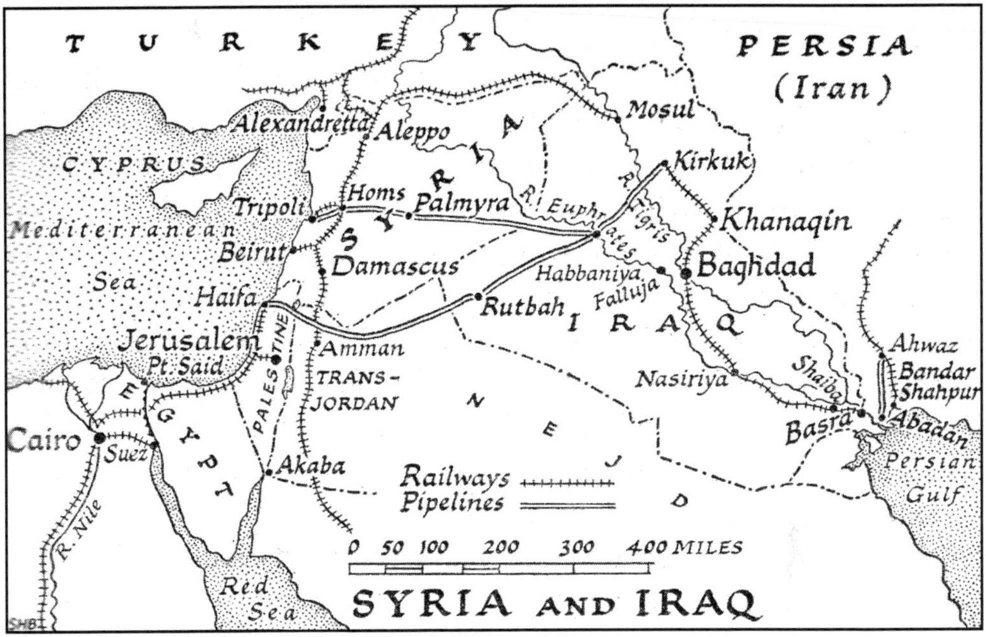

Map from Churchill, W. *The Grand Alliance*, p. 265. (Reproduced with permission of Curtis Brown, London on behalf of the Estate of Sir Winston Churchill. Copyright © Winston S. Churchill)

Chapter 14
Defeat in Crete

Hitler's directive for Crete

As the German Army were winding up their campaign in Greece, Hitler issued his Directive No. 28 for the conquest of Crete on 25 April 1941. This was to be known as *Operation Merkur*, and the capture of Crete was 'in order to have a base for conducting the air war against England in the Eastern Mediterranean.'

Hitler entrusted command of the operation to Commander in Chief of the Luftwaffe, and instructed him to 'principally draw upon the Air-borne Corps and the Luftwaffe units that are employed in the Mediterranean.' Once the island had been captured, then the specialised Air-borne Corps would be withdrawn for deployment elsewhere.[1]

Preparations in Crete

The vulnerability of the Allied position in the Eastern Mediterranean was now only too evident and the defence of Crete became even more imperative. Although some Allied troops were already in Crete, these were reinforced by the evacuees from Greece. Together they consolidated a defence line, especially around the port of Suda Bay and the three major cities of Heraklion, Retimo and Caneans on the northern coast. The prime strategic locations though were the various airfields, especially at Maleme in the west.

These strategic areas would naturally be the prime focus of a German assault. The defence of Crete was entrusted to the great New Zealander, General Freyberg VC, who, like Blamey in Greece, was extremely sceptical of the possibility of success against overwhelming German forces. He contacted his government and asked them to pressure the highest authorities to back up the defence of Crete with naval and air support.[2]

The evacuees from Greece arrived for the most part under-equipped, tired and demoralised. After being deposited at Suda Bay Arthur Leggett and the men of 2/11th Battalion made their way to the nearby airfield at Retimo and began to dig in under the olive trees. He wrote of the state of his battalion:

> The whole battalion was in a bad way and our platoon was no different to the rest. Our clothing was dilapidated and, whilst causing no problem during the day, it afforded little comfort against the cold at night.
>
> We still had a rifle but ammunition was in very short supply…

1 Fuhrer's Directive, 25 April 1941, Document No. 403, Directive No. 28, ibid, Vol. XII, p. 636.
2 Sandford, K. ibid, p. 62.

Food was terribly scarce and cooking equipment 'make-shift'. The battalion was so spread out that company cooking became a problem. Our platoon appointed its own cook and we cooked for ourselves. Our principal cooking utensil was a 4 gallon petrol tin into which was tossed our rations of bully beef accompanied by occasional fresh vegetables purchased under the barter system from the local villagers.[3]

Shortly after arrival General Freyberg visited Leggett's position, and he 'told us' Leggett stated 'what to expect. It wasn't good news. We were to be bombed and strafed by enemy aircraft before an eventual paratroop landing designated to capture the airstrip.'[4]

The Allied troops dug in and waited for the inevitable invasion. While the remnants of the British Expeditionary Force made preparations as best they could, an intense battle was already being fought in the air and on sea, and in many regards the first phase of the battle of Crete took place between the Mediterranean Fleet and the numerous transport ships, against the superior numbers of the *Luftwaffe.*

The battle for Crete

The Germans assaulted Crete with the biggest airborne assault in history on 20 May 1941. The two main objectives were the airfield at Maleme and the port at Suda Bay. Later that day further assaults took place at other strategic positions, especially Retimo and Heraklion. Arthur Leggett wrote:

Enemy aircraft patrol and machine gun attacks increased on the morning of 20th May as a group of some twenty Junkers troop-carriers came in from the sea. We thought they were heading for the airstrip but before the coast they turned away and headed for the western end of the island. Another mob came in around mid-day but they turned east; apparently heading for Heraklion.

It wasn't hard to work out where the next lot was going to land.[5]

The New Zealanders bore the brunt of the initial landings, as they were securing Malema airfield. This area likewise had received a real hammering in the morning, then, as Sandford writes, 'Black dots suddenly fell from the bellies of the low-flying planes. In an instant the dots were blossoming into parachutes, hundreds upon hundreds of them, swaying earthwards, filling the sky with their different colours.'[6]

These dots and parachutes were none other than Hitler's favourite airborne troops. When the suddenness of this spectacle died away the New Zealanders began to fire at the incoming German troops. Although many died, many others who were out of reach of

3 Leggett, A. ibid, pp. 150-51.
4 Leggett, A. ibid, p. 151.
5 Leggett, A. ibid, p. 153.
6 Sandford, K. ibid, p. 65.

the firing, landed safely, formed up, took their supplies and went into action.[7]

Shortly afterwards the Junkers bombers came in lower than usual pulling behind them up to six gliders full of German troops. The New Zealanders in and around Maleme airport were in for a horrid time. Charles Upham and the men of the 20th Battalion were in the reserve area closer to the town of Hanea (Canea) and were observing the proceedings further west. Suddenly they were informed that some German troops had landed nearby. Although still suffering from severe dysentery Upham moved out and personally dealt with some of the paratroopers. This was the first of numerous acts during this campaign which was soon to make Upham a legend throughout the Allied forces.

Meanwhile at Maleme more German troops continued to land on the western end of the airfield. The New Zealanders wanted desperately to counter-attack, but for some inexplicable reason they were not released to do this. It later became known that the German troops were expecting a counter-attack, and doubted their ability to withstand it.[8] German paratroopers and glider troops were now landing all over the island, especially at the strategic locations. From his position near the airfield at Retimo Arthur Leggett recalls:

> Around 4 pm a whole swarm of fighters and light bombers began to pay considerable attention to our area by intense bombing and strafing; but we were dug in and stayed under cover … and the whole battalion waited.
>
> They first appeared as black dots superimposed above the horizon separating the blue sky from the blue ocean.
>
> Not just a few planes but a whole armada of Junkers three-engined troop-carriers…
>
> They … commenced flying along the coast towards the airstrip directly in front of the battalion's position.
>
> It was an awesome sight as doll-like figures began jumping out of the planes to fall a short distance before their 'chutes opened and floated them to the ground.[9]

While Leggett, other Australians, British and Greek troops fought against the German paratroopers and glider-borne troops at these locations, the key location was Maleme. After fighting against heavy odds and out-equipped, this airfield fell on 21 May, thereby allowing more German troops to land in Crete. The fighting on land was tough and often hand to hand, with the Anzacs and British, alongside Greeks and local Cretans not giving an inch. The battle for Crete though was really won, as it was in Greece, in the skies. The German *Luftwaffe* held the advantage, especially after it captured the airfield at Maleme.

It was imperative that Maleme be retaken. Early in the morning of 22 May the 20th and 28th New Zealand Battalions (the Maori Battalion) went forward to recapture this

7 Sandford, K. ibid, p. 66. Of the 10,000 German paratroopers who landed, some 4,000 died.
8 Sandford writes that later the commander of the 4th Brigade, Brigadier L. M. Inglis asked General Student, the German commander of the invasion, what would have happened if the New Zealanders had counter-attacked that day, and he responded, 'If you had done so, I could not have held Crete.' Sandford, K. ibid, p. 68.
9 Legget, A . ibid, p. 153.

strategic position. Upham's platoon was suddenly pinned to the ground by machinegun fire. Charles Upham single-handed silenced that machine-gun post and the eight German paratroopers manning it. This was merely the first of many similar exploits of this extraordinary man over the following days in Crete, heroics which won him the Victoria Cross. Yet as heroic as the New Zealanders were, they were overwhelmed by the numbers of Germans who had now landed at Maleme. They had to withdraw.

Similar events were occurring elsewhere. Once the Germans secured a position they were able to bring in more air-borne troops, as well as utilise the airfield they had secured at Maleme. Leggett's position near Retimo was also overrun , and he too was informed that they were withdrawing. His commanding officer, Captain Sandover told the men of the 2/11th Battalion, 'The island has capitulated…I'm afraid its every man for himself. You can stay here and be made a prisoner of war or you can follow me. I'm heading over the mountains to the other side of the island.'[10] Leggett and his mates headed for the mountains.

A general withdrawal from Crete was called for on 28 May. Except for some of the troops fighting near Heraklion, the remaining soldiers would need to withdraw over the high mountain ridge in the centre of the island and then reach the small port of Sfakia on the south coast. This withdrawal was another test of endurance for the Allied troops, and there were numerous accounts of bravery. While most men clamoured to get aboard a Royal Navy ship, one man was distraught at having to leave Crete, especially having to leave behind some of his men. This was Charles Upham, who by now was a walking and wounded skeleton. Sandford wrote:

> That he was already physically far past the point of effective soldiering he did not accept.
>
> Den Fountaine said: 'I actually had to hold Charlie and literally drag him off.'[11]

By 1 June 1941 the Royal Navy Mediterranean Fleet had succeeded in taking some 16,500 Allied soldiers to safety in Egypt. Unfortunately about 5,000 were unable to be evacuated. Many of these then fled to the hills, where they were sheltered by the locals, or survived according to their own whims.[12] Leggett and his mates had managed to trudge over the mountains, but they were not picked up by the British Navy. Instead they were surrounded one day by a heavily armed German unit and had no choice but to surrender.

Thereafter began a terrible ordeal as they were moved to various locations on foot to the northern coast. Then they were transported by a dirty ship to Thessalonica. Until this

10 Leggett, A. ibid, p. 159. Leggett then stated how the 2/11th Battalion had lost 53 men killed, 126 wounded, and ultimately 426 prisoners of war at Crete.

11 Sandford, K. ibid, p. 103.

12 In October 1996 I spoke with Andreas Broas at Sfakia who told a moving story of how his uncle had sheltered several New Zealand soldiers. The Germans later located the hill, apprehended the New Zealanders, and on a hill near Sfakia Harbour, executed the uncle. He showed me the spot where the execution took place.

point the German guards were mostly those who had initially captured him and his mates, and they were quite lenient in their treatment of the Allied POW's.

Once their ship reached Saloniki, however, their guards were older men, of whom he wrote, 'Most of them had a moustache like Adolf Hitler and they were all bad. Once the seemingly endless counting and checking was over, and we commenced to move off through the streets of Saloniki rifle butts to the ribs became regular aids to progress. If a man dropped through pain or malnutrition he was kicked to his feet and pushed on by a shouting, abusive Hun.'[13]

This was the type of German soldier who now controlled the city of Thessalonica, and it did not augur well for the local inhabitants.

Although the withdrawal from Crete was mostly successful, the defeat was a huge morale loss for the Allies and this defeat caused further concern for the Jewish communities in the Mediterranean region. There was however one small silver lining from the battle and loss – those crack German paratroopers had been so decimated that they could not be effectively used elsewhere in the Eastern Mediterranean region.

13 Leggett, A. ibid, pp.162-63.

CHAPTER 15

THE SYRIAN CAMPAIGN

Vichy France joins the Axis

As soon as the Vichy French regime openly collaborated with Nazi Germany in its quest to send arms and personnel to Iraq, the British realized they had no choice but to invade Syria and neutralize any potential future threat from this region. General Wavell informed Churchill on 22 May 1941:

> This Syrian business is disquieting, since German Air Force established in Syria are closer to the Canal and Suez than they would be at Mersa Matruh. The [Vichy] French seem now wholly committed to the Germans. I am moving reinforcements to Palestine ... because we feel we must be prepared for action in Syria, and weak action is useless.[1]

Wavell's view was also that of Australian Prime Minister Robert Menzies, who cabled to Churchill on 29 May 1941 concerning the situation in Syria:

> I again emphasize to you that Australia and New Zealand have a large stake of four divisions in the Middle East, subject to the deductions in Greece and Crete, in addition to their vital interest in the preservation of one of the great Empire bastions. A defeat around the Suez would be a calamity of the first magnitude.[2]

Germany was also pressuring Turkey to forego her neutrality. If the Germans took control over Syria, thereby forming an Axis link across the Aegean and Eastern Mediterranean, it may have influenced Turkey. Despite the recent victory in Iraq the situation in the Eastern Mediterranean was still very critical for the Allies.

Formation of the *Palmach*

At this critical time when so many of the young Jewish men were in various service units with the British Army, and with a German invasion from any direction now a real possibility, the Jewish leadership established a special or elite force (similar to a commando unit) on 14 May 1941 from within the *Hagana.* This elite unit was named *Palmach* - an acronym for 'Shock Companies'.

The basic aim of the *Palmach* was to defend the Jewish community against an Axis invasion, and against an Arab attack upon them in conjunction with the Axis invasion. It

1 Wavell to Churchill, 22 May 1941. Quoted in Churchill, W. *The Grand Alliance,* pp. 325-326.
2 Quoted in Laffin, J. *Greece, Crete and Syria,* p. 124.

was commanded by Yitzhak Sadeh. Uzi Narkiss stated that the role of the *Palmach* was 'to fight against the Germans', but, he added, 'Everyone was naïve [including] the President, Mr. Ben Zvi, our leader, who thought that a Jewish guerrilla army would be able to stop and fight the famous German Army, during the peak of its victories' [3]

The impending German attack forced the Jewish community of Palestine to lay the foundations for a very resourceful armed unit, which would greatly benefit them in the future. They would have their first forays during the upcoming conflict in Syria.

Complications in Syria

The defeat of the Iraqi forces once again changed the geo-political dynamics in the Middle East. The Vichy French authorities were now very concerned that the presence of German military personnel in Syria would provide the British with a pretext to attack. On 1 June 1941 Admiral Darlan, informed the German Ambassador in Paris that he wanted all German personnel in Syria to leave.[4] This request was reinforced by the High Commissioner in Syria, General Dentz who also wanted all Germans out of Syria before the same mistake happened in Syria as had happened in Iraq.[5]

The Jewish communities in Syria and nearby Palestine were perturbed by all these movements. In Palestine the Jewish newspapers were daily reporting the atrocities inflicted upon their brethren in Europe. On 4 June 1941 another 5,000 Palestinian Jews volunteered for the British Army and at their induction service Chief Rabbi Uziel said:

> … since the destruction of the Second Temple the Jewish people had never been engaged in a holy war as today.[6]

The composition of the opposing forces

An Allied conquest of Syria was imperative. The invasion force would be commanded by the British General Maitland Wilson, and would be comprised of the 7th Australian Division minus the troops in Tobruk, as well as Free French, British and Indian troops. Later, components of the 6th Australian Division that did not get taken to Crete from Greece were also involved, and an Arab Legion force of some 3,500 led by Major John Glubb.

Opposing them was a large Vichy French force of some 60,000 including French Legionnaires, and many from French colonies in Africa.

When the 7th Australian Division was transferred from Egypt they found themselves scattered through the Galilee region. The 2/5 Field Regiment, including Roden Cutler was located near to Nazareth. The biographer of Cutler, Colleen McCullough wrote

3 Interview with General (reserve) Uzi Narkiss, on *The Battle for Zion*.

4 The Embassy in Paris to the Foreign Ministry, 1 June 1941, Document No. 581, telegram No. 1690, ibid, Vol. XII, p. 936.

5 The Embassy in Paris to the Foreign Ministry, 1 June 1941, ibid, p. 937.

6 *Palestine Post,* 5 June 1941.

concerning this time:

> On 30 May the regiment moved up to Jdiede, ten miles to the west of Nazareth. Here was country surely not unlike that Jesus Christ had looked across, fertile timeless fields dewed with forested hills. The inhabitants of Jdiede were Jewish and lavishly hospitable, even to offering bunches of flowers. It was a land of milk and honey.
>
> Training intensified. Peculiar shivers ran down the spines of men like Roden who were acquainted with the Bible, for most of the exercises took place on the plain of Armageddon. An omen, or merely a coincidence? Those who knew their Bible wondered.[7]

Jewish involvement

While preparing for the invasion the British authorities required intelligence concerning the terrain and disposition of the French forces, and also some capable saboteurs who could blow up the Vichy communications system, and who knew the lay of the land and who knew Arabic. The Arab department of the SOE (Military Intelligence), had recruited some Arab men for this task.

Three or four days before the invasion these Arab men suddenly disappeared. The head of the department, Group Captain Donville, was in a quandary. Then Julian Amery, whose father Leo Amery had been an active proponent of the Balfour Declaration, offered to speak to the Jewish leadership about the problem.[8]

The Jewish leadership was more than willing to step in, offering to raise two companies of specialists, who mostly knew Arabic, but who could also operate as sappers and guides.

Prior to this the *Haganah* had already experienced one failed operation. On 18 May a group of twenty-three young Jewish men set out in a small boat to destroy the oil refineries at Syrian Tripoli. The boat disappeared and there was no trace of these men. This event caused tremendous grief throughout the Jewish community in Palestine.[9]

Numerous other Jewish men were accepted as a company of guides, commanded by two leading *Haganah* men, Yigal Allon and Moshe Dayan. While stationed at Kibbutz Hanita on the Lebanon border, Dayan's small groups made numerous spying trips over the border, supplying the British with invaluable information.

Dayan also made trips through the land looking for recruits. At Kibbutz Ramat Yochanan he met a young Yitzhak Rabin, son of a Jewish Legion soldier, and a future Prime Minister of Israel. Dayan asked Rabin if he could fire a rifle, throw a grenade, operate a machine-gun, drive a car and a motorcycle. Despite only being able to do half of these, Dayan nevertheless signed him for active service. Rabin was co-opted into 'Company B.'

Not long after Dayan met a friend Zalman Mart in Moshav Nahalal and asked him, 'Do

7 McCullough, C. *Roden Cutler, V.C.* p. 98.

8 As testified by Julian Amery and quoted in Lossin, Y. *Pillar of Fire*, p. 305.

9 HaCohen, D. ibid, pp. 133-39.

you want to see the Australians fight?' Mart said he did, so he jumped into Dayan's car and became another recruit.

The Allied troops began moving towards the borders of Lebanon and Syria on 6 June 1941 for what hereafter would be colloquially called the 'slouch hat invasion.' Of this movement the Reuters correspondent, Desmond Tighe wrote:

> Many Australians are fresh from their home country while others have seen service in Greece and the western Desert. Several senior officers who served in Palestine in the last war with Allenby know every inch of the terrain. The "Diggers" are thoroughly at home in Palestine.'[10]

The two Jewish companies of guides were active in the days before the major invasion. Yigal Allon's Company A was working at the north eastern border in the central and eastern sectors of the invading force going into Lebanon, in the region of Marjayoun. Moshe Dayan's Company B was operating closer to the coast, north of Rosh Haniqra.

The young Yitzhak Rabin was given some timely advice. He was told to 'watch out for the French Senegalese (fighting for the Vichy) who were brutal, and for the advancing Australians who shoot first and ask questions later.'[11] There was some sense to this advice as the guides were also sometimes dressed as Arab civilians.

The task of these leading groups of guides was to destroy telephone communications between Sidon and Tyre, and Rabin, being the youngest and most agile of the three in his small unit, was instructed to climb the telephone pole and cut the wire. He later recalled, 'I must admit that my part was very simple in that invasion: a lot of walking, no fighting, though you had to get up a telephone pole – that wasn't easy.'[12]

The invasion begins

The British Government informed the Vichy authorities on 8 June 1941, that because of 'their policy of collaboration with the Axis Powers' and because of German infiltration into Syria, 'Free French troops have, therefore, with the support of Imperial forces, entered into Syria and Lebanon at an early hour this morning.'[13]

In a later communique the British impressed upon Marshal Petain 'to offer no opposition to the measures which the Allied forces are taking in order to prevent the enemy from using Syria as a base of operations against them.'[14]

The invasion which began early on 8 June was a three-pronged attack: One thrust

10 *Palestine Post,* 10 June 1941, p. 1.

11 Comments by Rabin to the author in a meeting at the Ministry of Defense on 5 November 1992. At that interview (when I accompanied Lord Gerald Balfour) Rabin spoke for almost fifteen minutes about the role of the Anzacs in the region. He, like Uzi Narkiss and many other Israelis had the greatest admiration for the Anzac soldiers.

12 Slater, R. *Rabin of Israel*, p. 41.

13 *The Times*, 9 June 1941, quoted in Kirk, G. ibid, p. 97.

14 *The Times,* 14 June 1941, quoted in Kirk, G. ibid, p. 98.

headed for Beirut along the coastal road; a second thrust aimed for Marjayoun and the Bekaa Valley in the centre of the country with their object being the large Rayak airfield; while the third aimed for Damascus, through both Kuneitra and up the railway line to Deraa. The first two thrusts were carried out primarily by the 7th Australian Division, while the thrust aiming for Damascus was comprised primarily of the Free French and the Indian troops, and later reinforced by men from the 6th Australian Division.

From the outset the Axis Powers offered assistance to France, but Admiral Darlan 'did not want to appeal for German assistance at this time because he wished to show that the British attack lacked any pretext.' [15]

Moshe Dayan's injury

Moshe Dayan and his reconnaissance group which was comprised of ten Australian soldiers, four Jewish 'guides' and a local Arab man, managed to experience some fighting before the actual invasion began.

Their task was to secure two bridges on the coastal road some ten kilometers north of the border. Arriving at their target late in the evening of 7 June 1941 they found the bridges had not been damaged by the Vichy French, and knew they had to stay and secure these bridges until the main invasion arrived.

Meanwhile the group decided to attack a nearby police station that they suspected was poorly manned. They were mistaken, and as they approached the French soldiers opened fire with machine guns. The combined Australian-Jewish force then charged the station and took it.

The firing alerted Vichy French troops nearby and soon reinforcements arrived. As the fighting intensified the Allied group realized they had to survive until the main invading force arrived in a few hours' time. It was during this period of time that a bullet hit a pair of binoculars which Dayan was using, shattering his eye.

Bleeding quite profusely, Moshe Dayan's only hope of survival was to be evacuated to a hospital in Palestine as soon as possible. Later with the arrival of the invading force, Dayan was placed on a French truck and driven south passing thousands of Australian troops moving north. Finally he was rushed to a hospital in Haifa in a British ambulance and operated upon. Moshe Dayan survived his ordeal, and later rose to be the Israeli Chief of Staff for the 1956 Suez War and Minister of Defense for the 1967 Six Day War.

Meanwhile there was elation in Palestine as news reached them of the invasion of Lebanon and Syria. The *Palestine Post* wrote:

There was no mistaking the dominant feeling yesterday when the news came through

15 The Embassy in Paris to Foreign Ministry, 11 June 1941, Document No. 616, footnote 5, citing Telegram No. 1730 of 8 June 1941, ibid, Vol. XII, p. 1009. Rudolph Rahn wrote that deliberations concerning an impending French-German military collaboration had been in progress since at least 31 May involving Admiral Darlan. See *Memorandum by Minister Rahn*, 30 July 1941, Document No. 165, ibid, Vol. XIII, p. 252-53. Rahn also mentioned 'The attack of two German Stuka formations was enough to scatter the British fleet and force it to observe the utmost caution' (page 254) indicates that there was some minimal German military involvement.

of the Allied advance into Syria and Lebanon: it was of great relief...Considering what is at stake – Iraq and the road to the east, on one side, Palestine and the road to Suez on the other, the British and the Free French have only taken the course imposed upon them.[16]

Towards the objectives

The invasion force meanwhile made its way towards the three objectives, Beirut, Marjayoun and Damascus. In many areas the fighting was very intense. The Vichy French then began to bomb civilian targets in Palestine itself, and on 10 June Haifa endured a four-hour bombing by enemy planes. Worst was to follow. On 12 June enemy aircraft flew further south to Tel Aviv and one bomb landed on an Invalids Home, killing twelve and injuring twenty-four people. These raids prompted the editor of the *Palestine Post* to write:

> ...it does show what a deadly danger to all neighbouring countries the presence in Syria of German air planes would become if the process were not checked.[17]

Early in the fighting the Axis Powers offered their assistance, but on 11 June the Vichy Minister of War informed General Dentz that such assistance would only be accepted on certain conditions; one of which was that there would be no direct *Luftwaffe* involvement. When, however, the Royal Navy seriously challenged the Vichy Navy along the coast, permission was sought by the French Navy for the involvement of *Stuka* dive-bombers. On several other occasions there were similar requests, but the Vichy leadership recognized that there would be dire consequences if they permitted such direct German involvement.

Most of the work of the Palestinian Jewish guides was ended shortly after the invasion occurred. They had successfully fulfilled their allotted task. But for Yigal Allon there was a nice bonus.

His 'Company A' had captured four Vichy French prisoners and brought them back to the border. At this point he met an officer belonging to the Australian 7th Division, who, Allon wrote:

> ... was very pleased with us and said he would recommend us for decorations. We said that that was no good, because we were not enlisted in the British forces, but could we share the spoils of victory? He would take the prisoners and we would take their arms. He agreed, gave us the arms and invited us to help ourselves from a pile of other arms he had captured from the French. We loaded them into a van, took them away, and used them against the British years later.[18]

16 *Palestine Post,* 9 June 1941, p. 4.

17 *Palestine Post,* 11 June 1941, p. 4. Indeed this situation is reminiscent of situations facing Israel many decades later when Hizbollah missiles landed on Haifa.

18 Bethell, N. *The Palestine Triangle*, p. 104.

The capture of Damascus

The advance to Damascus was hard fought, and many Allied soldiers died in the first thrust. Wavell then sent in reinforcements from India that had recently arrived in Iraq, and men of the 6th Australian Division, who had been evacuated from Greece.[19] With the arrival of these men, General Lavarack, commander of the 7th Australian Division, was now promoted to commander of 1 Australian Corps.

Bob Holt was one of the 6th Australian Division reinforcements who made their way by train onto the Transjordanian plateau and then onto Damascus. Outside Damascus they encountered the large Vichy French fortress of Goybet, the storming of which he wrote:

> It was quiet, peaceful and pleasant looking at the cool white buildings in the distance … Our undermanned sections did not worry too much about digging in – that is until the first shell came whistling over and then we must have looked like a company of beavers.[20]

That evening Holt and his company had the difficult task of capturing the fortress. They had to make their way through barbed wire entanglements, at which time, Holt recalled:

> The French held their fire till we were in the middle of the entanglement and then they blasted shit out of us with everything they had – rifles, machine guns, mortars – the lot.[21]

Holt was hit twice during this attack, first in the leg and then in the chest. The stretcher-bearers managed to extricate him from the field of fire, and some time later he was taken into Damascus for attention.

Some of the men of the 2/3rd Australian Battalion then headed towards the Damascus-Homs road to stop any Vichy forces entering into Damascus from that direction. In the process they overtook trucks full of Free French soldiers – who were supposed to enter Damascus first. A British liaison officer serving with the Free French, Colonel Bernard Fergusson, wrote that the entrance into Damascus was:

> Marred unfortunately, by the sudden appearance on the road of hordes of Australian vehicles crowded with Diggers all imbued with one ambition: to be the first into Damascus. I still don't know where they came from, nor to whom, if anyone, they owed allegiance.[22]

19 *Habforce* also struck out from Iraq aiming for Palmyra in the north.

20 Holt, B. ibid, pp. 117.

21 Holt, B. ibid, p. 118.

22 Laffin, J. *Greece, Crete and Syria,* p. 151.

On 21 June 1941 city officials of Damascus surrendered the ancient city to an Australian officer, Colonel A.S. Blackburm, VC. Blackburn and his staff were then given a sumptuous luncheon.[23] It was all very reminiscent of the 1918 official surrender to the men of the 10th Light Horse Regiment. Then in similar circumstances to 1918, the Free French later repeated the surrender, in order to announce that they had first entered Damascus.

The celebrations in Damascus were marred several days later when Vichy planes bombed the city, killing 70 people. From Damascus Allied troops then headed towards the Bekaa Valley aiming for the strategic Rayak airfield. Meanwhile the other two thrusts were experiencing strong resistance, but slowly their objectives were being met.

Ironically, negotiations between the French and Germans had stalled and none of the German promises which were given which paved the way for France permitting German use of the bases in Syria, had been fulfilled. This caused Dentz at one point to comment to Rahn, "Tell me, what are we fighting for here anyway?"[24] Dentz's comment in many ways sums up this entire campaign in the minds of many of the soldiers on both sides: 'What was the real purpose of this campaign?'

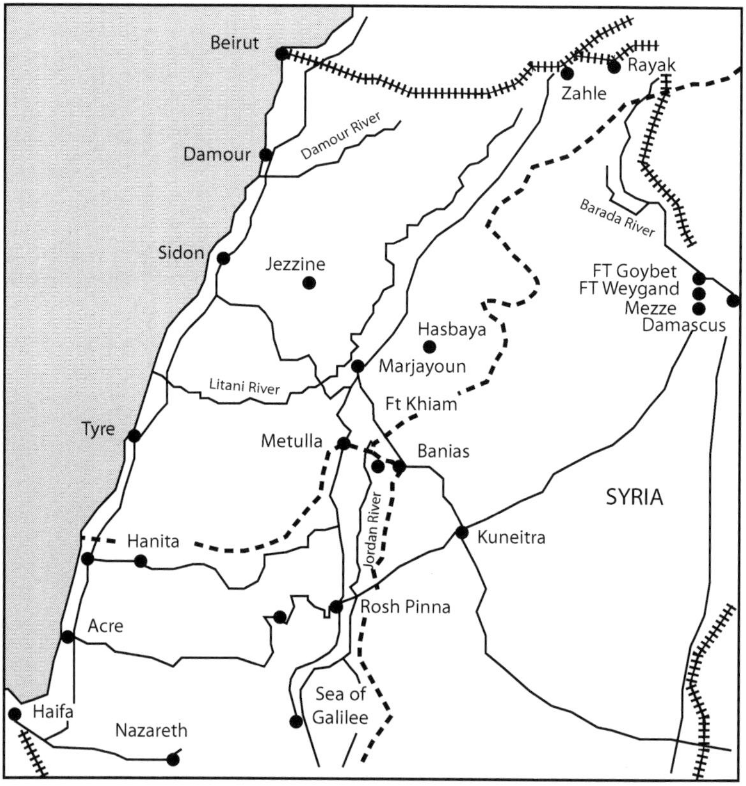

23 Laffin, J. *Greece, Crete and Syria,* p. 150.
24 *Memorandum by Minister Rahn,* 30 July 1941, Document No. 165, ibid, Vol. XIII, p. 255.

Deadlock at Marjayoun

The thrust through the central route also experienced very tough battle conditions. The first objective was Marjayoun, which sat astride the Litani River. In the initial thrust this large town was captured, and the Australians then headed through very steep mountainous terrain to the next objective, Jezzine. While en-route the Vichy French made a successful counter-attack on Marjayoun and after the garrison troops fled, they recaptured the town. While some of the troops continued towards Jezzine, the men of Roden Cutler's 2/5th Regiment had to quickly turn around and come back in case they were cut off altogether.

Thereafter a great deal of the fighting took place in the vicinity of Marjayoun.[25] Finally, after two weeks of intense fighting, Marjayoun was finally captured on 28 June. While the Allied troops then headed north again towards their objective, Cutler's 2/5th Regiment was transferred to the coastal movement in time for a key battle at Damour.

Possible German involvement

While tough fighting was taking place at Damour, the Vichy commander, Dentz, removed his headquarters north to Aleppo and there awaited the arrival of reinforcements. He had been promised four battalions of men and forty planes of supplies.[26] It would take eight days to arrive, so the Vichy forces had to continue fighting for that period.

When the situation became desperate in Syria, the French sought for a legitimate way to receive German assistance. The French Government wanted to ascertain that such German assistance would involve a "declaration cleared for publication that, in contrast to England, Germany does not call in question French rights in Syria."[27]

This was a very delicate issue for the Germans, as they had to ensure the Arab nations did not construe Germany as abetting the French presence in Syria. Thus while the German and French Governments were now deliberating about possible involvement, and possible wording of a German declaration, the situation on the ground for the Vichy forces became desperate.

There was a limited German involvement at this stage. *Habforce* and the reinforcements from India were attacking Palmyra in the north, and Rahn states, '... the Luftwaffe had attacked the English columns near Palmyra at quarter-hour intervals and in large dispersed them ... The small garrison of Legionnaires was holding Palmyra and had thus far victoriously repelled all attacks.'[28]

From Damour to Beirut

From the Allied perspective the capture of Damour on the coast now took on extra significance, even though they were probably oblivious to the political deliberations then

25 It was in this fighting that Cutler showed exceptional courage and leadership qualities, which were later recognized and he was awarded the Victoria Cross. Cutler was later the Governor of New South Wales.

26 *Memorandum by Minister Rahn*, 30 July 1941, Document No. 165, ibid, Vol. XIII, p. 258.

27 *Memorandum by the Director of the Political Department*, Berlin 25 June 1941, Document No. 19, ibid, Vol. XIII, p. 22.

28 *Memorandum by Minister Rahn*, 30 July 1941, Document No. 165, ibid, Vol. XIII, p. 258.

taking place between the Germans and the French. If Damour was captured before any aid, or reinforcements, arrived for the Vichy forces, then the campaign would virtually be over.

When Damour was finally captured on 7 July without reinforcements eventuating, Dentz delivered his initial requests to the Allies for an armistice. As could be expected with a complicated campaign such as this one, the negotiations were suitably complicated. The Vichy Government did not want any Free French involvement at all, while, naturally, the Free French did want involvement.

From the Allied perspective they also wanted to occupy as much of the country as possible before the full Armistice went into place, so they delayed their response to the requests of Dentz. Finally on 11 July 1941 the British agreed to commence negotiations. By that time the Allied troops were in Beirut, and the Syrian Campaign was over. Negotiations and the signing of the Armistice thereafter occurred at Acre in Palestine. On 15 July men of the 7th Australian Division paraded through the streets of Beirut to a heroes' welcome.

Despite neutralizing Syria, the Germans were still a threat, especially if they managed to defeat the Russians and break through the Caucasus Mountains, and thereafter reach the oilfields of Mosul. Thereafter Australian, New Zealand, British and Indian soldiers would be on garrison duties in Syria when not in the fighting zone in North Africa, as part of the Ninth Army.

The 1941 campaign in Syria confirmed the apprehensions of British officials in 1917 of the vulnerability of the Suez Canal if a belligerent power was in control in the land of Israel. Additionally it confirmed to the Jewish people in Palestine their vulnerability if hostile forces were located so close by. The capture of Syria eliminated one possible avenue of a Nazi threat to their existence.

CHAPTER 16

BARBAROSSA AND BRUTALITY

Operation *Barbarossa* and reactivation of the *Einsatzgruppen*

Whatever evil had thus far happened in Nazi-occupied Europe was soon to be overshadowed. At 3.30 am on 22 June 1941 Hitler launched his most extensive and boldest assault thus far: the invasion of Soviet occupied Europe. This was Operation *Barbarossa*, the largest military assault in history.

This massive military campaign stimulated the reformulation of the *Einsatzgruppen*. While in Poland the *Einsatzgruppen*, and then later other Nazi formations, did murder and execute thousands of Poles and Jewish people when they first invaded the country. The vast majority of the Jewish people however, were then moved to concentration points in major cities, which then became vast ghettos. The most significant was the Warsaw Ghetto, which ultimately was home to over 400,000 Jewish people.

During the weeks before the launch of Operation *Barbarossa* the commander in chief of the German army, General von Brauchitsch, had given instructions that specialised units would be attached to the *Wehrmacht* as they entered into the Soviet Union. The responsibility of these units was to 'execute measures against the civilian population.'[1]

These units were to be the reconstituted *Einsatzgruppen*, who would operate in four distinct areas as units A,B,C and D. Each *Einsatzgruppe* was then divided into several smaller units, known as *Sonderkommandos* or *Einsatzkommandos*. These units then received specialised training at a police training school in Germany before the invasion.

The leaders of these units were most often intelligent and educated men, so they knew full well what they were being commissioned to do. One such leader, Otto Ohlendorf, was the 'chief of Einsatzgruppe D.'[2] After he was captured he was interrogated, and asked how many 'men, women and children did your group kill.' Ohlendorf immediately responded, 'Ninety thousand.'[3] When he was then asked what instructions he had received, Ohlenberg responded:

> "The instructions were that the Jews and the Soviet political commissars were to be liquidated."[4]

Ohlenberg then described how an average 'action' took place:

1 *Einsatzgruppen*, www.deathcamps.org/occupation/einsatzgruppen.
2 Shirer, W. *The Rise and Fall of the Third Reich*, p. 958.
3 Harris, W. *Tyranny on Trial*, p. 349-50, quoted in Shirer, W. ibid, p. 958.
4 Ohlendorf's testimony on trial at the Nuremberg Trials, quoted in Shirer, W. ibid, p. 959.

The *Einsatz* unit would enter a village or town and order the prominent Jewish citizens to call together all Jews for the purpose of "resettlement." They were requested to hand over their valuables and shortly before execution to surrender their outer clothing. They were transported to the place of execution, usually an antitank ditch, in trucks – always only as many as could be executed immediately. In this way it was attempted to keep the span of time from the moment in which the victims knew what was about to happen to them until the time of their actual execution as short as possible.

Then they were shot, kneeling or standing, by firing squads in a military manner and the corpses thrown into the ditch. I never permitted the shooting by individuals, but ordered that several of the men should shoot at the same time in order to avoid direct personal responsibility. Other group leaders demanded that the victims lie down flat on the ground to be shot through the nape of the neck. I did not approve of these methods.[5]

The *Einsatzgruppen* operated in all the regions captured by the *Wehrmacht.* In most locations they were assisted by local collaborators. On most occasions the 'action' was local and small in number, but on many occasions there were also very large Jewish communities which were murdered. Perhaps the highest number in one location was at Kiev, the capital of the Ukraine, where on 29 and 30 September 1941, some 33,771 people, mostly Jewish, were murdered.[6]

What was happening in the Soviet Union was bestial. Although there may not have been a specific Directive from Hitler or the Nazi leadership specifically stating that all the Jewish people, men, women and children were to be murdered in such a way, what was happening was the logical outcome of Hitler's own statements, in *Mein Kampf* and in his various speeches, as well as the known sentiments of his henchmen, particularly Himmler.

It was not only the Jewish people who experienced the bestiality of Operation *Barbarossa.* Millions of ordinary Russian speaking people were either murdered outright, or died as a result of starvation when the big cities were put under German siege. In addition, millions of soldiers died in conflict, and up to three million Soviet prisoners of war were purposely starved to death.[7]

To press on further with the subject matter is well outside the scope of this book, but the subject matter is more than relevant, for all this despicable treatment of fellow human beings was a precursor to the next phase in the proposed genocide of the Jewish people, Hitler's 'Final Solution to the Jewish Problem' and the possible introduction of this program into the Middle East.

5 Ohlendorf's testimony on trial at the Nuremberg Trials, quoted in Shirer, W. ibid, p. 959.

6 I have read various estimates to the number of Jewish people murdered through the operations of the *Einsatzgruppen* in the Soviet Union. William Shirer quotes a figure of 633,000 by 23 March 1943, (Shirer, W, ibid, p. 963). Other figures go over the one million mark.

7 For further reading see Shirer, W, ibid, and Snyder, T, ibid.

Chapter 17
Operation Battleaxe

Hitler's long term objectives

Hitler was so convinced that he would conquer and subdue the Soviet Union that he was already planning for the furtherance of the campaign in the Mediterranean for afterwards. On 11 June 1941 he sent out a Directive No. 32, part of which stated 'The possibility of exerting strong pressure on Turkey and Iran improves the prospects of utilizing these countries, too, for the fight against England, either directly or indirectly.'[1]

In this directive he dedicated considerable detail for how he intended to defeat 'the English.' One avenue, he stated, was, 'In order to facilitate the difficult attack on Egypt from the west, one should also consider exercising German pressure in the direction of the Suez Canal from the east.' Then, he stated, 'At the very least the English defensive forces will thereby be divided.' To achieve this goal, he stated:

> … provision should be made for concentrating in Bulgaria as soon as possible forces strong enough to make Turkey politically compliant or to break her resistance by force of arms.
>
> Within the framework of this army and also in the Caucasus when the collapse of the Soviet Union has created the conditions for such, motorised expeditionary corps are to be established in order later to open the way through Turkey and Syria into Palestine and through Iran to Basra.[2]

In a later version of this Directive (to which a number of additions were made) Hitler stated, 'In North Africa the important thing is to eliminate Tobruk and thus to establish the basis for continuing the German-Italian attack against the Suez Canal. The attack is to be prepared for approximately November with the proviso that the German Africa Corps will be reinforced with regard to man power and material to the greatest possible extent and that adequate reserves of all kind will be placed at its disposal.'[3]

Apart from these German military moves, Hitler also sought to utilise internal uprisings, stating:

> Utilization of the Arab liberation movement. In the case of larger German operations,

1 Draft Fuhrer's Directive, 11 June 1941, ibid, p. 1012.
2 Draft Fuhrer's Directive, 11 June 1941, ibid, p. 1014.
3 Draft Fuhrer's Directive, 11 June 1941, ibid, pp. 1013.

the situation of the English in the Middle East will be all the more difficult the more forces are tied down *at the proper time* by centers of unrest and insurrectionary movements. All military, political, and propaganda measures serving this purpose must be harmonized very closely with one another in the preparatory period. I designate *Special Staff F [Sonderstab F]*,which will make its headquarters in the area of the Wehrmacht Commander, Southeast, as the central office in the field to participate in all planning and measures in the Arab area. It is to be given the best experts and agents.[4]

No doubt Haj Amin was greatly pleased to know how his propaganda efforts were being utilised.

Operation *Battleaxe*

While the Axis leadership was formulating its plans, Wavell was formulating his own for the relief of Tobruk. The British plan involved breaking through the German defensive line at Sollum and Halfaya pass and pressing on post-haste to Tobruk. The forces to be used were the 7th Armoured Division (commanded by General Creagh), the 4th Indian Infantry Division and the 22nd Guards Brigade (under General Messervy). Operation *Battleaxe* was to be commanded by General Beresford-Peirse. The first objectives of the British attack were the strong Axis positions behind the Halfaya Ridge, primarily Fort Capuzzo and Sidi Omar.

The involvement of the 7th Armoured Division, the members of which were known as the 'Desert Rats', meant that this division would fight in yet another North African battle. By November 1942 this division had seen action in all of the major battles that were fought in this see-sawing campaign.

General Beresford-Peirse launched a two-pronged assault early on 15 June 1941, one along the coastal plain aimed at Sollum and the other from behind the Halfaya Ridge aimed at Fort Capuzzo, Mussaid and Sidi Omar. The key position was the Halfaya Pass.

The main forces opposing them apart from Italian infantry, were the 5th German Light Division and the 15th Panzer Division. By that evening the British had captured Fort Capuzzo, while a tank duel took place north of that strategic position.

The crucial day of Operation *Battleaxe* was 16 June 1941. That morning Rommel wrote to his wife:

There was heavy fighting in our eastern sector all day yesterday ... To-day – it's 2.30 am – will see the decision. It's going to be a hard fight, so you'll understand that I can't sleep. These lines in haste will show you that I'm thinking of you both. More soon – when it's all over.[5]

4 Draft Fuhrer's Directive, 11 June 1941, ibid, pp. 1014-15.
5 Rommel, E. *The Rommel Papers*, p. 144.

In the morning Rommel's attack upon Fort Capuzzo ended in failure, and the loss of many of his valuable Panzers. But, to the north-west near a place called Sidi Azeiz another tank duel took place between the 5th German Light Division and the 7th British Armoured Brigade. On this occasion the Germans were victorious, and then they continued on eastwards to Sidi Suleiman, and were later joined by the remnants of the 5th Panzer Division at Fort Capuzzo.

The battle concluded on 17 June 1941, with the Axis forces reaching Halfaya and then proceeding north to encircle the British. The British force, however, had already withdrawn from Fort Capuzzo and other locations, and made a retreat south and then around the base of the Halfaya Ridge, thereby avoiding the Axis force. Despite Rommel's exaggerated reports (the losses on the British side were not as he had stated[6]), the Axis had indeed won a convincing victory.

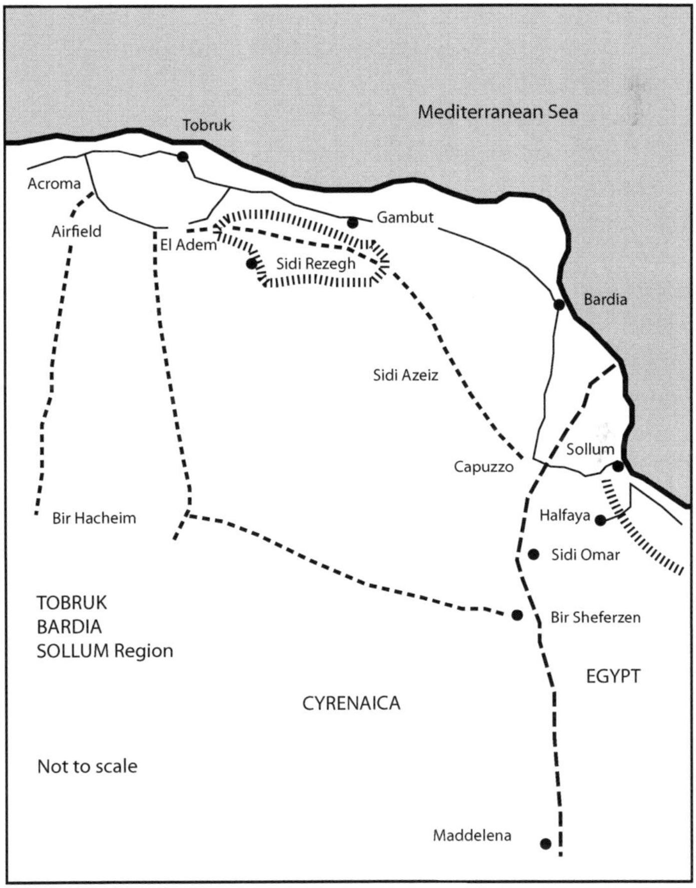

6 Rommel, E. *The Rommel Papers*, pp. 145-6.

Wavell replaced by General Auchinleck

A victory for Rommel meant a defeat for Wavell. This defeat was the last of his many (too many) challenges in his vast realm of the Middle East command. Churchill informed him on 21 June 1941 that he would be replaced by General Claude Auchinleck, and that he would replace Auchinleck as C-in-C of India.[7]

With Auchinleck's arrival several important changes were made: Western Desert Force was hereafter named Eighth Army and would be commanded by General Alan Cunningham. William Gott now took over command of the 7th Armoured Division.

Auchinleck too had a mammoth task to perform. Ever since the BEF headed out to Greece the Eastern Mediterranean had been rife with military disasters and potential military disasters. Thousands of Allied soldiers had died in Greece, Crete and Syria, many more thousands had been wounded, and over ten thousand had been taken prisoner. Now, following the beginning of Operation *Barbarossa* and with the capture of Syria, Auchinleck had to supervise and garrison the northern border of Syria and Iraq.

In the midst of all these immense challenges, there was one bright light: the 'Rats of Tobruk' were still keeping the Axis forces at bay. While they were doing this, all of those other Axis victories were incomplete. But, if Rommel captured Tobruk there was every chance the goal of capturing the Suez Canal would be completed.

During this period also, the remnants of the badly bruised New Zealand Division returned to their camps at Maadi in Egypt, and shortly later they were sent forward to Baggush Box to improve the defences there. It was there in October 1941 that the BBC declared, 'The Victoria Cross has been awarded to an officer of the New Zealand Military Forces, Second Lieutenant Charles Hazlitt Upham, for gallantry in Crete.'[8]

Movement of South African Divisions

After a number of months at the camp near Alexandria, Ron Turrel and the 2nd South African Division moved towards the front line, and their second stop was El Alamein. Of this new position Turrel wrote:

> The three or four square mile area that was occupied by the 2nd Division was ground that was only slightly raised above the level of the country to the west, but this was marginal. Inland was the railway line linking Alex and Mersa Matruh, and past that an almost featureless plan which stretched south to the edge of the Quattara Depression. The latter was a place where no sensible person ventured, and was reputed to be completely impassable. It was never my business to go near there, and I was quite happy to leave it that way…
>
> It seemed to us at first that the purpose of sending our Division to Alamein was that it should create a strong defensive position there in case of need. At the time, all

7 Churchill to Wavell, 21 June 1941, in Churchill, W. *The Grand Alliance*, pp. 345-46.
8 Sandford, K. ibid, p. 107.

the digging and concreting seemed so pointless – why, the enemy was far off on the Libyan border, several hundred miles to the west, and moving away at that. A more probable explanation was that our Division was being moved forward to be available when needed…

We were there for almost three months.[9]

During those three months these colonial soldiers, endured the monotony of army life in the North African desert. During the same period the battle-weary 2nd New Zealand Division was also brought forward to Mersa Matruh. As these colonial troops moved forward, another colonial division prepared to move back.

Many Australian troops replaced at Tobruk

It was expected that Rommel would soon unleash a new and devastating assault against Tobruk. The Australian commander and government were concerned that their men were too weakened after five months on the front line, and called for their withdrawal for rest and recuperation.

This began from September. Among those replacing the 9th Division men were many Polish soldiers, part of General Wladyslaw Anders Polish Army, which had arrived in the Middle East after a long and circuitous journey.[10] This was to be their first taste of action in their new sphere of conflict, and they became an integral part of the Eighth Army henceforth, and went on to fight in Sicily and Italy.

The surviving men of the 9th Australia Division then returned to their camp at Julis and were feted by the Jewish people of Palestine. The 2/13th Battalion however remained at Tobruk. Moses Mosenson was also relieved after enduring an equal amount of time at Tobruk. Soon after, while stationed in Transjordan, and on hearing of the news of the progress of the war, he reflected:

When I listen to the radio I am sometimes overcome by sad and painful thoughts. The fate of the world is being decided now on the battlefields of Russia. Millions of people are dying there and thousands of villages are being turned into mounds of destruction … the fate of the Jews looms at us out of all this. When you listen to the awful news of our ruin and the menace of the horror to come, we know that our going [to fight in Tobruk] was not in vain, but a solemn duty to the children. For their sakes we must create a world completely different from the one we have today.[11]

9 Turrel, R. ibid, pp. 203-04.

10 Anders was imprisoned by the Soviets in 1939 but after Operation *Barbarossa* he was released in order to establish a Polish Army to fight alongside the Soviets. Due to numerous difficulties however Anders received permission to take his troops and many Polish civilians out of the Soviet Union in 1941, and these people (perhaps as many as 100,000) entered Iran. The soldiers then made their way via Iraq and Palestine to the Western Desert in 1942.

11 Mosenson, M. *Letters from the Desert,* p. 80.

Egyptian contact with Nazi Germany

The failure of Operation *Battleaxe* once again affected the geo-politics of the Middle East. In early October 1941 an Egyptian named Dr. Samir Zoulfakir Bey (who was related to the former Egyptian Prime Minister Zoulfakir Bey) spoke to the German Ambassador in Istanbul, Von Papen, on behalf of the Egyptian King and the three leading Egyptian political parties, *Wafd* (the fatherland party), *Hisb el Watani*, and the liberal-constitutional party *Ahrar Dusturiye.*[12]

Von Papen wrote to the Foreign Ministry on 6 October 1941 that Dr. Zoulfakir was instructed:

> ... to clarify the question of what fate Germany envisaged for Egypt, in case the German attack in Libya, which the English and Egyptians envisaged in the immediate future, should be successful. They desired an assurance that Egypt would not be allotted to the Italian Lebensraum, but that she would be recognized as a completely independent state on condition of her cooperation with the Axis.
>
> Furthermore the circles mentioned above wish to make an agreement with the Axis to the effect that Cairo will no longer be bombarded. The latest attack resulted in an exceedingly large number of casualties among the civilian population, whereas no English soldiers had lost their lives....The latest attack is being strongly exploited by the English against the Axis, whereas it is the principal desire of the circles mentioned to promote a favourable atmosphere for an occupation by the Axis and, if possible, even to come to the aid of the Axis troops at the decisive moment.
>
> In this connection it should be noted that the English have made every preparation to evacuate Egypt. The transhipment port for English supplies is today Port Sudan.[13]

Challenges for Rommel

This it would seem was the beginning point of discussions between Germany and King Farouk and various Egyptian delegates concerning a possible Axis (especially German) Egyptian collaborative relationship.

Ironically, though, at this very time the German relationship with their Italian ally was being severely strained. A glimpse of these relational challenges is provided by Rommel's diary entry for 31 August 1940:

> It's damned hot again, so hot that one steams even in the early morning. Otherwise

12 *The Ambassador in Turkey to the Foreign Ministry*, 6 October 1941, Document No. 385, ibid, Vol. XIII, p. 618. The main purpose of the visit to Turkey was to seek Turkish asylum for the Persian Crown prince Mohammed Riza Pahlevi and Princess Fewzieh, King Farouk's sister, due to the possibility that the British would exile him.

13 *The Ambassador in Turkey to the Foreign Ministry*, 6 October 1941, Document No. 385, ibid, Vol. XIII, p. 619. An accompanying footnote, No. 4, stated that similar requests for Cairo not to be bombed had been made via the Swedish Minister in Cairo, but were rejected by the Germans, as they believed such requests should be addressed to the British "which, by its military measures, has made Egypt and her cities a theatre of war."

> there's nothing doing, except that the Italian High Command is dissatisfied at having so little to say in things here. They mess us about over all manner of petty details, but we don't take any of it lying down. Maybe they're working for a real bust-up, in order to get me, or perhaps the whole German force, out of the way. I for one wouldn't be sorry to have a change of theatre.[14]

Yet despite his negativity towards his ally, Rommel remained committed to his task at hand, and wrote again on 12 October 1941, that, concerning the British, 'Once we've taken T. [*Tobruk*], there'll be precious little hope for them here.'[15] Taking Tobruk was an obsession for him and indeed for the Axis High Command. Planning now began in earnest to launch another offensive to take this festering sore.

14 Rommel, E. *The Rommel Papers*, p. 150.
15 Rommel, E. *The Rommel Papers*, p. 152.

Chaim Weizmann – never gave up pressuring the British Government to permit a Jewish Division to be formed (Zionist Archives)

New Zealanders arrive in Egypt and are greeted by Anthony Eden

Australian soldiers marching in Jerusalem on Anzac Day, 25 April 1940

British and Commonwealth soldiers dancing the hora with Jewish kibbutzniks (Zionist Archives, Jerusalem)

Jewish volunteers enlisting for service in the British Army (Zionist Archives, Jerusalem)

New Zealanders training in Egypt (NZ Army Museum, DA 2099)

The Royal Navy and RAF – the campaign could not have succeeded without them (Schick Archives Christ Church, Jerusalem)

Walter Ellingham and Bruce Ballantyne, Long Range Desert Group - LRDG (Picture Post, 21 June 1941). The LRDG played an important role throughout the campaign

Alexander Olive and men of the 6th Australian Division prepare for battle (Courtesy Ross Olive)

Field Marshal Erwin Rommel, commander Panzer Army Africa (Courtesy Ted Pritchett, who found it in a deserted German hospital in Tobruk)

John Marriott, 1st South African Division (courtesy Kim Weatherston)

Churchill and General Freyberg, August 1942 (NZ Army Museum DA 2598)

Alexander Olive and mates from the 6th Australian Division digging in near Mount Olympus, Greece (Courtesy Ross Olive)

Maleme, Crete, scene of harsh battles

German War Cemetery, Crete

Veteran of the North African campaign Frank Beech, 2/7th Field Regiment, 9th Australian Division (Courtesy Craig Beech)

George Charleston, 20 Anti-Tank Company – died and buried at Tobruk (Courtesy Ernest Eagleton)

Allied troops in Tobruk

British Crusader tanks (IWM 018971)

Life with the 'Desert Rats' during the North African Campaign (Courtesy Ian Paterson, 'Desert Rats' history website)

Charles Upham, the most decorated infantry soldier in the history of the British Empire, being the winner of two Victoria Crosses during the campaign (NZ Army Museum DA 69810)

Two of the stalwarts of the campaign: Winston Churchill, who gave unstinting support to the Middle East campaign, and General Morshead, undoubtedly the hero of the siege of Tobruk (AWM PO 1997)

Alexander Olive and his mates in Syria (Courtesy Ross Olive)

Moshe Dayan, Yitzhak Sadeh and Yigal Alon of the *Palmach* (Zionist Archives, Jerusalem. This picture was taken in 1938)

Plaque at Nehr el Kelb (Dog River) south of Beirut (From collection of Sapper Frederick Button, in possession of daughter Jill Ross)

Haj Amin el-Husseini, the Mufti of Jerusalem, with Adolf Hitler, November 1941 (Bundesarchiv Berlin 146-1987-004-09A)

Jewish population being registered, Thessalonica, 1942 (Bundesarchiv Berlin, 101i-168-0894-21a)

2o.7.1942 startete er bereits zum ersten Mal nach T o b r u c k und erhielt von Generalfeldmarschall Rommel die notwendigen Instruktionen für den Einsatz.

Entry in Walter Rauff's military record concerning his visit to Tobruk to meet with Rommel (Bundesarchiv Berlin, Rauff R70-1 Italien Fol.1)

Prime Minister Winston Churchill, General Jan Christian Smuts, General Sir Alan Brooke (CIGS) and Air Chief Marshal Sir Arthur Tedder, Cairo, August 1942 (Imperial War Museum E51223)

Churchill inspects his old regiment, the 4th Hussars, August 1942 (NZ Army Museum, DA 2604)

General Bernard Law Montgomery, Commander Eighth Army. (NZ Army Museum, DA 10815)

The Battle of El Alamein – the terrible aftermath

Photographs from collection of Malcolm Graham McLeod, a 'Rat of Tobruk', courtesy of his daughter, Helen Ardente.

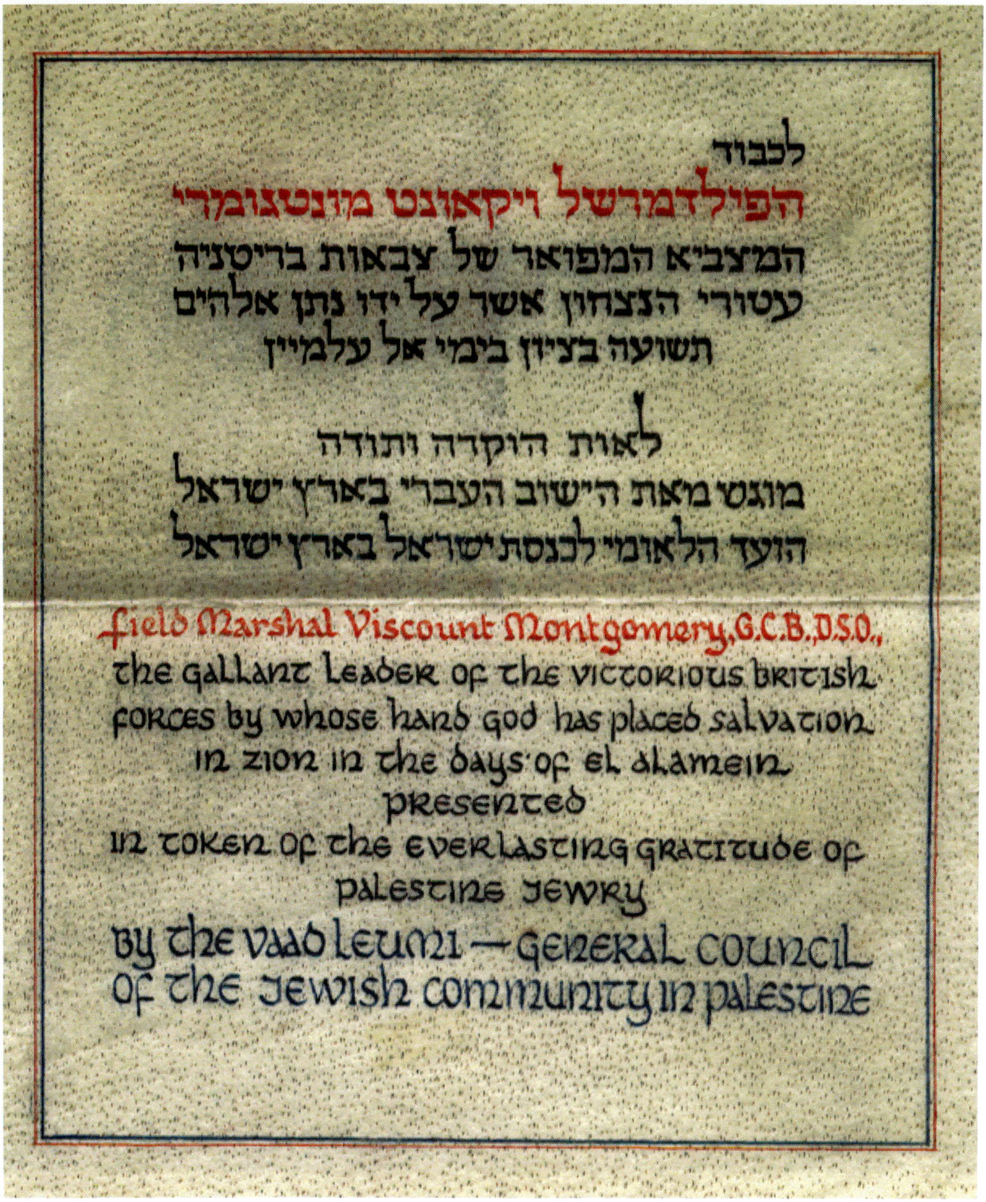
לכבוד
הפילדמרשל ויקאונט מונטגומרי
המצביא המפואר של צבאות בריטניה
עטורי הנצחון אשר על ידו נתן אלהים
תשועה בציון בימי אל עלמיין

לאות הוקרה ותודה
מוגש מאת הישוב העברי בארץ ישראל
הועד הלאומי לכנסת ישראל בארץ ישראל

Field Marshal Viscount Montgomery, G.C.B., D.S.O.,
the gallant leader of the victorious British
forces by whose hand God has placed salvation
in Zion in the days of El Alamein
presented
in token of the everlasting gratitude of
Palestine Jewry
by the Vaad Leumi — General Council
of the Jewish Community in Palestine

Inscription accompanying the Bible presented to Field Marshal Viscount Montgomery by the Jewish leadership of Palestine – *Eretz* Israel.

El Alamein Commonwealth War Cemetery

German War Memorial

Sollum-Halfaya Commonwealth War Cemetery

Pte. John Crombie, 6th Australian Division, died at Tobruk 1941

The author at his uncle's grave in Sollum-Halfaya War Cemetery, 1992

CHAPTER 18

THE MUFTI PARTNERS WITH HITLER

Haj Amin 'suddenly' arrives in Rome

When the Mufti arrived in Iran from Iraq he came under the shelter of the Japanese Legation in Tehran. He was well received in Iran, as the leader, Reza Shah Pahlavi was actively pro-German. Haj Amin then set about to further ties with Nazi Germany as best as he could.[1] During this same period both the Soviets and Britain were becoming concerned by the strengthening relationship between Iran and Germany, and pressured Iran to break off this relationship. When the Shah refused, British and Soviet forces invaded in September 1941. Reza Shah abdicated the throne in favour of his son Mohamed Reza Shah, who was more pro-British.

Haj Amin knew the British authorities were seeking him, so he sought shelter with the Italian Legation. He then disguised himself, and managed to escape Iran via Turkey, and suddenly appeared in Rome on 13 October 1941.[2] Although he had wanted to go to Germany, he had no choice but to accept the Italian offer.[3]

Two weeks later, on 27 October 1941, the Mufti's arrival in Italy was published in the Italian newspapers, creating somewhat of a sensation. On that same day he met with Mussolini, and, according to Ciano's aide, Filippo Anfuso, 'the Grand Mufti's personality had made a very favourable impression on the Duce.' Prince Otto Bismarck from the German Embassy recorded, obviously from discussions with Anfuso, that he 'seemed to know exactly what he wanted, and the discussion between the two 'revolved exclusively around the Arab problem.' The Grand Mufti, Bismarck reported:

> ...had told the Duce that his political aim was the independence of Palestine, Syria and Iraq. He had further indicated that at the proper time he would ask the Italian and German Governments for a statement in which they would identify themselves with his political endeavors, to which the Duce had given his consent.[4]

1 See Edwin Black, 'Denial of Holocaust nothing new in Iran: Ties to Hitler led to plots against Britain and Jews', *San Francisco Chronicle,* 8 January 2006, on www.bankingonbaghdad.com

2 *The Charg'e d'Affairès in Italy to the Foreign Ministry,* 13 October 1941, Document No. 399, ibid, Vol. XIII, p. 641.

3 *Memorandum by Minister Grobba,* 6 November 1941, Document No. 452, ibid, Vol. XIII, p. 747. He later informed German officials, 'he was fully aware that Germany was of greater military and political importance than Italy and that the misgivings of the entire Arab world regarding Italian intentions also stood in the way of close cooperation of Arab circles with Italy.'

4 *The Charg'e d'Affairés in Italy to the Foreign Ministry,* 28 October 1941, Document No. 428, ibid, Vol. XIII, pp. 704-5. Bismarck also quoted Alfuso as stating that once Gaylani arrived in Rome then Haj Amin would travel with him to Berlin.

Mussolini's and Haj Amin's joint statement

On 5 November 1941 the provisional text agreed to between Mussolini (and Ciano) on behalf of Italy and Haj Amin, representing the Arab nationalist movement, was given to the German Embassy in Rome for German consent.[5] The initial document (which was later adapted, and which still awaited Hitler's final approval) stated:

> "Amin al-Husayni, the Grand Mufti of Palestine and one of the leading representatives of the independence movement of the Arab peoples, has had a frank and cordial exchange of views with the Duce and the Fuhrer.
>
> In this conversation he was told the following:
>
> (1) That the two Axis Powers will give every possible support to the Arab countries, which are now suffering under British domination and oppression, in the fight for their freedom.
>
> (2) That the Axis Powers, supporting the aspirations of the Arabs, are prepared to recognize the full sovereignty and complete independence of the Arab countries of the Near East which are now occupied or controlled by the English. Pursuant thereto, the Axis Powers are prepared to give their consent to the elimination of the Jewish national home [*judisch-nationalen Lebensraumes*] in Palestine.
>
> Their readiness to do this will be set down in the near future in a formal agreement that will seal the sincere friendship and close cooperation between the Axis Powers and the Arabs in the future. The negotiations for the conclusion of such an agreement will be started as soon as possible.
>
> In the course of the discussions the intention of Italy and Germany, to respect, as before, to the full extent, the sovereignty and the independence of all Arab countries that are now sovereign and independent was again confirmed."[6]

Haj Amin arrives in Berlin

Having obtained Mussolini's endorsement, Haj Amin then continued on to Berlin, arriving there on 6 November 1941. He was warmly welcomed by officials from the Foreign Ministry and provided lodgings at the prestigious Bellevue Castle.[7] The head of the welcoming delegation was Minister Fritz Grobba.[8]

5 *The Ambassador in Italy to the Foreign Ministry*, 5 November 1941, Document No. 449, ibid, Vol. XIII, p. 742.

6 The Ambassador in Italy to the Foreign Ministry, 5 November 1941, Document No. 449, ibid, Vol. XIII, p. 742-3. Footnote 2 reveals that the Germans did not like the German word *Lebensraumes* and this was changed.

7 Schloss Bellevue is in the Tiergarten suburb of Berlin and has been the residence of the President of Germany since 1994. See www.wikipedia.

8 Fritz Grobba (1886-1973) served briefly in the German Consulate in Jerusalem. While serving as a German soldier on the Turkish front during World War One he married a Syrian Arab woman. He began working in the German Foreign Service in 1922 and served for many years in the Middle East Department. In 1932 he became Ambassador to Iraq. While there he became more involved in Arab nationalism, and even serialised a version of *Mein Kampf* for Arabic radio, and arranged for Iraqi army officers to be trained in Germany. Thereafter began a close relationship between the Iraqi Army and Germany. He was German Ambassador to Saudi Arabia from 1937 till the outbreak of the War.

Haj Amin, Grobba and the other delegates then discussed the declaration which he was seeking from Italy and Germany, and Haj Amin mentioned the adaptations which the Italians wanted. It was apparent that to obtain a joint Axis statement endorsing the requests of the Mufti would not be so straightforward. He may have received an endorsement from Mussolini, but, it was Hitler's endorsement he was really seeking. Grobba stated that the:

> Grand Mufti attaches great importance to being received by the Fuhrer. Since this statement is based on an exchange of views between the Duce and the Fuhrer, he would be especially grateful if the Fuhrer would express his approval of the proposed statement to him personally, as the Duce had done. Moreover, he hopes that his reception by the Fuhrer will have a great propaganda effect on the entire Arab world and, beyond that, the Islamic world.[9]

No doubt stimulated by the arrival of Haj Amin in Berlin, Ribbentrop requested the Foreign Ministry to prepare a Memorandum on German interests in the Middle East for discussion with Hitler. The core of this Memorandum was based around this statement, 'It goes without saying that as regards this region our policy must first and foremost be guided by military needs and therefore must serve the purpose of defeating England.'[10]

Although the Arab world was grateful for the radio message on 21 October 1940 of German sympathy for Arab independence, the Arabs now sought, so the Memorandum stated:

> A new statement of policy by Germany and Italy in favour of the Arab world appears absolutely indispensable because its absence is an obstacle to loyal cooperation with the Arabs. It seems all the more necessary to issue such a statement soon, as according to the Arab states with a view toward the formation of a Greater Arab federation.[11]

The Memorandum stated that the basis for such a fresh statement of support was the text proposed by the Mufti and 'approved by the Duce.' Naturally, it continued, French reaction was a factor, as the region proposed for Arab independence included Syria. The Memorandum concluded:

> From the standpoint of German policy there would be no objections if after the war Iraq, Syria, Palestine, and Transjordan were united into a greater Arab federation which would then enter into a relationship of friendship and alliance with Germany and Italy. Given their military and financial weakness, these countries would in all circumstance be

9 Memorandum by Minister Grobba, 6 November 1941, Document No. 452, ibid, Vol. XIII, p. 748.
10 Memorandum by the Foreign Minister, 13 November 1941, Document No. 468, ibid, Vol. XIII, p. 775.
11 Memorandum by the Foreign Minister, 13 November 1941, ibid, p. 775.

dependent upon such support by the Axis Powers.[12]

The German Foreign Ministry also proposed the establishment of a council of Arab leaders in Berlin, including the Mufti, the Syrian independence fighter Fawzi al-Qawuqchi and possibly the former Iraqi Prime Minister, al-Gaylani. Part of the work of this council would be to make daily Arabic radio broadcasts as well as other forms of propaganda on behalf of the Axis among the Arabic speaking and Muslim peoples.

Hitler read the Memo put out by the Foreign Ministry and was of the opinion that matters connected to the Arab world should be in the Italian sphere of influence, but this was countered by the fact that there was more prestige if the centre of such operations was from Berlin and not Rome.[13]

Ribbentrop's meeting with the Grand Mufti

Haj Amin's goal of meeting personally with Hitler took a big step forward when Ribbentrop agreed to meet with him on 28 November 1941. Haj Amin stressed to the Foreign Minister 'that the Arabs were naturally friends of Germany because both were fighting three common foes: the English, the Jews and Bolshevism. It had been a great deed on the part of Germany to have proceeded against these three enemies.'

Although Haj Amin admitted that the insurrection in Iraq had not succeeded, this nevertheless was just a beginning of an Arab insurrectionist movement. Such a beginning amounted to insurrection and sabotage, as well as mobilizing positive forces, such as an Arab legion to fight for the Axis cause.

The Mufti emphasised on several occasions the great importance the Arabs gave to collaboration with the Germans, and for the urgent need of a clear statement of German endorsement and support for Arab independence.

Concerning the three common enemies of Nazi Germany and the Arab nationalist movement (Britain, Bolshevism and the Jews), Ribbentrop stated, concerning the Jews:

> 'As a sworn enemy of the Jews, Germany understood the troubles of the Arabs in this field …'[14]

As a result of the failed *coup d'etat* in Iraq and the defeat in Syria, Ribbentrop reiterated to Haj Amin that 'it was now necessary to proceed very cautiously and prudently'[15] in regards to precipitating action against the British. Despite the need for caution, the Foreign Minister

12 *Memorandum by the Foreign Minister*, 13 November 1941, ibid, p. 776.

13 Brief by Walter Hewel, personal representative of Foreign Minister to Hitler, 15 November, 1941, Document No. 475, ibid, Vol. XIII, p. 786-87.

14 *Record of the Conversation of the Grand Mufti with the Foreign Minister* in Berlin on 28 November 1941, Document No. 514, ibid, Vol. XIII, p. 878.

15 *Record of the Conversation of the Grand Mufti with the Foreign Minister,* ibid, p. 879.

gave the Mufti optimism by stating that 'his cause would receive support.'[16] Exactly how this would happen, was still to be determined.

Ribbentrop emphasized that when the Germans made such a statement of support it would need to be at the appropriate time, and at a time when tangible German support would be available; in other words, 'if an announcement were made, it had to be backed up by the power to carry it out.'[17] The Fuhrer, Ribbentrop stated, 'did not wish a declaration to be made to be followed by inaction. He feared that the Arabs would in that case only lose confidence, and he thought that the declaration had better be made at a time when we were ready to strike and expel the English from the Suez Canal.'[18]

The opportune time for this open and clear statement of support Ribbentrop stated, echoing Hitler's words, would be when the German Army had reached the Black Sea and made it a base of their further operations.

Despite the numerous times that Ribbentrop echoed Hitler's desire to delay the issuing of such a statement until a more appropriate time, the Mufti kept re-stating that such a declaration was needed now, for he 'considered it important for the declaration to be issued immediately in order that popular support might be retained and confidence bolstered. He wished to prepare the Arabs by such a declaration for a later operation, so they would not again be taken by surprise, as was the case with the Iraq venture.'[19]

In addition to relaying to the Mufti the concerns and decisions of Hitler concerning the Arab nationalist movement, Ribbentrop himself, as the Foreign Minister, also had to consider how the issuing of such a statement of support of the Arab independence movement would affect Germany's relationship with both Turkey and France, which was still the legally Mandated authority in Syria. The Grand Mufti sought to allay Ribbentrop's concerns on both these matters.

Hitler meets the Mufti in Berlin

Both Grobba and Ribbentrop were clearly satisfied that Haj Amin, the Muslim spiritual leader of Palestine and quasi-official spokesman of the Arab nationalist movement, could be of benefit to the cause of Nazi Germany. Through their influence Hitler agreed to meet the Mufti on 30 November 1941. In his opening remarks Haj Amin stated that:

> He wished to … convey to the Fuhrer of the Greater German Reich, admired by the entire Arab world, his thanks for the sympathy which he had always shown for the Arab and especially the Palestinian cause, and to which he had given clear expression in his public speeches. The Arab countries were firmly convinced that Germany would win the war and that the Arab cause would then prosper. The Arabs were Germany's natural

16 *Record of the Conversation of the Grand Mufti with the Foreign Minister,* ibid, p. 879.

17 *Record of the Conversation of the Grand Mufti with the Foreign Minister,* ibid, p. 879.

18 *Record of the Conversation of the Grand Mufti with the Foreign Minister,* ibid, p. 879.

19 *Record of the Conversation of the Grand Mufti with the Foreign Minister,* ibid, pp. 879-80.

friends because they had the same enemies as had Germany, namely the English, the Jews, and the Communists. They were therefore prepared to cooperate with Germany with all their hearts and stood ready to participate in the war, not only negatively by the commission of acts of sabotage and the instigation of revolutions, but also positively by the formation of an Arab Legion. The Arabs could be more useful to Germany as allies than might be apparent at first glance, both for geographical reasons and because of the suffering inflicted upon them by the English and the Jews. Furthermore, they had close relations with all Muslim nations, of which they could make use in behalf of the common cause. The Arab legion could be quite easy to raise. An appeal by the Mufti to the Arab countries and the prisoners of Arab, Algerian, Tunisian, and Moroccan nationality in Germany would produce a great number of volunteers to fight. Of Germany's victory the Arab world was firmly convinced...

In this struggle, the Arabs were striving for the independence and unity of Palestine, Syria, and Iraq. They had the fullest confidence in the Fuhrer and looked to his hand for the balm on their wounds which had been inflicted upon them by the enemies of Germany.[20]

At this point Haj Amin alluded to the letter of 8 April, 1941 from the German Foreign Ministry which alluded to the fact that Germany held no Arab territories, and that Germany 'understood and recognized the aspirations to independence and freedom of the Arabs, just as she supported the elimination of the Jewish national home.'[21]

Haj Amin stated that a public declaration 'would be very useful for its propagandistic effect on the Arab peoples at this moment.' 'It would' he continued 'rouse the Arabs from their momentary lethargy and give them new courage. It would also ease the Mufti's work of secretly organizing the Arabs against the moment when they could strike. At the same time', he continued, 'he could give the assurance that the Arabs would in strict discipline patiently wait for the right moment and only strike upon an order from Berlin.'[22] As he had done previously with Ribbentrop, Haj Amin pressed again and again for a quick German statement of support.

Hitler responded that:

... Germany's fundamental attitude on these questions, as the Mufti himself had already stated, was clear. Germany stood for uncompromising war against the Jews. That naturally included active opposition to the Jewish national home in Palestine, which was nothing other than a center, in the form of a state, for the exercise of destructive

20 *Memorandum by an Official of the Foreign Minister's Secretariat*, 30 November 1941, Document No. 515, ibid, Vol. XIII, pp. 881-2.

21 *Memorandum by an Official of the Foreign Minister's Secretariat*, 30 November 1941, Document No. 515, ibid, Vol. XIII, pp. 882. The letter is from 8 April 1941, ibid, Vol. XII, No. 293.

22 *Memorandum by an Official of the Foreign Minister's Secretariat*, 30 November 1941, Document No. 515, ibid, Vol. XIII, pp. 882. Haj Amin also spoke of the situation in Iraq, as well as Turkish and French hesitancy.

influence by Jewish interests. Germany was also aware that the assertion that the Jews were carrying out the function of economic pioneers in Palestine was a lie. The work there was done only by the Arabs, not by the Jews. *Germany was resolved, step by step, to ask one European nation after the other to solve its Jewish problem, and at the proper time direct a similar appeal to non-European nations as well.*[23]

At this stage it was clear, even without the public statement that Haj Amin was seeking, that Hitler purposed uncompromising war against Jewish people, both in Europe and outside of Europe, which involved:

- the solving of the Jewish problem, and
- the destruction of the Jewish national home.

Concerning his attitude towards the Jewish people Hitler further stated:

> Germany was at the present time engaged in a life and death struggle with two citadels of Jewish power: Great Britain and Soviet Russia. Theoretically there was a difference between England's capitalism and Soviet Russia's communism; actually, however, the Jews in both countries were pursuing a common goal. This was the decisive struggle; on the political plane, it presented itself in the main as a conflict between Germany and England, but ideologically it was a battle between National Socialism and the Jews. It went without saying that Germany would furnish positive and practical aid to the Arabs involved in the same struggle, because platonic promises were useless in a war for survival or destruction in which the Jews were able to mobilize all of England's power for their needs.[24]

Hitler then mentioned that German aid to Iraq had been insufficient, and that 'Iraq was overcome by the power of Britain, that is, the guardian of the Jews.' In view of this, he, as the leader of Germany had to not only assist the Arabs, but also he had to do so as a rational man. His rationality was that the Arab situation needed to be viewed within the bigger context, which included the struggle in the northern Caucasus region; and the possible ramifications that such a declaration could make with the French, especially those allied to de Gaulle, who could 'interpret the Fuhrer's declaration as an intention to break up France's colonial empire and appeal to their fellow countrymen that they rather make common cause with the English to try to save what still could be saved.' Within this broader context, Hitler further stated:

> A German declaration regarding Syria would in France be understood to refer to the

23 *Memorandum by an Official of the Foreign Minister's Secretariat*, 30 November 1941, Document No. 515, ibid, Vol. XIII, pp. 882-3. Italics the author's.
24 *Memorandum by an Official of the Foreign Minister's Secretariat*, 30 November 1941, ibid, p. 883.

> French colonies in general, and that would at the present time create new troubles in western Europe, which means that a portion of the German armed forces would be immobilized in the west and no longer available for the campaign in the east.[25]

It was clear that although Hitler had support for the Arab position, its needs at that time were subservient to the need to maximise German military involvement on the Eastern Front. Germany could not at that time have any complications with France which would entail transferring valuable troops from the Eastern Front (or elsewhere).

Then the German dictator clearly summarized his thoughts and views, 'enjoining' the Mufti 'to lock it in the uttermost depths of his heart'. These views, he stated, were:

> 1. He (the Fuhrer) would carry on the battle to the total destruction of the Judeo-Communist empire in Europe.
> 2. At some moment which was impossible to set exactly today but which in any event was not distant, the German armies would in the course of this struggle reach the southern exit from Caucasia.
> 3. As soon as this had happened, the Fuhrer would on his own give the Arab world the assurance that its hour of liberation had arrived. Germany's objective would then be solely the destruction of the Jewish element residing in the Arab sphere under the protection of British power. In that hour the Mufti would be the most authoritative spokesman for the Arab world. It would then be his task to set off the Arab operations which he had secretly prepared. When that time had come, Germany could also be indifferent to French reaction to such a declaration.[26]

Thus in conclusion, Hitler reiterated to the Mufti that with the bigger picture in view, it would be better to hold off with such a statement for a few months, stating, 'The moment that Germany's tank divisions and air squadrons had made their appearance south of the Caucasus, the public appeal requested by the Grand Mufti could go out to the Arab world.'[27]

Despite this concluding statement from Hitler, the Mufti again sought for a clear assurance, 'secretly at least. To enter into an agreement with Germany of the kind he had just outlined for the Fuhrer.' Hitler's response ended the discussion:

> The Fuhrer replied that he had just now given the Grand Mufti precisely that confidential declaration.[28]

25 *Memorandum by an Official of the Foreign Minister's Secretariat*, 30 November 1941, ibid, pp. 883-4.
26 *Memorandum by an Official of the Foreign Minister's Secretariat*, 30 November 1941, ibid, pp. 884.
27 *Memorandum by an Official of the Foreign Minister's Secretariat*, 30 November 1941, ibid, pp. 884.
28 *Memorandum by an Official of the Foreign Minister's Secretariat*, 30 November 1941, ibid, pp. 884.

This assurance, hereafter in written form in the Minutes of this meeting, revealed the clear commitment of Hitler. The two representative arch enemies of the Jewish people and of the Jewish national home had met and entered into an, albeit unwritten, agreement.

Repercussions

One of the stated reasons why the German authorities wanted Haj Amin in Germany was the use he could be there for their propaganda purposes – to create a pro-German and pro-Axis position in the Arab-Muslim world to rise up against the British. It was, though, a two-way street. Haj Amin, as a representative of the Arab nationalist movement, and as the Muslim spiritual leader of Palestine (albeit in exile) had a two-fold agenda:

1) the ousting of the British and the French from the Middle East so that independent Arab nations could arise and,

2) the complete destruction of the Jewish national home in Palestine.

The Nazi Government now placed Haj Amin in charge of the 'Arab Office'.[29] He thereafter became active in fomenting anti-British and pro-Nazi propaganda through numerous channels, including Arabic radio. He was also responsible for raising awareness for an Arab military unit in the *Wehrmacht*, which was named 'Free Arabia'. This was in effect the Arab Legion that he had stated he wanted to raise, and on one occasion he stated, "... the day would soon arrive when he would lead an army to liberate Palestine".[30] If Haj Amin el-Husseini was involved in liberating Palestine in any way, it was very clear from his track record what he intended to do with the Jewish people who lived there.

Also while in Berlin the Mufti addressed the opening of the Islamic Central Institution, of which he became the honourary chairman. This position, like his previous role as head of Supreme Arab Committee in Palestine, provided him with much prestige. Although there were only about 3,000 Muslims in Germany, there were many more whom he could reach in Europe, including in Bosnia.[31]

Due to his prestige, though, Haj Amin stood to influence millions more in the Islamic world through propaganda work beamed out by radio from Berlin. Haj Amin's presence in Germany was indeed an ominous sign for the Jewish people everywhere, including those living in the Middle East.

29 He was seemingly granted a salary of 50,000 Reichsmarks a month as well as living expenses. Breitman, R and Gouda, N. *Hitler's Shadow*, 2001, on www.archives.gov.iwg/reports/hitlers-shadow.pdf

30 Lossin, Y. *Pillar of Fire*, p. 335.

31 Later, in 1943, he was involved in raising an armed unit of Muslims in Bosnia.

CHAPTER 19

OPERATION CRUSADER AND THE RELIEF OF TOBRUK

German and Allied Plans

According to a letter from the German War Office to the generals in August 1941, it was anticipated that, following the defeat of the Soviet Union, German assistance would then be given to 'rendering possible the capture of Tobruk.' In addition attacks upon Malta would be resumed.

The Memorandum also stated that 'Should the campaign in the East be over, and Turkey comes to our side, an attack on Syria and Palestine in the direction of Egypt is contemplated... [1]

Rommel, however, was not willing to wait until certain events transpired in the East before attempting to break through in North Africa. Following the failed Allied Operation *Battleaxe* he began planning a new offensive, which he aimed to launch on 23 November 1941.

Auchinleck, the new C-in-C Middle East and the new commander of the Eighth Army, General Cunningham, were also planning a new attempt to break through to Tobruk, which was due to be launched on 18 November 1941, just before Rommel's planned attack.

In the intervening months, the British Mediterranean Fleet and submarines operating out from Malta managed to destroy a very high percentage of the supplies required for Rommel's upcoming offensive. This advantage forced the German High Command to transfer a number of U-Boats from their Atlantic work to the Mediterranean. When one such U-Boat rammed a torpedo into *HMS Ark Royal* and sank her on 12 November 1941 it was clear that a change in the balance sheet was about to happen.

Operation *Crusader*

Auchinleck and Cunningham had two Corps at their disposal, the 13th Army Corps (4th Indian Division; New Zealand Division; 1st Army Tank Brigade) and the 30th Army Corps (7th Armoured Division; 4th Armoured Brigade group; 1st South African Division; and 22nd Guards Brigade Group). In addition the Western Desert Air Force was to play a significant role. The overall objective was to liberate Tobruk, capture Cyrenaica, and if possible, also capture Tripolitania. The 30th Corps was to aim towards Tobruk from the desert route, while the 13th Corps was to attack the Axis coastal garrisons (the areas between Sollum, Halfaya and Bardia) and then move towards Tobruk along the coastal route. As these

1 Churchill, W. *The Grand Alliance*, p. 554.

two movements were taking place, the garrison force at Tobruk was to break-out and encounter the Axis forces.

Interestingly the New Zealander's left their most accomplished warrior behind. Kippenberger felt that Upham was not in the correct frame of mind to be thrust into this foray. Upham was understandably upset at his omission, but being the soldier he was, he ultimately accepted his fate.[2]

The Axis force included the 15th and 21st Panzer Divisions, the 90th German Light Division, and seven divisions of Italian infantry. As Rommel had intended launching his attack on 23 November, he was in Rome at the time when Cunningham launched his attack.[3]

The attack began as scheduled on the morning of 18 November. The 30th Corps made their thrust in the direction of Tobruk. The main objective was the Sidi Rezegh Ridge to the south-east of Tobruk. This ridge is higher than the surrounding countryside and offers a clear view, and close by was an airfield. Rommel understandably had placed a strong force in this location.

The Sidi Rezegh Ridge was the key to breaking through into Tobruk. The forces of both sides, especially the armoured divisions, were locked in battle there for several days and the Eighth Army could claim some minor victories. Following these initial victories both Auchinleck and Air Marshal Tedder informed Churchill that all was going well.[4] Initially the ridge was captured by the 30th Corps, but then due to a spirited counter-attack, the Axis recaptured it on 22 November. The 30th Corps had suffered tremendous casualties, and, as Auchinleck wrote, it 'was compelled to retire, having lost two-thirds of its tanks and leaving the garrison of Tobruk with a huge salient to defend'.[5] General Norrie ordered a withdrawal eastwards of some thirty kilometres.

The 13th Corps then began its offensive on 21 November, with the 4th Indian Division heading towards Sidi Omar from Halfaya, and the 2nd New Zealand Division circumventing the Halfaya Ridge and heading towards Fort Capuzzo and then Bardia. After securing the outskirts of Bardia, and thereupon cutting off the frontier Axis troops, General Freyberg then headed towards Sidi Rezegh.

While the 13th Corps was moving forward, the *Afrika Korps* on the night of 22 November heavily assaulted the 30th Corps positions, and, as Auchinleck said, 'practically annihilated the 5th South African Infantry Brigade.'[6] On the same day the garrison forces inside Tobruk began their breakout.

During these days the 7th Armoured Brigade and 7th Support Group were continually in

2 Sandford, K. ibid, pp. 120-21.

3 While in Rome the British landed a commando force led by Colonel Laycock along the Axis controlled coast on 17 November in order to disrupt their communication lines, and also to assassinate Rommel. The attempt failed, as he wasn't there, but much damage was done. In the ensuing fight at Rommel's HQ Lieutenant-Colonel Keyes was killed. He was later awarded the Victoria Cross posthumously. The LRDP was also involved.

4 Churchill, W. *The Grand Alliance*, pp. 561-62.

5 *Gazette*, 1948, quoted in Churchill, W. The Grand Alliance, p. 564.

6 *Gazette*, ibid, p. 564.

the midst of the very intense fighting. One man amongst many who exemplified extreme courage under fire was Brigadier John 'Jock' Campbell. Campbell was continually in the forefront of fighting, exhorting his men, either on the ground, on a transport vehicle or astride a tank, especially on 21 November when his men stopped two Panzer divisions from capturing the airfield. His bravery was a great example to his men, and he was later awarded the Victoria Cross.[7]

Rommel had now taken control of the situation from the Axis side, and on 24 November made a thrust for the border in order to cut-off the Eighth Army. Rallying his remaining armour, Rommel headed towards the border along the inland El Abd Track towards Bir Sheferzen on the border. From there he sent some of his forces south, while the bulk headed north adjacent to the border.

There was now a strong possibility that apart from the *Afrika Korps* cutting off the Eighth Army, they might also totally destroy the Eighth Army armour, thereby endangering Egypt itself. The situation was now critical, so critical in fact that Auchinleck intervened. Sensing that General Cunningham was beginning to think defensively instead of maintaining an offensive attitude (the object was the relief of Tobruk), Auchinleck replaced him with General Neil Ritchie. During this period of intense fighting the New Zealanders and the 4th Indian Division played very significant roles.

While all this was happening the Western Desert Air Force and the Mediterranean Fleet were doing their utmost to upset the Axis supply lines and destroying as much of their stockpile, especially of fuel, as possible.

Relief of Tobruk

While the 4th Indian Division was battling in the Sollum area, fighting in and around Sidi Rezegh continued unabated and the New Zealand Division was heavily involved. On 26 November contact was made with the Tobruk garrison, with the 19th New Zealand Battalion 'joining up with men from the Essex Regiment patrolling out from town.'[8] This news greatly perturbed Rommel, who immediately returned from Derna and attacked the New Zealanders and 7th Armoured Division in force and recaptured Sidi Rezegh.

The Allied forces were severely hammered, with the New Zealanders suffering some three thousand casualties and contact with Tobruk was severed. Lieutentant-General Fritz Bayerlein recorded that on 1 December 1941 'a concentric attack was launched which resulted in the destruction of the greater part of the New Zealand Division.'[9]

At this point Rommel made another attempt to relieve his garrisons near the border (the Sollum, Halfaya and Bardia enclave), while Ritchie regrouped his heavily pressed forces and made a last ditch effort to sever the Axis communications line at El Adem west of

7 'Jock' Campbell would be, alongside Charles Upham, a legend from the North African campaign. Before he was tragically killed in a motor accident in February 1942, he was the holder of the DSO and Bar and the Military Cross..
8 Sandford, K. ibid, p. 121.
9 Rommel, E. *The Rommel Papers*, p, 169.

Sidi Rezegh and south of Tobruk. If Ritchie's attack succeeded then Rommel would have been cut off.

Operation *Crusader* was now reaching its zenith. On 29 November the Eighth Army took El Adem and General Godwin-Austin's 30th Corps linked up with Tobruk. After some 242 days the siege of Tobruk was over.

Yet even with the link-up, and with the Italians not being involved as expected, Rommel kept pressing on with the offensive. Finally by 7 December 1941 he had to face the inevitable. Bayerlain wrote:

> In view of the great numerical superiority of the enemy and the condition of our own troops, Rommel now decided to give up Tobruk completely and beat a fighting retreat to the Gazala position. It was a painful decision to have to take, for the German troops had fought successfully and inflicted heavy losses on the enemy. But to have stayed any longer at Tobruk would merely have led to the steady attrition of our already weakened forces, and thus ultimately to the loss of Libya.[10]

Rommel withdraws from Gazala

The fall back line for the Axis forces was at Gazala west of Tobruk. Rommel succeeded in reaching Gazala on 12 December and established a strong defensive line running inland. General Godwin-Austin's 13th Corps continued to attack Rommel there. Rommel's situation was precarious, as revealed in a letter to his wife on 13 December 1941, 'The situation has been made very extremely critical by the failure of a major Italian formation. However, I hope to be able to hold on. Otherwise, I'm very well, in fixed quarters.'[11]

His optimism was short lived. Rommel had two choices at this stage. If he stayed at Gazala there was every likelihood that the Allied forces would take Mechilli and proceed by the inland route towards the Gulf of Sirte, and thereby cut off the Axis forces completely; or he could quickly retreat from Gazala before this scenario had occurred, and reach the Gulf of Sirte before the Eighth Army did. This way he could regroup and hold the position, which was closer to his supply base at Tripoli.

He chose the latter option, despite opposition from the Italian High Command and Field Marshal Kesselring. These dignitaries looked at the withdrawal from the political perspective – the damage such a withdrawal would have upon both Italian and German prestige. Rommel looked at the situation pragmatically: if he stayed he would lose his force and Cyrenaica and potentially Tripolitania, while if he withdrew he would retain his force, and potentially retain Tripolitania.

The withdrawal began on 16 December, with the Eighth Army in hot pursuit. The *Afrika Korps* and Italian Motorised Corps under the command of General Cruewell withdrew through the central route via El Abiar, while the Italian infantry divisions withdrew via

10 Rommel, E. *The Rommel Papers*, pp. 171-71.
11 Rommel, E. *The Rommel Papers*, p. 174.

the coastal route. Rommel was extremely distraught by this turn of events, and wrote to his wife Lu, 'Retreat to A-----! You can't imagine what's it's like...Little ammunition and petrol, no air support...[12]

When his forces reached Benghazi, Rommel, fully aware of the danger of being trapped, quickly moved on to Agedabia, where he arrived by 25 December 1941. Elements of the 22nd British Armoured Brigade then attacked his positions there on 27 December 1941, but much of this force was either destroyed or captured after three days of intense tank warfare.

Back at El Agheila

When realising that his defensive position at Agedabia was not strong enough, Rommel slowly withdrew the Axis forces further west, to the Mersa el Brega and El Agheila line, where the bulk of the Axis army arrived on 7 January 1942. There, on the Gulf of Sirte, Rommel consolidated his line.

Auchinleck desired to pursue Rommel, but poor weather, Axis air interference and the inability to repair the harbour at Benghazi greatly hindered him. Supplies had to be brought forward from the port at Tobruk.

Churchill had anticipated that the Axis force would be stopped before getting to this defensive line. His long-term plans involved either a joint operation with French forces in North Africa or an American force, to move from the west towards Tunis and thereby destroy all Axis forces in North Africa. This forestalment went contrary to his plans.[13] Then to add difficulties to the situation, a large German convoy managed to reach Tripoli with supplies and reinforcements for the Axis force on 19 December.

The weakened Axis force managed to strengthen a defensive line running some fifty miles from el Agheila inland to the edge of the Libyan Sand Desert. The Allied force facing him was spread out over a considerable area and was not strong enough at the same time to make a concerted assault upon this weak, yet ever strengthening Axis line of defence. Auchinleck was of the opinion that Rommel was in no position to attack, and if he did, the Allied force would withdraw to a defensible line.[14]

Simultaneously with these developments, the *Luftwaffe* based in Sicily had strongly attacked the RAF based in Malta and hindered their activities. This then ensured successful sailing for Axis supply convoys from Italy to reach Tripoli. The arrival of each new convoy strongly bolstered Rommel's forces and confidence, and, realising the weakness of the British forces opposing him in the border region between Tripolitania and Cyrenaica, he began preparing for a break-out – before the Eighth Army managed to regroup and pursue him.

12 Rommel, E. *The Rommel Papers*, p. 175. 'A' refers to Agedabia.
13 Churchill, W. *The Hinge of Fate*, pp. 22-23.
14 Churchill, W. *The Hinge of Fate*, p. 25.

2nd South African Division moves to the battle zone

The casualties in the Eighth Army were high, and those involved in the fighting were now rested. Turrel and his mates in the 2nd South African Division were about to move forward to the front line. He recorded of the trip forward:

> There was only one tarred road running all the way from Alexandria through Mersa Matruh, Sidi Barrani, up the Sollum Pass and on to Tobruk, carrying a single line of traffic in each direction. To avoid total chaos and keep traffic moving either way there must have been some pretty nifty timing arrangements.[15]

While en-route they came across a couple of Kiwis looking the worse for wear, who had 'been part of the New Zealand Division which had been roughed up at Sidi Aziz.' One of them then opened up and gave the raw South Africans some sobering reflections:

> "We were in the Western Desert, and Jerry kicked us out. We re-grouped, were sent to Crete, and Jerry kicked us out. We re-grouped again, went up into the desert, and Jerry gave us another kicking. He's a better man than we are, that's all. You guys can go up there and do your stuff if you like, and I wish you luck...."

Turrel's reflection was sobering, 'It was hardly morale-building stuff for men who, up to then, had never had a shot fired at them in anger, but who were anticipating that experience right soon.'[16] The New Zealand soldier's comments were quite common – the Allied soldiers held the German soldiers in high regard as fighting men.

The route of the 2nd South African Division was through the desert route at Bir Sheferzen, the reason being, as Turrel stated, 'A fairly large pocket of Germans and Itis[17] had been left behind in the area at the top of Halfaya and Sollum Passes, and stretching from there to the Libyan coast at Bardia.'[18] The Axis garrison force in the Sollum-Halfaya-Bardia pocket continued to hold out against the Eighth Army.

While camped adjacent to the Halfaya Ridge, and in the meal queue on their first Sunday the cook had just given the call 'come and get it.' Then they heard the 'sound of a solitary aircraft high in the sky.' Turrel, like the other soldiers had no doubt it was an Allied plane. Then it began to fly low towards them, and he recalls 'I looked up in time to see three little black dots emerge from the plane, and I believe I was the first to grasp their significance. "Scatter! I shouted, "those are bombs!"

'The queue' he continued 'melted away faster than butter on hot toast. There was no shelter anywhere, no place to hide, so I ran for the stores tent ... I looked around for my

15 Turrel, R. ibid, p. 217.
16 Turrel, R. ibid, pp. 218-19.
17 Itai's was a term used for Italians.
18 Turrel, R. ibid, p. 220.

tin hat. Nowhere to be found. Never mind, I grabbed the "cardboard" helmet which the army had given me, jammed it on my head, and lay flat in the dirt. Curious how so many inhibitions disappear under such circumstances. Seconds later' Turrel continued 'the ground shook … from the two explosions … The bombs had exploded right in the middle of our camp, but miraculously, not a soul had been hurt. [19]

The 2nd South African Division had now entered into the reality of the war front. Shortly later they moved forward to Sidi Omar, overlooking the Axis forces who were still bottled up in the area. Turrel recalled of the move, 'This time the move was a short one, to a place called Sidi Omar, a dusty, god-forsaken spot if ever there was one.'[20]

The two South African divisions were now adjacent to each other, and shortly afterwards Halfaya and Sollum fell. The South Africans then were involved in the final assault on Bardia. It was while in the area of Bardia that one of those humorous incidents happened which occasionally gave the soldiers a break from the mundane. Attached to the South Africans were some eighty Africans, primarily in the service units as drivers. Although supposedly non-combatants, along the way they had received some old Italian rifles. These they replaced when they found abandoned Lee Enfield rifles from the battlefields around Sidi Rezegh.

Good quality rifles, however, wasn't the only thing they found. The white South Africans had been issued with a 25-gallon cask of issue brandy, a treasure which was usually 'kept under supervision in the stores tent.' One night, however, it was left unattended. Unattended maybe, but not untouched. The Africans had found it, and downed the whole lot!

The next day their CO, Captain van Rensburg had a real challenge getting them onto parade. One by one, van Rensburg managed. Some had to be carried there, others just 'sat with happy looks on their faces.' The incident almost turned sour though when one drunk man with rifle draped across his knees flatly refused to attend parade. It took some quick thinking on behalf of Mo 'Raphael' and Turrel to bring the man to the ground.[21]

While the Africans were enjoying the fruits of war – rifles and brandy – the Axis garrison in the pocket finally surrendered, Bardia the first on 2 January 1942, and the Halfaya-Sollum area next, on 17 January 1942. Together some 14,000 Axis soldiers were taken prisoner, 4,000 of whom were crack German troops. Operation *Crusader* proved to be very expensive to both sides. Altogether some 33,000 Axis soldiers were taken prisoner (including 10,000 Germans). During the period 18 November till mid-January 1942 the Allies lost some 2,908 men killed, 7,339 men wounded and 7,457 men missing, as well as losing some 278 tanks.[22]

19 Turrel, R. ibid, p. 221.
20 Turrel, R. ibid, p. 225.
21 Turrel, R. ibid, pp. 237-38.
22 Churchill, W. *The Grand Alliance*, p. 575.

Tobruk (or Tobruch)

It was not long before the 2nd South African Division received its commission to become the garrison at Tobruk. On the way, Turrel, explains he noticed that 'Some of the signposts read "Tobruch", and I felt like asking people to make up their minds about the spelling, until I remembered that the name was really an Arabic one, and its spelling probably only a few squiggles.'

While the South Africans were acclimatising themselves to their new locale at garrison Tobruk (or Tobruch), further south at Mersa el Brega General Rommel was already planning for his next thrust eastwards – and these very same South Africans were in his sights.

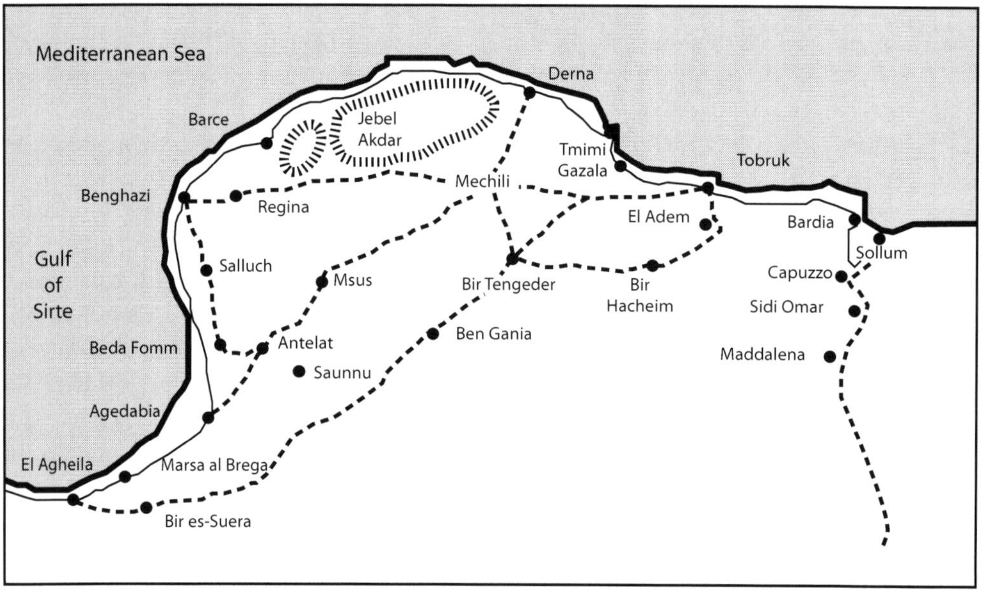

CHAPTER 20

THE FINAL SOLUTION TO THE JEWISH PROBLEM

Several thousand kilometres away from Tobruk, another group of Germans had others than South African soldiers in their sights. While the *Einsatzgruppen* were to the best of their ability exterminating potential political problem makers in the regions under German influence, Hermann Goring instructed Reinhard Heydrich on 31 July 1941:

> I herewith commission you to carry out all preparations with regard to … a total solution of the Jewish question in those territories of Europe which are under German influence …
>
> I furthermore charge you to submit to me as soon as possible a draft showing the … measures already taken for the execution of the intended final solution of the Jewish question.[1]

The term 'final solution' was often used by senior Nazi leaders, and was synonymous to 'extermination.' This was the logical outcome of what Hitler meant in his 1939 Reichstag speech. Shirer states:

> What became known in high Nazi circles as the "Fuehrer Order on the Final Solution" apparently was never committed to paper – at least no copy of it has yet been unearthed in the captured Nazi documents. All the evidence shows that it was most probably given verbally to Goering, Himmler and Heydrich, who passed it down during the summer and fall of 1941. A number of witnesses testified at Nuremberg that they had "heard" of it but none admitted ever seeing it.[2]

Shirer then provides evidence from one convicted Nazi, Hans Lammers, who testified, 'I knew that a Fuehrer order was transmitted by Goering to Heydrich … This order was called "Final Solution of the Jewish Problem."'[3]

A start had already been made on fulfilling this 'final solution' through the work of the *Einsatzgruppen* and through the various concentration camps and ghettos. But as new territories opened for Hitler's forces, and as these areas were filled with Jewish people, the need was felt to dispose of the 'Jewish problem' more quickly.

1 NCA, III, pp. 525-26 (ND 710, PS), quoted in Shirer, W. *The Rise and Fall of the Third Reich*, p. 964.
2 Shirer, W. *The Rise and Fall of the Third Reich*, pp. 964-65.
3 TMWC, XI, p. 141, quoted in Shirer, W. ibid, p. 965.

It was with this perspective in mind that the deputy commander of the SS, Herman Heydrich was commissioned to determine a plan to complete the task, quickly and efficiently.

Meeting in Wannsee

Heydrich accordingly summoned fifteen senior German officials to a meeting on 20 January 1942 at a luxurious house in the exclusive Berlin suburb of Wannsee. The purpose of the meeting was not to discuss the issue of exterminating the Jewish people from Europe, but how to achieve this goal more effectively. In an opulent home, over a sumptuous lunch, these men came to discuss and decide upon the final solution – the physical extermination – of an entire people, all eleven million Jews of Europe.

Those attending fell into two categories: SS affiliated, and Reich (Government) affiliated. Together these men represented every spectrum of German political control related to the occupied enemy territories and the Jewish people, and represented the governmental bureaucracy of Nazi Germany. Any decision made at this level would be expected to be fully instituted.

Heydrich was the deputy chief of the SS, and had himself been given the written statement in 1941 by Goring, the *Reichsfuehrer*, (deputy to Hitler). He carried with him the full weight and authority of the Nazi German system.

The Minutes of the meeting

Heydrich's deputy, Adolf Eichmann, took notes of the meeting. These were later edited by Heydrich, who replaced the direct statements with euphemisms which were known and understood by all present.[4]

Heydrich provided a brief summary of his job description until that point, which was:

a) The expulsion of the Jews from every sphere of life of the German people,
b) The expulsion of the Jews from the living space of the German people.

His task, Heydrich stated, was to 'cleanse German living space of Jews in a legal manner.' This process began, so he stated, with the emigration of Jewish people out of Germany, Austria and the Protectorate of Bohemia and Moravia.

Following some further information relating to financing that emigration, Heydrich then came to the core of the meeting:

> Another possible solution of the problem has now taken the place of emigration, i.e. the evacuation of the Jews to the East, provided that the Fuhrer gives the appropriate approval in advance.
>
> These actions are, however, only to be considered provisional, but practical experience is already being collected which is of the greatest importance in relation to the future

4 For example 'transported to the East' meant extermination.

final solution of the Jewish question.

Approximately 11 million Jews will be involved in the final solution of the European Jewish question, distributed as follows among the individual countries....[5]

Heydrich then continued:

Under proper guidance, in the course of the final solution the Jews are to be allocated for appropriate labor in the East. Able-bodied Jews, separated according to sex, will be taken in large work columns to these areas for work on roads, in the course of which action doubtless a large portion will be eliminated by natural causes.

The possible remnant will, since it will undoubtedly consist of the most resistant portion, have to be treated accordingly, because it is the product of natural selection and would, if released, act as a seed of a new Jewish revival (see the experience of history.)

In the course of the practical execution of the final solution, Europe will be combed through from west to east...

The evacuated Jews will first be sent, group by group, to so-called transit ghettos, from which they will be transported to the East.[6]

Further information was then provided concerning the Jewish people then still living in Germany and Austria, whereupon Heydrich then stated:

The beginning of the individual larger evacuation actions will depend on military developments. Regarding the handling of the final solution in those European countries occupied and influenced by us, it was proposed that the appropriate expert of the Foreign Office discuss the matter with the responsible official of the Security Police and SD.[7]

The issue of determining who was Jewish, Heydrich stated, would be based upon the Nuremberg Laws. Thereupon follows a lengthy explanation concerning who was and who was not classified as Jewish. Joseph Buehler, representing the central government of Poland had one request, 'to solve the Jewish question in this area as soon as possible.'[8]

Other matters were obviously discussed, but according to the Minutes, the meeting then concluded with Heydrich requesting of the participants 'that they afford him appropriate support during the carrying out of the tasks involved in the solution.'

5 *Minutes of Wannsee Conference*, 20 January 1942. Source www.historyplace.com/worldwar2/holocaust/h-wannsee.htm. At this point Heydrich provides numbers for the Jewish populations of Europe, mentioning some 35 political entities. For Greece he gives the number at 69,600.

6 *Minutes of Wannsee Conference*, 20 January 1942. Source www.historyplace.com/worldwar2/holocaust/h-wannsee.htm

7 *Minutes of Wannsee Conference*, 20 January 1942. Ibid.

8 *Minutes of Wannsee Conference*, 20 January 1942. Ibid.

Consequences of these decisions

Until this point most of the killing of Jewish people (and indeed other 'non-desirables') had been through shooting, and this primarily through the *Einsatzgruppen*. In addition there were numerous concentration camps in Germany, as well as in other countries since occupied by the German forces where most of those who were executed were shot.

Some concentration camps had already been built in Poland. The first was at Chelmno near Lodz, where thousands of people, mostly Jewish, were murdered even before the Wannsee Conference. Many of these were from the nearby Lodz ghetto. The murders were mostly in specialised vans whose exhaust fumes were channelled into a compartment where the victims were sealed in. Many experiments took place at Chelmno which assisted the Nazis to determine the most effective form of execution: gassing.

Another camp was established near the village of Treblinka in June 1941 and was used initially as a labour camp. A new section was then built following the Wannsee Conference, and began to operate from 11 July 1942. It's first 'inmates' were 6,500 Jewish people from the Warsaw ghetto, who arrived on 22 July 1942. The following day the majority of these people were sent to specially constructed gas chambers, and were gassed to death. Thereafter each day there were approximately 5,000 arrivals.[9]

In 1940 a former Austrian cavalry barracks at Auschwitz near Krakow was converted into a prison camp, and over the following years it was expanded. In 1941 a separate area was built, named Birkenau. Gas chambers were installed there in March 1942, and thereafter Auschwitz-Birkenau became by far the worst of the death camps where Hitler's 'Final Solution to the Jewish Problem' was to be carried out in full. During 1943 almost the entire Jewish population of Thessalonica was transported and murdered at Auschwitz.

Numerous other camps fulfilling a similar function were established, namely Belzec, Sobibor, Mathausen and Majdanek. All of these places became specialised murder camps.

With such a sophisticated murder system now in place, and in view of Hitler's statement to Haj Amin el-Husseini on 30 November 1941, that 'Germany was resolved, step by step, to ask one European nation after the other to solve its Jewish problem, *and at the proper time direct a similar appeal to non-European nations as well*',[10] the issue now was 'how long it would be before this "Final Solution to the Jewish Problem" would be transported outside Europe, to areas where German soldiers were now treading.'

As far as the Middle East was concerned this was merely academic, as German attempts to enter into Iraq had been thwarted, and there were very few Jewish people in the Gulf of Sirte. Matters, though, were soon to drastically change in North Africa which could potentially bring the Holocaust to the very precincts of the Middle East.

9 Possibly about 780,000 Jewish people were murdered at Treblinka.

10 *Memorandum by an Official of the Foreign Minister's Secretariat*, 30 November 1941, Document No. 515, ibid, Vol. XIII, pp. 882-3. Italics the author's.

CHAPTER 21

ROMMEL BREAKS OUT

Consolidation

While the Axis forces at Mersa el Brega and El Agheila continued to consolidate, Auchinleck did little to fortify his line opposite them, despite bountiful supplies arriving at Benghazi port. The Panzer Army Africa was able to consolidate its position due to the loss of Allied supremacy in the air at Malta and the loss of ships by Admiral Cunningham. These set-backs allowed several Axis convoys to reach Tripoli with much needed reinforcements and supplies. Apart from the convoy in December 1941, another arrived on 5 January 1942. The arrival of these two convoys in particular permitted Rommel to already contemplate a renewed counter-attack – even so soon after a prolonged and exhausting withdrawal.

The Axis attack from El Agheila

On 21 January 1942 Rommel sent a small reconnaissance force out from behind his line, and these three attacking columns managed to get through the gaps in the Eighth Army lines. This Axis force was anticipating an Allied attack against them, but when Rommel realised there was little by way of an Allied force opposing them, he decided to press forward. The small Allied force opposite him now retreated in haste.

Initially Auchinleck was not overly concerned with this break-out, as he did not consider Rommel had sufficient supplies to proceed very far. On this matter he seriously misjudged the situation. Rommel's forces captured Agedabia on 22 January 1942, and then soon afterwards his *Afrika Korps* destroyed and captured a large part of the 1st British Armoured Division, the remnants being pursued in the direction of Msus. It all seemed *déjà vu* from the break-out the previous year.

When Churchill received a message from the Eighth Army on 24 January that preparations were being made to evacuate Benghazi, he for the first time understood the gravity of this latest Axis breakout.[1] Auchinleck rushed forward to the front line and met with General Ritchie. There he too understood the gravity of this new development. Emboldened by his easy breakout, Rommel now sent two attacking columns forward, one to Msus and the other to Benghazi. Benghazi was evacuated on 29 January 1942, and the men of the 13th Corps were ordered to fall back to a line stretching from Gazala to Bir-Hacheim.

General Bayerlein wrote:

> … on the 28th January, he launched a surprise attack on Benghazi itself. The fortress was

1 Churchill, W. *The Hinge of Fate*, p. 28.

first sealed off to the north and then to the south, and by the 29th was in our hands. The vast quantities of vehicles, arms and material which fell into our hands served to equip and motorise many of our own units.

After this victory, Rommel decided to embark on a long-range thrust to the east.[2]

Concerning this deteriorating situation Auchinleck wrote to Churchill, 'It must be admitted that enemy has succeeded beyond his expectations and mine, and that his tactics have been skilful and bold.'[3] Indeed Rommel had been bold, and his boldness shocked both Auchinleck and Churchill. Such was Rommel's brilliance that Churchill stated to Parliament on 27 January, 'We have a very daring and skilful opponent against us.'[4] The set-back caused Auchinleck to admit the absolute superiority of the German armour, and that if this situation was to be reversed they needed to double their own armoured forces. The earlier loss of over 100 tanks from the 1st Armoured Division was a bitter blow for the Allies, as these tanks had been brought to Egypt via the Cape and prepared as best as possible for desert conditions.

Rommel wrote to his wife on 4 February 1942, 'On the move since the 2nd. But we have got Cyrenaica back. It went like greased lightning. I hope to be home in 10 days and to get quite a bit of leave. But there's still a lot to do until then.'[5]

General Ritchie's forces withdrew all the way back to Gazala, west of Tobruk, where they were consolidated, and a defensive line established from the coast inland through to Bir Hacheim and then back to Tobruk. Rommel's goal was now to break open this defensive position.

Hitler endorses all-out assault in North Africa

Basically until this point Hitler's interest in the Mediterranean was about helping his Italian ally. Yet according to Churchill on 13 February 1942 Admiral Raeder was able to convince Hitler of the possibility and importance of defeating the British in the Middle East. Raeder stated to Hitler, 'Suez and Basra are the western pillars of the British position in the East. Should these positions collapse under the weight of concerted Axis pressure the consequences for the British Empire would be disastrous…'[6]

Hitler thereafter gave more support to the North Africa campaign than he hitherto had done. Malta was the first to feel the brunt of this new German offensive. The Germans threw everything they had at destroying and subduing Malta. Their intention was to obliterate the island garrison and capture it. Rommel planned his next offensive around the expected fall of Malta, thinking that he would be in the best position by June.

2 Rommel, E. *The Rommel Papers*, p. 183.

3 Auchinleck to Churchill, 29 January 1942, quoted in Churchill, W, *The Hinge of Fate*, p. 31.

4 Churchill, W. *The Hinge of Fate*, p. 67.

5 Rommel, E. *The Rommel Papers*, p. 183. The Axis forces considered Cyrenaica to be the western part of what the Allies called Cyrenaica. The section from Tobruk through to Sollum they called the Marmarica district.

6 Quoted in Churchill, W, *The Hinge of Fate*, p. 296.

The Axis supplies that did manage to get through from Italy were offloaded at Benghazi, but if Rommel was going to defeat the British in the Middle East, it would be imperative to capture Tobruk in the first instance in order to cut down the length of his supply line. Rommel was intent on attacking as soon as he was supplied.

During the following three months the situation deteriorated for the Allies. The Axis vigorously renewed their aerial assault on Malta, thereby hindering the British garrison there from interfering with the Axis convoys taking supplies and reinforcements from Italy to Libya. The aerial assault on Malta became so intense that the actual survival of the island fortress itself was imperilled.

Political ramifications in Egypt

Although a relative calm had descended over Egypt, there were still apparent tensions under the surface, especially within the political sphere where there were numerous parties with quite distinct perspectives and objectives.

Rommel's new offensive, coupled with the renewed Axis bombing of Malta, and news of Japan's capture of British dominions in Asia, re-ignited pro-German sentiments in Egypt.[7] Prime Minister Hussain Sirri came under extreme pressure from anti-British elements. On 1 February 1942 extremist students began demonstrating in the streets. The following day the pro-British Sirri, resigned.

As a result of the situation in Iraq in 1941 when a pro-Axis Government came into power, the British Government was fully aware of the ramifications if a less than sympathetic government came into power in Egypt – especially with a reinvigorated German-led army heading towards Egypt.

Accordingly on 3 February 1942 the British Ambassador to Egypt, Sir Miles Lampson, visited King Farouk and stated that the:

> … co-operation of the well-intentioned Sirri Government with the British had been prevented by intrigue in other quarters; Axis propaganda had not been adequately checked; pro-Axis elements had been left at liberty; the students had been encouraged to demonstrate in favour of Rommel; now that the enemy was advancing in Cyrenaica, the strategic situation was full of dangerous possibilities for Egypt, Britain's vital base in the Middle East.[8]

Ambassador Lampson insisted that the King install a government which commanded a majority, and which could control the internal situation, preferably led by Mustafa an-Nahhas, the leader of the Wafd Party. King Farouk replied that he would consult with his senior politicians. The senior Egyptian politicians however refused to accept the British

7 There were other issues as well, including food shortages and the recent severing of diplomatic relations with Vichy France.
8 Kirk, G. *The Middle East in the War*, p. 209.

ultimatum, at which point the Ambassador informed the King that he would visit him at nine pm. This the Ambassador did accompanied by General Stone, commander of British troops in Egypt, and three tanks and infantry.

At this point the King recalled his senior politicians, and then agreed to invite Nahhas to be the prime minister and form a new Cabinet. Nahhas accepted the position. He thereafter formed a new government and on 7 February 1942 'a proclamation was issued dissolving Parliament so that new elections might be held.'[9]

This unpleasant incident ensured that in this unpredictable time, when there was every likelihood of a renewed German-led thrust towards Egypt, there was less likelihood of political insurrection within Egypt, triggered off by pro-Axis elements within the Government and the Palace.[10]

Ultimatum from Churchill

Churchill pressured Auchinleck to attack Rommel as quickly as possible and not wait any longer, otherwise the Axis forces would become too reinvigorated.[11] Auchinleck responded that he was in no hurry and had established a firm defensive line around Gazala, Tobruk and Bir Hacheim. He was looking for an offensive in early June 1942.

Auchinleck's waiting strategy irked Churchill and the Chiefs-of-Staff, who had to view the North African campaign within the bigger picture of the conduct of the War. Malta was close to collapse, and the British required airbases close enough to be able to fly sorties there. There were such air-bases in eastern Cyrenaica, and it was these which the Chief of Staff wanted secured.[12] Besides this, millions of Soviet soldiers were fighting against the Germans on the Eastern Front under adverse conditions.

Auchinleck's seeming procrastination continued to irk Churchill, who requested that he return to Britain. Auchinleck refused, so instead Churchill sent two emissaries, Sir Stafford Crisps who was en-route to India, and General Nye, to Cairo to discuss the matter with Auchinleck.

Auchinleck however continued to procrastinate concerning an attack, a matter which increasingly frustrated Churchill and the General Staff. Churchill was forced to give him an ultimatum – attack in order to draw off some of the flak upon Malta – or be relieved.[13]

Auchinleck's challenges

Auchinleck agreed to bring his plans forward and to attack in early June. The New Zealanders had already been transferred north to Syria, as too had the 9th Australian Division, on garrison duties. Auchinleck decided to leave the New Zealanders in Syria as he was unsure of the stability of the northern region, and also concerned about the Turks,

9 Kirk, G. ibid, p. 210.
10 Kirk, G. ibid, p. 211.
11 Churchill to Auchinleck, 26 February 1942, in Churchill, W. *The Hinge of Fate*, p. 291.
12 Kirk, G. ibid, p. 213.
13 Kirk, G. ibid, p. 215.

'whose attitude' he stated 'I am not too sure.' [14] Sandford described the new locale of the New Zealanders:

> This is the Djedeide Box. In Syria. It is astride the Bekaa valley and will stop the Germans from penetrating south down the valley. The enemy may come swiftly through Turkey and sweep into Syria. He will find a number of sympathizers here. Once through Syria he is at large in the Middle East and can put an intolerable squeeze on the Suez Canal.[15]

Auchinleck did though bring the 4th Indian Division from Iraq, now that the situation there was quieter. On a later occasion Auchinleck again expressed his concerns about the northern border, his concern that he did not have enough troops 'to face a German attack through Anatolia or to defend Persia.'[16] The garrison in Syria was known as the Ninth Army and that in Persia (Iran) as the Tenth Army.

The Eighth Army was now bolstered. The front line from Gazala inland to Bir Hacheim was manned by the 1st South African Division in and near Gazala and then further south by the 50th British Division and then an extensive belt of some 500,000 mines down to Bir Hacheim, which became a fortress manned by the Free French. Tobruk was garrisoned by the 2nd South African Division.

Both sides observed each other building up their supplies and strength. Writing to his wife Lu on 12 May 1942 Rommel recorded:

> Nothing much to report. Heat and lots of dust. The main road is a sea of pot-holes with the amount of traffic on it.
>
> There's a certain nervousness on our front. The British are expecting us and we them. One day the two forces will measure their strength. You'll hear about it soon from the papers. We're all hoping that we'll be able to bring the war to an end this year. It will soon have lasted three full years.[17]

The Biltmore Programme

Those very same years had presented the Jewish people with immense challenges, primarily 1) the Nazi-led desire to annihilate them as a race, and 2) the British Government's decision to deny them the right to have a national home in Palestine.

Due to the War situation it was difficult for the full executive of the World Zionist Organisation to meet. So the American Zionists convened a meeting from 6-22 May 1942, at the Biltmore Hotel in New York. Over 600 delegates attended from eighteen nations.

At the conclusion the delegates passed an eight point resolution, in which it was stated:

14 Auchinleck to Churchill 22 May 1942, in Churchill W, *The Hinge of Fate*, p. 311.

15 Sandford, K. ibid, p. 127.

16 Auchinleck to Churchill, 10 June 1942, in Churchill, W. *The Hinge of Fate*, p. 364.

17 Rommel, E. *The Rommel Papers*, p. 188.

> Point 6. The Conference calls for the fulfillment of the original purpose of the Balfour Declaration and the Mandate which recognizing the historical connection of the Jewish people with Palestine was to afford them the opportunity, as stated by President Wilson, to found there a Jewish Commonwealth. The Conference affirms its unalterable rejection of the White Paper of May 1939 and denies its moral or legal validity …
> Point 8. The Conference declares that the new world order that will follow victory cannot be established on foundations of peace, justice and equality, unless the problem of Jewish homelessness is finally solved … and that Palestine be established as a Jewish Commonwealth integrated in the structure of the new democratic world.

This statement, later endorsed by the Zionist leaders in Palestine laid the foundation for a new attitude within the Zionist movement. Hereafter the Jewish people looked less to Britain for guidance in fulfilling their hopes and vision, but more to the United States.

It also established a very clear mandate: the Jewish people were going to fight for the establishment in Palestine of a Jewish Commonwealth, which meant nothing less than statehood. But before they could even get that far they first would need to survive, not just in Europe, but also in Palestine.

Operation *Venezia* begins

After three months of waiting and preparing Rommel broke-out on 26 May 1942 in what was called Operation *Venezia*. The Axis forces gained the initiative the quickest. Still fuming at his previous failure to take Tobruk, Rommel lashed out with all that he had, and his major objective was at the southern end of the Gazala Line, at Bir Hacheim, guarded by the 1st Free French Brigade, and then later by punching a hole through the Allied minefields in the midst of the 50th British Division.

Although some Allied troops were quickly overrun, many others held up his thrust, and his plan for easy victory was not attained. The evening of the first day Rommel was somewhat worried as he lost too many of his precious tanks, primarily as a result of the effectiveness of the new Grant tanks being used by the Eighth Army.

During the following days an intense battle continued in and around Bir Hacheim and the bridgehead through the mine field. Rommel's biggest challenge was the 150th British Brigade, whom he made the focus of his attack, and wrote of the assault on this brigade:

> The attack was launched on the morning of the 31st May. German-Italian units fought their way forward yard by yard against the toughest British resistance imaginable. The defence was conducted with considerable skill and, as usual, the British fought to the last round.[18]

The heavy fighting had now been going on for nearly a week when early on 2 June the Axis

18 Rommel, E. *The Rommel Papers*, p. 212.

forces attacked Bir Hacheim. The key to this position were the extensive fortifications and minefields which the Free French had established. While this battle was in progress the Eighth Army made a strong counter-attack on 4-5 June, but when this ended in failure, the initiative passed to the Axis.

Rommel then concentrated upon the Bir Hacheim position and the resilient Free French finally surrendered on 11 June 1942. The Axis force now aimed north towards the coast with the intention of cutting off the Allied forces which stretched up to Gazala. In the process the Axis forces destroyed many of the valuable Allied tanks. Rommel wrote of this time, 'The battle, which had begun so badly for us, was now taking an increasingly favourable turn. All this we owed to the courage of the German and Italian soldiers.[19]

The Axis forces were now encircling the bastion of Tobruk itself.

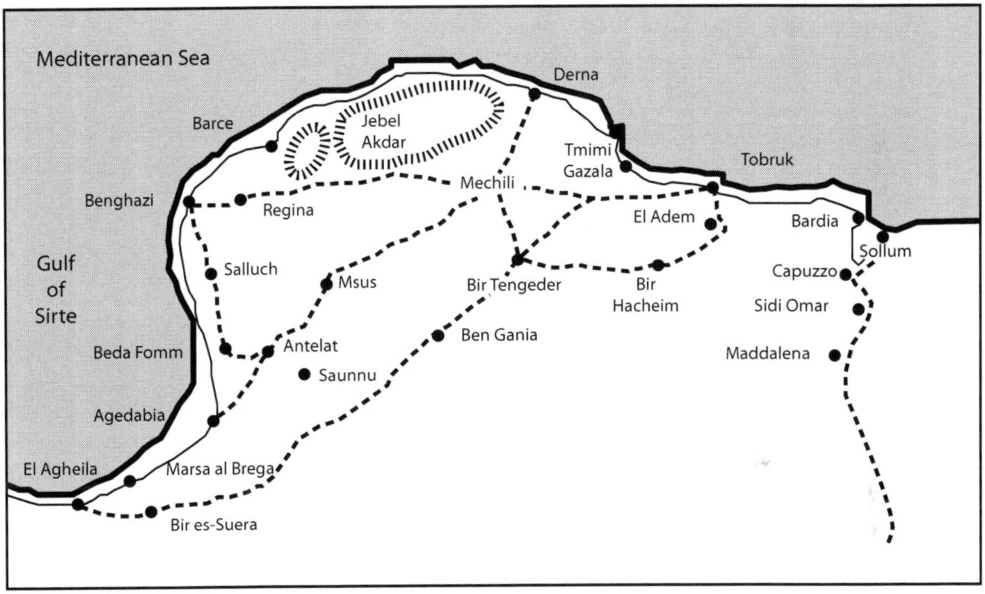

19 Rommel. E. *The Rommel Papers*, p. 222.

CHAPTER 22
TOBRUK FALLS

The defence of Tobruk

Now for the third time in the North African campaign Tobruk was at the centre of operations. On 12-13 June 1942 intense battles were fought to the south of Tobruk for possession of several strategic ridges known as Knightsbridge and El Adem. As these were taking place the beleaguered 1st South African Division and remnants of the 50th British Division were successfully extricated before they were fully encircled and cut off by the Axis forces.

Life for the garrison forces through the months January to June was one of waiting. The waiting came to a sudden end in the middle of June 1942. Ron Turrel wrote, 'The news from the Gazala Line, not more than fifty miles west of us, was not at all comforting. We heard how the Free French had been chopped up at a place called Bir Hakeim on the southern end of the Line, and this was a matter of concern for us.'[1]

Turrel recorded again soon afterwards:

> The news from the front grew steadily worse, until on Saturday 13th June the big gallop through Tobruk of the troops from the Gazala Line commenced. By mid-morning there were three solid columns of men in trucks, cars, gun limbers, ambulances, all streaming through the town, all converging on the solitary road leading out. The chaos on each of the three roads was notable, but at the confluences of all three columns it could have been catastrophic. Fortunately, all had the same idea in mind – to go East – and that as quickly as possible; this single-mindedness did help.[2]

The situation looked ominous, and Churchill instructed Auchinleck on 14 June to 'fight it out to the end.'[3] Churchill needed to clearly reiterate to Auchinleck that General Ritchie was not to consider withdrawing at all from Tobruk. Auchinleck instructed Ritchie on 14 June, 'Tobruk must be held and the enemy not allowed to invest it.'[4] As in 1941, Tobruk was to be held at all costs.

The defence of Tobruk was entrusted to General Klopper, commanding the 2nd South African Division, and together with administrative, transport and other personnel, there were some 35,000 Allied troops stationed there. Klopper had provisions for three months

1 Turrel, R. ibid, p. 251.
2 Turrel, R. ibid, p. 251.
3 Churchill to Auchinleck, 14 June 1942, in Churchill, W, *The Hinge of Fate*, p. 369.
4 Auchinleck to General Ritchie, 14 June 1942, in Churchill, W, *The Hinge of Fate*, p. 414.

if a siege developed as it had in 1941.

Turrel continued:

> By Sunday evening, the Gazala Gallop was over. Not only had the 1st S.A Division, the 50th British Div. and the 151st Brigade, plus lots of ancillary troops, disappeared into the east, but quite a sizeable portion of the Tobruk garrison as well. The ack-ack guns, all the armour, much of the artillery, had flown. On Monday, the ring around Tobruk snapped shut.[5]

When the Axis armour of the 15th Panzer Division reached the Mediterranean on 15 June the ring indeed had snapped shut. General Erwin Rommel could write to his wife:

> The battle has been won and the enemy is breaking up. We're now mopping up encircled remnants of the enemy. I needn't tell you how delighted I am. We've made a pretty clean sweep this time. Of course it's cost us some sad losses here and there.[6]

Rommel's assault

The battle of Gazala had indeed been won, but if Tobruk was not captured, then there would be no real fruits of victory. Rommel was not at all interested in another siege of Tobruk. He was intent on complete subjugation, evident in this description:

> To every man of us, Tobruk was a symbol of British resistance and we were now going to finish with it for good.[7]

With this clear intention he renewed his offensive on 16 June and quickly captured the crucial positions of El Adem, Belhamed and Acroma which formed the outer protection of Tobruk. This was followed by the crushing defeat of the 4th Armoured Brigade at Sidi Rezegh to the south east on 17 June. At this point the Tobruk garrison was cut off from effective armoured assistance. Inside the Tobruk perimeter were two South African brigades, one Indian Brigade, two Coldstream Guards Brigade Battalions, and the 32nd Army Tank Brigade had two battalions of infantry tanks.[8]

From this position of strength Rommel then began a concerted assault on the actual perimeters of Tobruk garrison on the morning of 20 June. The 11th Indian Infantry Brigade received the bulk of this assault as Rommel positioned the 15th and 21st Panzer Divisions together with other forces, against this Allied position. They soon overwhelmed the Indians and penetrated into the heart of Tobruk garrison.

5 Turrel, ibid, p. 252.

6 Rommel, E. *The Rommel Papers*, p. 224.

7 Rommel, E. *The Rommel Papers*, p. 225.

8 Commentary inserted into text by B.H. Liddell-Hart in Rommel, E. *The Rommel Papers*, p. 228-29.

Part of the reason for the easy penetration of the Panzer tanks is provided by Turrel, who wrote:

> What we didn't know was that the mines in the "minefield" protecting the only easy entrance into the fortress had largely been removed some months back and sent up to the Gazala Line, and the "minefield' was now almost completely innocuous; the tanktraps protecting the "minefields" were almost completely filled with drifting sand.[9]

In desperation General Klopper then sent his remaining armoured units and part of the Coldstream Guards to the assistance of the Indians, but it was all to no avail. When the Axis force reached the strategic "Kings Cross" position they began to shell Tobruk town. Klopper informed Eighth Army HQ, "My HQ surrounded. Infantry on perimeter still fighting hard. Am holding out, but I do not know how long."[10]

While the infantry fought gallantly, the signallers and others like Turrel watched from a distance. All they could see, he wrote:

> ... was a procession of Stuka dive-bombers, which were running a shuttle service with bombs from the nearby El Adem airfield to where the fighting was taking place. As almost all the ack-ack guns had been removed, and as we had no air assistance whatever, those planes had it all their own way until someone must have found a gun somewhere.
>
> We were delighted when one of the Stukas was hit. Moving smoothly along to drop its next load of destruction on our chaos, suddenly tipped nose-down as a lucky shot hit him in the tail. That Stuka screamed vertically to the ground, ending in a huge flash as the bomb that it was carrying exploded ...
>
> By midday it became clear that affairs were going very badly for the defenders; the noises of battle were coming a good deal closer.[11]

Rommel's assessment was that, 'By nightfall two-thirds of the fortress was in our hands; the town and harbour had already been captured by the Afrika Korps in the afternoon.'[12] There were mixed reactions within Klopper's senior staff as to what course of action to now take: stand and fight, attempt a breakout, or surrender. It was clear that any further fighting would result in significant casualties. Ritchie desired for him to stand and fight, but instructed him, "I ... must therefore leave you to act on your own judgment regarding capitulation."[13]

The commander of Turrel's unit, Colonel Stevenson then addressed Turrel and his comrades for the last time, and stated:

9 Turrel, R. ibid, p. 253.

10 Klopper to Eighth Army HQ, 20 June 1942, in Churchill, W, *The Hinge of Fate*, p. 417.

11 Turrel, R. ibid, p. 255.

12 Rommel, E. *The Rommel Papers*, p. 231.

13 Ritchie to Klopper, radio conversation, 20 June 1942, in Churchill, W, *The Hinge of Fate*, p. 418.

> An attempt was to be made to make a last ditch stand with the Sixth Brigade on the western perimeter. Each man could choose for himself: either he could make his way there under his own steam, or he could attempt to escape.[14]

After considering all the options Klopper decided to surrender garrison Tobruk, and did so at 7.45 in the morning of 21 June 1942. Rommel recorded that at 09.40 'about four miles west of the town, I met General Klopper, G.O.C. 2nd South African Infantry Division and Garrison Commandant of Tobruk. He announced the capitulation of the fortress of Tobruk.'[15] He later wrote to his wife, 'Tobruk! It was a wonderful battle...I must get a few hours' sleep now after all that's happened.'[16]

Either before or soon after his sleep, Rommel issued an 'Order of the Day', part of which stated:

> During the long hard struggle of the last four weeks, you have, through your incomparable courage and tenacity, dealt the enemy blow after blow. Your spirit of attack has cost him the core of his field army, which was standing poised for an offensive. Above all, he has lost his powerful armour...
>
> Soldiers of the Panzer Army Afrika!
>
> Now for the complete destruction of the enemy. We will not rest until we have shattered the last remnants of the British Eighth Army. During the days to come, I shall call on you for one more great effort to bring us this final goal.[17]

While Rommel and his troops were exuberant, many of Klopper's troops were despondent. Some did make attempts to break-out, but only one significant attempt was successful, when 199 men from the Coldstream Guards and 188 South Africans broke through to the south.[18] For those approximately 35,000 men who remained, there awaited several years of Axis captivity before them. Among them were Ron Turrel and his brother Peter.

Reactions to the fall of Tobruk

Churchill was in Washington when he received news of the fall, and he stated that this was one of the heaviest blows he encountered during the war. President Roosevelt asked how he could help, and Churchill asked for the immediate shipping of the latest US Sherman tanks. Roosevelt agreed.[19]

In Egypt the fall of Tobruk 'received maximum publicity, and started many wild

14 Turrel, R. ibid, p. 256.
15 Rommel, E. *The Rommel Papers*, p. 231.
16 Rommel, E. *The Rommel Papers*, p. 231.
17 Rommel, E. *The Rommel Papers*, p. 232.
18 Churchill, W. *The Hinge of Fate*, p. 418.
19 Churchill, W. *The Hinge of Fate*, pp. 382-3.

rumours.'[20] Moses Mosenson wrote to his wife on 22 June:

> *Tobruk has fallen.* The heart is oppressed. There is something personal for me in this loss. It is as if I felt it on my own flesh. For this place had become a symbol of resistance to the storm.[21]

The Jewish community in Palestine was in shock. A member of the *Vaad Leumi* delivered a very sobering report on the Hebrew radio in Palestine. Mosenson wrote:

> Yesterday on the Jerusalem radio we listened to Moshe Shertok's call to the Jewish community. Listening to his grave apprehensions, thoughts arose in my mind concerning what is in store for the community and how it will face what must come upon it. I am afraid to express what I have been thinking…[22]

The fall of Tobruk on 21 June 1942 was the worst possible nightmare for the Jewish people living east of that small Libyan town. Coming events, both in Germany and in the actual fighting fully justified their apprehensions.

20 Kirk, G. ibid, p. 216.
21 Mosenson, M. *Letters from the Desert,* p. 122.
22 Mosenson, M. *Letters from the Desert,* p. 122.

Chapter 23

Race to the Suez Canal

Axis plans

Such was the euphoria with the fall of Tobruk and subsequent move eastward of the Axis forces, that the Allies feared that Alexandria and Cairo would soon also fall. Initially the German plan had been to capture Tobruk then subdue Malta before continuing on with the advance into Egypt. This plan was now jettisoned. Hitler sent the following communique to Mussolini:

> Destiny has offered a chance which will never occur twice in the same theatre of war … The Eighth Army has been practically destroyed. In Tobruk the port installations are almost intact. You now possess, Duce, an auxiliary base whose significance is all the greater because the English themselves have built from there a railway leading almost into Egypt. If, at this moment, the remains of this British Army are not pursued to the last breath of each man, the same thing will happen as when the British were deprived of success when they nearly reached Tripoli and suddenly stopped in order to send forces to Greece …
>
> The God of battles visits warriors only once. He who does not grasp her at such a moment never reaches her again …[1]

Mussolini agreed and then made preparations to fly out to Rommel's headquarters so as to march in the triumphal entrance into Egypt.[2] Rommel states that Mussolini gave permission for 'freedom of operation' and allowed the 'advance into Egypt.'[3] Not everyone though was excited about this change of plan. Field Marshall Kesselring warned Rommel that North Africa would never be secure while Malta remained unconquered.

A possible factor in this decision to press forward was over-optimism concerning the degree of active support in Egypt.[4] Had the British not intervened as they did in early February 1942, there may have been more likelihood of a local *coup d'etat*, but in June 1942 this possibility was considerably less.

Allied plans

What remained intact of the Eighth Army was quickly withdrawn back to the Egyptian

1 Quoted in *Comando Supremo*, by Cavallero, p. 277, in Churchill, W. *The Hinge of Fate*, p. 420.
2 Churchill, W. *The Hinge of Fate*, p. 393.
3 Rommel, E. *The Rommel Papers*, p. 235.
4 Kirk, G. ibid, p. 218.

border at Sollum. This they managed to do primarily because of the RAF, which constantly hassled and bombed the Axis forces.

On 21 June the Middle East Defence Committee in Cairo sent a telegram to Churchill outlining the two options available to them: to stand at Sollum or to withdraw to a more defensible position at Mersa Matruh. The telegram concluded, 'We have decided on the second course.'[5]

Both Churchill and General Dill disagreed with the decision to withdraw further east, as they knew key reinforcements were en-route to Egypt. In addition General Smuts confirmed that there was less danger confronting the Ninth and Tenth Armies in the north (because the feared German break-through from the Caucasus was not imminent), thereby three of the divisions east of the Suez could be returned. These considerations were relayed to Auchinleck, impressing upon him the need to hold on at Sollum. Churchill also informed him that Roosevelt was even willing to release an American armoured division which had been ear-marked for elsewhere.[6]

Auchinleck, however, resisted these instructions, and chose to retreat to the Mersa Matruh line. In Syria the 2nd New Zealand Division, recovering from its many battles, was quickly assembled and returned back to the front line. Blyth wrote:

> Everybody started rushing around bringing equipment up to a state of instant readiness. Word was out that the Division was returning post haste to Egypt because the 8th Army had suffered heavy defeat at the hands of Rommel, but as things had been going well in the desert we did not pay too much attention to this.[7]

The *Palestine Post* reported some time later:

> The dash of the New Zealand Division from Syria to the western desert was made under cover of the strictest secrecy and at a "bewildering" speed.[8]

As Rommel crossed the border into Egypt on 23 June, he was confronted by limited Allied forces at Sollum. The RAF again covered the retreat of the Eighth Army back to the Mersa Matruh line.[9] The Matruh line itself was not well defended, with the only 100 tanks available being those from the 7th Armoured Division. Reinforcements however began to pour in, including the New Zealand Division and the 1st Armoured Division.

When the New Zealanders arrived, General Freyberg requested that his, by now very experienced, soldiers not be kept in a static position, but be placed in 'a more fluid role.' They were placed south of Mersa Matruh in an area named Minqar Qaim. 'There'

5 Churchill, W. *The Hinge of Fate*, p. 421.

6 Churchill to Auchinleck, 22 June 1942, in Churchill, W. *The Hinge of Fate*, pp. 421-2.

7 Blyth, J. ibid, p. 31.

8 *Palestine Post*, 5 July 1942, p. 5.

9 Rommel, E. *The Rommel Papers*, p. 237.

Sandford stated 'it was to operate as a mobile force to hold the low ridges in that region, and wherever possible to use its mobility to attack and delay the enemy.'[10]

One of the first tasks of the Kiwis was to assist the engineers lay down some 9,000 mines in Rommel's expected pathway. Upham's 20th Battalion was involved in this delicate, but important, business.

The defence of Egypt was now entrusted to 10th Corps around Mersa Matruh, comprising the 10th Indian and 50th British Infantry Divisions. To the south was 13th Corps comprised of the 29th Indian Infantry Brigade and then the New Zealand Division, stationed at Minqar Qaim. Protecting the desert flank were the 1st Armoured Division and remnants of the 7th Armoured Division.

On 25 June Auchinleck came to the frontline and took over the direct command from Ritchie, a move which greatly pleased Churchill, who implored him to stand and fight as reinforcements were on the way.[11] Yet Auchinleck's next decision further upset Churchill: he decided to withdraw, all the way back to El Alamein, a further 120 miles east. This was a very courageous decision.

Churchill wasn't the only one to be concerned about this. Thomas Derrick, one of the survivors of the epic siege of Tobruk in 1941, wrote from his garrison duties in Syria, 'News from the Desert is not the best, Fritz being within 15 miles of Mersa Matruh, it now looks as though we are bound for ANOTHER ENGAGEMENT WITH MR ROMMEL.'[12]

Mersa Matruh and Minqar Qaim

As Rommel's Panzer Army Africa approached Mersa Matruh on 26 June 1942 he was hoping to bring the Eighth Army 'to battle at this point and attempt to destroy a major part of their infantry.'[13] He presumed that the 10th and 5th Indian Divisions, the 50th British Division and the 2nd New Zealand Division were all inside the perimeter. By this time some of the garrison had withdrawn, while the bulk of the New Zealand Division was located south east of Mersa Matruh at Minqar Qaim.

Before the withdrawal was complete, however, Rommel struck in force, on the evening of 26 June and broke through the position of the 29th Indian Brigade where the minefield was as yet incomplete. While Upham and his men of the 20th Battalion were in the open they heard the familiar screech of a Stuka dive-bomber, and all the men dived for whatever cover they could find. The Axis forces streamed through this opening and some reached the sea on the east side of Mersa Matruh.

The following morning, 27 June 1942, Axis armoured and infantry divisions began advancing against the New Zealand Division at Minqar Qaim. An intense artillery barrage

10 Sandford, K. ibid, p. 141.

11 Churchill to Auchinleck, 28 June 1942, in Churchill, W. *The Hinge of Fate*, p. 423.

12 Farquhar, M. *Diary of Thomas Derrick*, p. 92.

13 Rommel, E. *The Rommel Papers*, p. 236.

now ensued for several hours. One New Zealander soldier, John Blyth, wrote of this attack:

> Heavy artillery fire numbs the mind, which is just as well, but I was interested in my reaction. If this is war, and it undoubtedly was, it seemed to be the most stupid, scary, crazy business I had ever been involved in.[14]

In the afternoon it was noticed that these formations were endeavouring to completely surround the New Zealand position. The 27th June 1942 became one of the most significant days in New Zealand's military history, as it's only Division fought for its very survival. One man though seemed oblivious to the situation. Charles Upham kept encouraging his men and taking extraordinary risks upon himself.[15]

Despite their gallant stand against overwhelming odds during the day, it was clear that with the Axis forces encircling them (except the western side which led towards Libya) and with their ammunition running down, there was no chance that the New Zealanders would survive. Blyth wrote:

> Without ammunition it is absolutely certain the Division would not have survived another day, and that it faced extinction, a disaster that could not be contemplated for people in a small country like New Zealand.[16]

Freyberg took the decision to break-out during the night, but then he was wounded, and could not implement the decision. His deputy, General Inglis now took over. One brigade would approach the German line to the east, and when detected 'would charge ahead with bullet and bayonet.'[17] Their task was to open up a gap in the enemy line, and then the remainder of the division, who would already be in the transports, would then break through the gap. The 4th Brigade comprising the 19th, 20th and Maori battalions would lead the break-out.

When the time came, at 1.45 am, the section leaders assembled their men, and they began walking forward. Sandford writes, 'There was bright moonlight over the field, but the night seemed dark. It was all silence, just the rhythmic chuffing of men's boots against the sand and the stones, rifles held high, men walking forward with fear and hope in their hearts, wondering when the earth in front of them would awake and blaze. They were walking towards the enemy to punch the hole through the line…'[18]

After close to a kilometre of walking a shot came, then another and soon the line was hot. One New Zealander recalled afterwards that 'To a man the whole brigade

14 Blyth, J. *Soldiering On*, p. 38.
15 Sandford, K. ibid, pp. 144-45.
16 Blyth, J. *Soldiering On*, p. 42.
17 Sandford, K. ibid, p. 148.
18 Sandford, K. ibid, p. 149-50.

charged forward. No orders were given; no urging forward by officers and N.C.O.'s. With shouting, cheering, and war-cries every man broke into a run as if he knew exactly what was expected of him.'[19]

Every one of these men knew what was required, and what the consequences would be if they never broke through. It was absolute mayhem with hand to hand fighting, bombing, throwing of grenades, German trucks and vehicles going up in flames. As could be expected Charles Upham was in the midst of it all, urging his men of C Company forward, hurling grenades endlessly in total disregard for his own safety.

When the Brigade finally made it through the German lines, the flare went up to signal to the rest of the division that the way through was clear. The firing and confusion continued unabated, and Rommel himself wrote:

> A wild melee ensued, in which my own headquarters, which lay south of the fortress, became involved... The firing between my forces and the New Zealanders grew to an extraordinary pitch of violence and my headquarters was soon ringed by burning vehicles, making it the target for continuous enemy fire. I soon had enough of this and the headquarters ordered the staff to withdraw to the south-east. One can scarcely conceive the confusion which reigned that night. It was pitch-dark and impossible to see one's hand before one's face. The R.A.F. bombed their own troops, and, with tracer flying in all directions, German units fired on each other.[20]

The New Zealanders managed to extricate themselves from the web. Although an act of supreme heroism, it was nothing short of a miracle that they suffered so few casualties compared to the Germans. Upham summed it up, 'This show tonight will make bloody history.'

This withdrawal was one of the truly great Allied escapades of the War, and Freyberg received the following words from Churchill, 'Deeply moved to hear of your new wound and new glory. Trust that your injury is not serious and that you will soon be back commanding your splendid division. All good wishes to you and to them.'[21]

The Eighth Army divisions remaining inside Mersa Matruh attempted to break out on 28 June, and although sustaining heavy casualties, many did manage to extricate themselves and reach the El Alamein line. The Axis force broke into Mersa Matruh on 29 June and finally subdued all fighting, and ended up with 6,000 more Allied prisoners. Even in victory, though, Rommel was disappointed, and stated:

> Our men had once again fought with extraordinary courage. Unfortunately, the New Zealanders under Freyberg had escaped. This division, with which we had already

19 Sandford, K. ibid, p. 150.
20 Rommel, E. *The Rommel Papers*, p. 238.
21 Churchill to Freyberg, 4 July 1942, in Churchill, W. *The Hinge of Fate*, p. 425.

> become acquainted back in 1941-42, was among the elite of the British Army, and I should have been very much happier if it had been safely tucked away in our prison camps instead of still facing us.[22]

He wrote to his wife on 29 June, 'Now the battle of Mersa Matruh has also been won and our leading units are only 125 miles from Alexandria. There'll be a few more battles to fight before we reach our goal, but I think the worst is well behind us. I'm fine.'[23]

A new line at El Alamein

All the exhausted Allied forces who managed to escape Rommel's net formed a new defence line at El Alamein some sixty miles (one hundred kilometres) west of Alexandria, spreading from the Mediterranean coast inland to the Qattara Depression, which lay thirty eight miles (about fifty-five kms) south from the coast. This natural depression was impenetrable.

The defensive line had been developed in 1941, and Ron Turrel and the 2nd South African Division had spent considerable time there before moving up to the front line. Along this line there were established three defensive positions known as 'boxes'. One was in the area from El Alamein station through to the coast; another was further south and known as the Bab el Qattara box, while the third was on the edge of the Qattara Depression itself, and this was not well established.

To the south of El Alamein there were three major ridges which formed a second defensive line, these being the Miteirya Ridge, the Ruweisat Ridge and the Alam Halfa Ridge. These ridges provided good natural fortifications, and were intermingled between the 'boxes.' The Alam Halfa Ridge was behind the front line and was basically a fall-back position.

By 30 June 1942 almost the entire Eighth Army had withdrawn to this new position. One Division not yet present was the 9th Australian Division, which was now summoned for immediate departure from its garrison duties in Syria. Initially there was no indication of where they were moving to, and many hoped it was for Australia. But alas the reality soon caught up with them. Derrick, his mates in the 2/48th Battalion and all the other battalions, were moved in almost total secrecy southwards, via Gaza, then inland through Beersheba of 1917 fame, and then through the central Sinai route via the wells of Jif-Jaffa of 1916 fame, and over the Suez Canal.

The 'Rats of Tobruk' were off to the desert again.

Preparedness

The Allied leadership was now extremely concerned. Churchill informed Minister of State Casey in Cairo, that:

22 Rommel, E. *The Rommel Papers*, p. 240.
23 Rommel, E. *The Rommel Papers*, p. 239.

> While Auchinleck fights at the front you should insist upon the mobilisation for battle of all rearward services. Everybody in uniform must fight exactly like they would if Kent or Sussex were invaded. Tank hunting-parties with sticky bombs and bombards, defence to the death of every fortified area or strong building, making every post a winning-post and every ditch a last ditch. This is the spirit you have got to inculcate. No general evacuation, no playing for safety. Egypt must be held at all costs.[24]

While orders were given to hold Egypt at all costs, the sudden thrust of the Axis forces eastwards had alerted everyone in the Middle East to the possibility of an Axis victory. No one was more concerned than the Jewish communities, especially the 70,000 or so in Egypt, and the 500,000 or so in Palestine.

They had every right to be concerned.

Meanwhile the men who had played such a huge role in stopping the Panzer Army Africa were about to play another role in stopping Germany's soldiers entering Palestine. On 30 June 1942 Thomas Derrick wrote, 'Must not fail to mention that we were informed late last night of our coming task – one of action in the Western Desert.'[25]

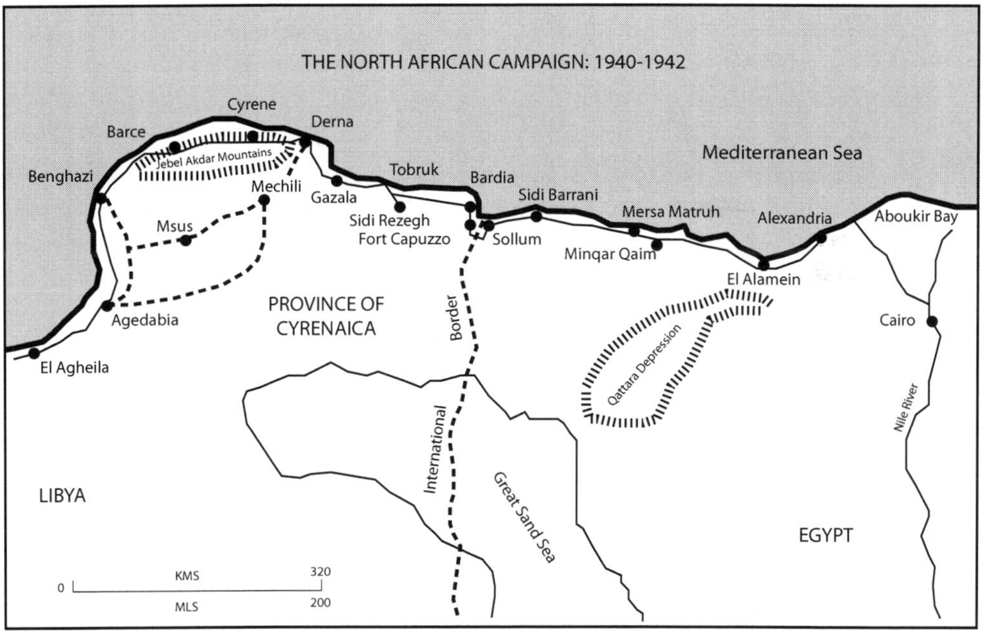

24 Churchill to Casey, 30 June 1942, in Churchill, W. *The Hinge of Fate*, pp. 426-6.
25 Farquhuar, M. ibid, p. 93.

Chapter 24

Jewish anxiety in Palestine and Egypt

Jewish anxiety in Palestine

On the same day that the Eighth Army withdrew from Mersa Matruh, *Haganah* commanders in Palestine were requested by the British to bring the 'First *Palmach* Company' to the Negev region and prepare for the German invasion. One of those men was Israel Galil, who wrote:

> Not all our boys were armed. There were not enough weapons for all members of the company. Some had pistols, rifles and submachine guns. Others in the company were armed with sticks.[1]

Uzi Narkiss, later to command the capture of the Old City of Jerusalem in 1967, said of this critical time:

> I think the most naïve thing that was done at that time was that our platoon commander, a kibbutznik took all of us to a British police station, [and said] 'If tomorrow or the day after tomorrow the Germans will show up we will do everything to occupy the British police post before them so that we will be able to defend the Negev here.' Nobody asked how are we going to do it because we did not have even one rifle. But naïve as we were with this sincerity and devotion for a certain cause which was defending the country now in order to establish a Jewish State, we said 'OK Sir'. We didn't have any arms but we were willing to do whatever [was needed].[2]

Moses Mosenson, back at the front line in North Africa, wrote on 2 July that one of the Jewish soldiers had received a newspaper from his kibbutz. One article related to how the situation was explained to the children:

> Yesterday morning, after a meeting of the *kibutz* concerning matters of security, we had a discussion at the school. We told the children that at first we hesitated to tell them that the Germans have a great many weapons and that they have pushed the English back and conquered part of Egypt. We did not know if they, the children, could help us.

1 Lossin, Y. *Pillar of Fire*, p. 337.
2 Interview with General Narkiss , April 1997, as shown on the documentary *The Battle for Zion*.

After explaining the Biblical story of Gideon and the Midianites, the few against the many, the correspondent continued:

> The children asked that they be allowed to drill and that they should be taught how to use guns and to shoot well. [Then the children were told there were few guns]. The discussion was tense, we ended by deciding to have them exercise in getting up quickly, aiming stones at targets, etc. We would also teach them how to overcome heat and thirst.[3]

Mosenson and the Jewish soldiers in the desert took heart from the resolve of the kibbutz children and became even more determined not to allow the Germans to break through. Everyone knew the dire consequences if they did. Senior Jewish leaders in the United States cabled Churchill in early July 1942:

> ... asking for immediate mobilization of all available Jewish manpower in Palestine, emphasizing that the German advance to Suez would threaten 550,000 Jews with annihilation.[4]

The *Statesman and Nation* journal in London emphasized the gravity of the situation extremely well:

> We will need every tank and gun we have got to hold Palestine and Syria ... the military case for holding Palestine has been reinforced by the duty to preserve the Jewish population from Himmler's gas chambers and firing squads.[5]

The tension was palpable in Palestine. David Horowitz from the Jewish Agency stated that the Jewish community at this time was almost certain:

> ... that what awaited them was a catastrophe from Rommel's army, which had come as close as El Alamein. We knew that what stood between us and Rommel was a very thin barrier of British forces.[6]

A debate now raged within the Jewish community in Palestine (known as the *Yishuv*) about the course of action to follow if the German forces entered into Palestine. Only the previous year at the height of the Syrian crisis, there were fears of a Vichy-German invasion from the north, and strategies were put into place for dealing with this possibility.

3 Mosenson, M. *Letters from the Desert,* pp. 124-125.
4 *Palestine Post,* 5 July 1942, p. 1.
5 Quoted in *Palestine Post,* 5 July 1942, p. 1.
6 Lossin, Y. *Pillar of Fire*, p. 337.

In addition, with each German advance in the Russian campaign, the threat of a northern invasion remained a distinct possibility, especially if Turkey revoked its neutrality.

Now the possibility of a German invasion returned, as it did in early 1941 at which time Rommel was stalled at Tobruk. The Jewish Agency debated that if the Nazis occupied, whether 'the inhabitants of the Yishuv should evacuate together with British forces eastwards towards British possessions in Iraq and India or undertake a Masada-like last stand in Palestine.'[7] Uzi Narkiss said again about this possible scenario:

> In Palestine itself our government, the Jewish Agency, was very anxious, and everybody felt it, anxious and pre-occupied for the future of the tiny Jewish minority living in Palestine...
>
> The British High Commissioner called the...President of the Jews living in Palestine, Mr. Ben Zvi, and announced to him, "Listen Mr. President, if and when the German Army will invade and capture Palestine, we the British...will withdraw all the way to India."... So our President was very shocked.

Ben Zvi, according to Narkiss, then reported the proceedings to the Jewish leadership and a debate took place as to the best course of action to follow for the beleagured Jewish community.[8]

Concerning the choice the leadership made, Narkiss stated:

> When our leaders came back from Mr. Ben Zvi [they] had several alternatives. One: that the women and children would withdraw with the British Army. The second, all the population would follow the British Army, and the last one; the entire population would remain and fight the Germans. And they chose the last one.
>
> But, in order to realize such an alternative you must have a fortress where you can get organized, fortified and from as a natural fortress as possible, you will be able to fight a superior power – that was the Germans. The choice was the Carmel or a certain part of it ... and to fight the German Army from there until the very end.[9]

Noted Israeli author Tom Segev wrote an article in the *Haaretz* newspaper on 20 January 2012 entitled *The makings of History/The Masada of the North* in which he reflected the view of historian Yoav Gelber about this period of time, stating:

> The Jewish public in the country would have been utterly helpless to block the German advance on their own. No one knew whether to prepare for an invasion from the south, through the desert, or from the north, through Syria, or from the sea.

7 Jewish Agency for Israel, Chapter 7, World War II, on www.jewishagency.com

8 Conversation with General Narkiss, April 1997.

9 Interview with General Narkiss, April 1997. This interview can be seen on the documentary *The Battle for Zion.*

There was no surety that the British would be able to regain control of the land, if it did fall into the Germans' hands, and there was no certainty that they would make its conquest a high priority. In the meantime, the leaders of the Haganah focused on the danger that the Arabs of the land would aid the Germans, more than on the German invasion itself.[10]

Haj Amin's activities

The danger presented by a combined German-Arab alliance was very tangible. Ever since he had arrived in Berlin Haj Amin had been sprouting forth anti-British and anti-Jewish propaganda over the Arabic radio station from Berlin.

According to the research of Mallmann and Cuppers there is tangible evidence that he was aware of the implementation of the 'Final Solution to the Jewish Problem' in Europe, and had met with senior Nazi leaders involved in the implementation of this plan, including Adolf Eichmann.[11]

Haj Amin desired nothing more than to see the destruction of the Jewish national home in Palestine. Mallman and Cuppers summarise his activities at this time:

> The capture of Tobruk at the end of June 1942, was the starting signal both for the RSHA[12] and el-Husseini to render the plan for the destruction of the Jews in Palestine into more concrete terms. While the Einstazkommando for the Panzer Army Africa was put together in Berlin and sent on to Athens to await further orders, the Mufti also intensified his activities to liberate Palestine. He offered to travel to Egypt and become active in propaganda work there in order to spur Arab collaboration. In this connection, he also called for dispatching the German-Arab Training Department to Egypt.[13]

Haj Amin's plan was to:

> Set up bands of Arabs as a fighting force and equip them. They will march to Egypt and other Arab countries in order to disturb and harass the enemy by destroying roads, bridges and possibilities for contact more generally, and to promote uprisings inside the country ... Set up regular Arab military units that will operate side by side together with troops of the Axis powers. These units will have a morally favourable impact in the Arab countries and will draw the volunteers in the British army to their side ... Dispatch weapons and munitions to Egypt behind enemy lines, and then to Palestine, Syria and

10 Segev, T. 'The Makings of History/Masada of the North', in *Haaretz Daily Newspaper*, 20 January 2012, www.haaretz.com/weekend

11 See Mallmann and Cuppers, ibid, pp. 26-28.

12 *Reichsichheithauptamt* (Reich Main Security Office)

13 Mallman K and Cuppers M, *The Einsatzkommando of the Panzer Army Africa, 1942*, wwwl.yadvashem.org, p. 28. The German-Arab Training Department was established through his initiative and came under the direction of General Helmut Felmy, and was comprised of armed units of Arabs who were trained by Germans 'and were to take part side by side with them in the fight against the British in the Middle East.' Ibid, p. 27.

Iraq – in order to lay the groundwork for uprisings and to harass the enemy.[14]

The average Jewish person in Palestine may not have been aware of what the Mufti of Jerusalem was involved in and planning, but they knew his track record, and there were many others who held similar perspectives among the Arab populations of the Middle East.

Renewed enlistment campaign

If the Jewish *yishuv* was to survive against the invading German-led army drastic measures would be needed. These measures were two fold. The first was to encourage enlistment in the British Army. On 4 July 1942 Moshe Shertok declared at an enlistment campaign in Tel Aviv:

> ... no nation was under a greater compulsion in facing the fateful necessity of fighting than the Jewish people, since the remnants of its hopes were concerned with this part of the world.[15]

The British authorities were now desperate. Their previous intransigence against Jewish volunteers slackened. They then recruited young Palestinian women into the Auxiliary Territorial Service (ATS). In all 3,150 Jewish women volunteered for this unit, compared to only 120 non-Jews, almost all of whom were Christian Arab and Armenian.[16]

By July 1942 there were some 27,000 Jewish men and women from Palestine enlisted in the British armed forces, mostly in service related formations.[17] In addition there was a much larger number involved in the Jewish *Haganah* force. Had the British further relaxed their opposition, many more Jewish people certainly would have joined the British Army. At this time nearly a third of the 8,000 Arab men in the British Army deserted with their rifles 'mostly during Rommel's advance.'[18]

The 'Carmel Plan'

The other commitment the Jewish leadership made for the survival of their people was for home defence. The British supported the Jewish authorities in forming a defence line running through the Judeo-Samarian mountain ridge through to the Carmel Range near Haifa. This was the next and most effective strategic position to make a stand.

According to a long standing geo-political and military principle, if an army invading

14 Niederschrift dess. V. 29.8.1942, ibid, R 27325; see Kriegstagebuch Amt Ausland/Abwehr II v. 13.7.1942, BA-MA, RW 5/498. Quoted in Mallman and Cuppers, *The Einsatzkommando of the Panzer Army Africa, 1942*, wwwl.yadvashem.org, p. 28.

15 *Palestine Post,* 5 July 1942, p. 5.

16 Lossin, Y. *Pillar of Fire,* p. 333.

17 Lossin, Y.*Pillar of Fire,* p. 333. I have read various estimates of numbers.

18 Bethell, N. *The Palestine Triangle*, p. 140.

from the south wanted to proceed further north, it would need to pass through the two main routes which bisected the Carmel Range and entered into the Valley of Jezreel. The main one of these was at Megiddo. The same principle applied for an army invading from the north, and until 1942 this scenario had been a distinct possibility.

It seems that ideas were discussed for developing a plan suitable for the overall strategic goal, that in the event of a German breakthrough into Palestine and of the link up with Arab nationalist forces, the entire Jewish population would be withdrawn to the Carmel Range. This was known as the 'Northern Plan' or colloquially as the 'Carmel Plan.'

Of this plan, David Horowitz said:

> The plans were to fight down to the last drop of blood, a new version of Masada – that's how you could define it. There was great fear.[19]

The late Professor Alex Carmel, a Jewish refugee from Nazi Germany, said of this plan:

> The plan was to take all the Jews of Palestine and to concentrate them on Mount Carmel and here ... we will fight till the end and we will not surrender to the Germans.[20]

On Mount Carmel they would be governed and administered by the Jewish leaders and would be, as much as possible, self-sustaining. Supplies would initially be stockpiled, but be replenished by RAF drops and by submarine.

This area would also be a staging ground for a guerrilla type of conflict against the invading force, especially by the *Palmach,* the elite force of the *Haganah.* Two special units were formed under the watchful eye of British intelligence agents.

One was a 'German' unit, comprised of young Jewish men who had been born in Germany or Austria, and who both looked Aryan and spoke fluent German. This unit was sent to Egypt to gain specialist training, with the view of ultimately being able to operate as spies behind German lines.

The other was a unit of Middle East looking Jewish men who knew Arabic fluently. These men were placed in neighbouring Arab countries where much pro-German sentiment abounded.[21]

Tom Segev, echoing Yoav Gelber, suggests that perhaps a myth grew up around the 'Carmel Plan' after the War of Independence by many who had lived in Palestine during the Second World War. Segev wrote, 'Most of them reconstructed the story after the War of Independence, and after Israeli mythology had internalized the Warsaw Ghetto Uprising. In the nature of things, the need arose to praise also the readiness of the Jewish

19 Lossin, Y. *Pillar of Fire,* p. 337.
20 Interview with Prof. Carmel, May 1997, which is featured in documentary 'The Battle for Zion'.
21 See Lossin Y. *Pillar of Fire,* p. 331.

public in Palestine to make a brave stand against the Nazis.'[22]

Apart from any debate there is in Israel today about the components of the 'Carmel Plan' one thing is for certain: there was genuine fear that the German-led Army could conquer Palestine, and together with the Arab nationalist movement cause considerable damage to the *Yishuv*; and that they the Jewish people could not rely upon the British to protect them, so they needed to take remedial measures themselves.

Jewish anxiety in Egypt

During the Second World War there was also a sizeable Jewish community of about 70,000 in Egypt, primarily in Cairo and Alexandria. These communities too were vulnerable if the German Army broke through.

Haj Amin sent Hitler a telegram in July 1942 congratulating him on his victories in North Africa, and endorsing the German and Italian acknowledgement of Egyptian independence.[23] At this point Arabs throughout the Middle East were encouraged to rise against the Allied command and welcome the German-led forces into their lands.

A pro-German group had been uncovered by the British authorities in Cairo, and included the future President of Egypt, Anwar Sadat. Sadat's motives, so he stated, were to aid in the independence of Egypt, and that if Germany was willing to assist in this then he would support them against the British.[24]

Thea Levinsohn was the head nurse of a surgical team at the Jewish hospital in Alexandria. During this critical period a foreign diplomat, whose daughter had been treated at the hospital, came one day to speak to the chief surgeon, Dr. Katz. Levinsohn recalls:

> Katz received him and a few minutes later called me into his room and showed me a document. It was a copy of a command to be obeyed immediately after Rommel and his advance detachment entered Alexandria, namely, to arrest the people named in the document for deportation to Germany. All our names and addresses, along with the German and Austrian refugees living in Alexandria, were listed.[25]

Shortly after this visit and information, the British governor in Alexandria also visited the hospital, and, according to Levinsohn he 'advised us, as Jewish refugees, to leave the town.'[26] It was clear that those whose names appeared on that list needed to leave Alexandria immediately.

This sense of despair among the Jewish people was also felt by the British civil authorities. Olivia Manning, whose husband, a civil servant, was being transferred to Jerusalem, stated:

22 Segev, T. ibid.
23 Sacher, H. *A History of Israel*, p. 229.
24 Lossin, Y. *Pillar of Fire*, p. 329.
25 Thea Levinsohn, quoted in *Jerusalem Post*, 23 October 1992.
26 Thea Levinsohn, quoted in *Jerusalem Post*, 23 October 1992.

When the Germans reached El Alamein, the sense of unease changed to incipient panic … Alexandria was shaken by the sounds of guns.[27]

The combination of all of these factors led to some confusion and panic in Egypt, what became known as 'the Flap.' The British Embassy in Cairo burned many of its documents, in what became known as 'Ash Wednesday', and all non-essential personnel were ordered out.[28]

Another eye-witness of the events in Egypt at that time was Edmund Stevens, who wrote an article which was published in the *Christian Science Monitor* on 24 July 1942. Stevens stated that there was relative calm and normality among the Anglo-American population in Cairo, and wrote:

The few instances of private individuals growing panicky became the objects of general derision and contrasted strongly with the exemplary conduct of the majority of the Anglo-American colony … The Egyptians and all other elements intently watched and weighed their every move…

Of the Anglo-Saxon civilian population those most vitally and personally affected by the military crisis were Jews, some of whom had personally fled from Nazi terror while others were all too clearly acquainted with the fate of their coreligionists under the Hitler heel to desire to repeat their experience.[29]

It would seem that the Jewish population in Egypt, as well as in Palestine, had every reason to be concerned with the German-led army so close.

27 Manning, O. *The Flap.* Quoted in *History of the Second World War,* (Purnell & Sons, Paulton, 1967), p. 1066.
28 *Purnell's History of the Second World War*, ibid, p. 1066.
29 Edmund Stevens, *Christian Science Monitor*, 24 July, 1942, quoted in Kirk, G. *The Middle East in the War*, pp. 219-20.

CHAPTER 25

EINSATZKOMMANDO AGYPTEN (EGYPT)

Formation of the *Einsatzgruppe Agypten*

At this very time the Nazi hierarchy was officially sanctioning the despatch to the Middle East of an *Einsatzkommando* to be attached to Rommel's forces, and which would enlist the active involvement of local collaborators. This force was to be known as the *Einsatzkommando Agypten* (Egypt). Of this unit, Mallman and Cuppers state:

> In the summer of 1942, while the world seemed to be waiting for Egypt to be conquered and for Rommel's divisions to cross the Suez Canal, the Germans had already completed secret preparations to deploy a security police and SD Einsatzkommando in the area. The decision to assign such an SS unit to Afrika Korps for the upcoming operations was made in June, based on the victories at Tobruk and Marsa Matruh, as well as the further advance, which exceeded all expectations. The RSHA had previously refrained from sending its own commando along during Rommel's journey through the Libyan desert. Now, however, such a step seemed essential given the "opposition potential" that could be expected when the troops reached the Egyptian capital and during the further movement into the Middle East – much like during the period prior to the assault on Poland in 1939 or the attack on the Soviet Union in 1941.[1]

Although there may have been previous discussions and planning concerning this formation, the official formation of the squad seems to have emanated from a discussion held on 1 July 1942 between Walter Schellenberg and Heinrich Himmler, in which Schellenberg mentioned the coming 'deployment in Egypt.'[2] Schellenberg was deputy to Heydrich in the SS (later becoming the deputy to Himmler), and 'In May 1941 he concluded an agreement with the German Army on the operation of the Einsatzgruppen (mobile killing units) in the Soviet Union.'[3] At that point Schellenberg was head of the SS intelligence.[4]

Any discussion therefore between Schellenberg and Himmler was of great importance. Later that same day Himmler met with Hitler for a considerable time. Mallman and Cuppers state of this meeting:

1 Mallman, K & Cuppers, M. *Nazi Palestine*, p. 116.

2 *Dienstkalender Himmlers*, p. 473, in Mallman & Cuppers. *Nazi Palestine*, p. 116-7.

3 *Encyclopaedia Judaica*, entry on 'Schellenberg, Walter', www.jewishvirtuallibrary.org. Interestingly, during much of the war there was competition between the intelligence branch of the SS (the SD) and the intelligence branch of the *Wehrmacht* (*Abwehr*).

4 From 1944 he was also head of Wehrmacht intelligence – Abwehr.

The decision concerning the Einsatzkommando must have been made at that meeting, because Obergruppenfuhrer Karl Wolff, chief of the personal staff of the Reichsfuhrer-SS, immediately contacted the OKH.[5]

The OKH stood for *Oberkommando des Heeres* – the ground forces. OKW and was the High Command of the German Armed Forces, and therefore involved all three branches of the forces - Army, Navy and Airforce and at that time was Field Marshal W Keital.[6] Until December 1941 the head of OKH had been Field Marshal von Brauchitsch, but in July 1942 it was Hitler.

Thus at this point, so it seems, the SS decision to establish an *Einsatzkommando* unit for Egypt was now to be delivered to the *Wehrmacht*, which in the North African context, would mean Panzer Army Africa.

Several days later, on 4 July 1942, Himmler recorded in his *dienstkalenda*r concerning the *Einsatzkommando* Egypt, that, 'Wehrmacht order to be issued tomorrow.'[7] The order for despatching the *Einsatzkommando* Egypt to North Africa was only issued on 13 July. The instructions were haunting in its scope:

> "With the approval of the Reichsfuhrer-SS and the chief of the German police, the deployment of the SS unit with Afrika Korps will be regulated as follows: (1) The SS Einsatzkommando receives its technical instructions from the chief of the security police and SD and carries out its assignments under its own responsibility. It is entitled, within the scope of its mission, to take executive measures against the civilian population on its own authority.[8]

The wording of this communication was very similar to the general instructions given to the *Einsatzgruppen* which had been operating in the Soviet Union.

Walther Rauff appointed as commander

The man ultimately chosen to lead the *Einsatzkommando Agypten* was Walther Rauff. Rauff had joined the German Navy (*Reichsmarine*) in 1924 and by 1936 was a lieutenant. During the earlier part of his naval service he befriended Reinhard Heydrich, who from 1931 worked for Heinrich Himmler as the 'head of the SS counter-intelligence system.'[9] Heydrich ultimately became deputy to Himmler.

5 Mallman & Cuppers, *Nazi Palestine*, p. 117.

6 In reality the OHW (*Oberkommando des Wehrmacht*) often had more authority that the OKH.

7 *Dienstkalender Himmlers*, p, 477, in Mallman & Cuppers, ibid, p. 117.

8 OKW/WFst/Qu.I to Dt.Gen.b.HQu.It.Wehrm., July 13, 1942, BA-MA, RW 5/690, in Mallmann and Cuppers. *Nazi Palestine*, p. 117.

9 Walter Rauff, in German intelligence officers, information released by M15 Security Service on 5 September 2005. Quoted in Wikipedia. The SS counter-intelligence department was the SD.

Rauff left the Navy in 1937 and worked thereafter for Heydrich in the SS headquarters in Berlin, in the security service department, the *Sicherheitsdienst* (SD), preparing for ultimate war. When Germany invaded Norway in 1940 he took up a position as head of the security police there for three months (the Reich Security Main Office – RSHA).

Obviously drawn to the sea, Rauff then returned to the *Kriegsmarine* between 1940-41 and even commanded a small fleet of mine sweepers. Heydrich, however, knew his capabilities and drew him back into the SS and then when Heydrich was appointed as governor of Czechoslavakia, Rauff followed and became his technical assistant.

Following Heydrich's assassination on 4 June 1942 Rauff then became the head of the SS Technical Department and became involved in pioneering a new and callous method of exterminating living people. He ' was responsible for the project of extermination using gas vans. After Jews and others were herded into the back of a gas van, the vehicle was sealed and the exhaust pipe introduced into the back. When the engine was turned on the fumes killed everyone in the back of the vehicle.'[10]

This was the man the SS chose to head up its specialised unit which was due to be despatched to North Africa, (and perhaps in time into Palestine).[11] Alongside Rauff were seven other SS officers: Wilhelm Beisner, Hans-Joachim Weise, Franz Hoth, Herbert Werth, Kurt Loba and Waldemar Menge. In addition to these men were another seventeen men from the SS.

The main reason there were so few men in the *Einsatzkommando Agypten* was that according to the experience in Eastern Europe, the SS was quickly able to recruit local collaborators to assist in the gruesome task of rounding up and shooting Jewish people.

Who would be the local collaborators that the *Einsatzkommando Egypt* would recruit in order to assist with their task? This aspect became evident when looking at the special tasks assigned to several of the SS officers in the group. Beisner was involved in Arabian affairs and was appointed as 'a Middle East expert.'[12] Weise had served as RSHA liaison officer for Haj Amin el Husseini, and his 'primary task would now involve establishing communications with Arab collaborators, whom he was to recruit in large numbers to work for the Germans.'[13]

***Einsatzkommando* Egypt travels to Athens and Libya**

Following the formation of *Einsatzkommando* Egypt, Rauff flew to Tobruk on 20 July 1942

10 Shraga Elam and Dennis Whitehead, *In the service of the Jewish State,* Ha'aretz newspaper, 31 March 2007, www.haaretz.com/weekend/magazine/in-the-service-of-the-jewish-state. Although involved in this cruel form of murder at the beginning, Rauff later transferred out of this unit. It is estimated that between 70,000-200,000 people, mostly Jewish, were murdered in this way. (See Elam and Whitehead, *In the Service of the Jewish State.*)

11 The National Archives, wrote under the title 'Opening of CIA Records under the Nazi War Crimes Disclosure Act' that 'there is a post-war report in the file that he tried to arrange the extermination of Jews in Egypt during late 1942.' See www.fas.org/sgp/news/2002-2005.

12 See also Mallman, K and Cuppers, M. *Halbmond und Hakenkreuz. The Third Reich, the Arabs and Palestine.*(Darmstadt, 2006).

13 Mallmann and Cuppers, *Nazi Palestine*, p. 120.

in order to liaise with Rommel concerning the implementation of his orders.[14] Mallman and Cuppers, who are the undoubted experts on this subject, state:

> Rommel was in the process of leading his troops, almost 500 kilometres to the east of Tobruk, in the decisive final phase of the First battle of El Alamein; any transport facilities would have been more urgently needed for supplies than for the conveyance of the Obersturmbannfuhrer. Instead, Rauff was probably officially assigned to one of the Afrika Korps staff officers during the visit to Tobruk.

The Israeli newspaper, *Haaretz* wrote an article on this event on 29 March 2007, and stated:

> The German journalist Wolfgang Loehde interviewed Rauff's assistant, Theodor Saevecke, who confirmed that Rommel opposed the plan. According to an American memorandum in the CIA files, Rauff flew to Rommel's headquarters to discuss the annihilation of Cairo's Jews but Rommel was disgusted by the plan and sent Rauff packing.
>
> In their first article the German historians did not refer to the memorandum, and in their detailed book they decided, without providing a reasonable explanation, that it was not credible.
>
> Rauff's file in Britain, which was recently declassified, contains a report of his interrogation by the British in Italy following his arrest at the end of the war. According to the report, Rauff said he had flown to Tobruk in July 1942 for a talk with Rommel, in which it was agreed that the arrival of the Einsatzkommando in North Africa "had been too long delayed to be of any value." This is diplomatic language attesting to Rommel's objections as well as to the cancellation of the mission.[15]

The original wording in the report concerning this trip is perhaps a bit ambiguous. It read:

> 20.7.1942 startete er bereits zum ersten Mal nach. Tobruck und erhielt von Generalfeldmarschall Rommel die notwendigen Instruktionen fur den Einsatz.[16]

14 Recommendation for decoration by HoSSPF Italy, Feb. 25, 1945, BAB, R 70 Italien/19; British intelligence service summary, Oct 23, 1942, NARA, RG 226, entry 11.9A, box 25, folder 637, in Mallman and Cuppers, Nazi Palestine, p. 117. There is a lack of consensus between the academics if Rauff actually met with Rommel at this time.

15 Shraga Elam and Dennis Whitehead, *Rauff vs. The Yishuv*, 29 March 2007, *Haaretz* Daily newspaper, www.haaretz.com/weekend/magazine/rauff-vs-the-yishuv.

16 Der Hochste SS und Politzeifugrer in Italien, OU den 25 February 1945, Bundesarchiv R 070/1 No 95, Italien, Bundesarchiv Berlin. Two translations of these instructions are: *'On the 20th of July 1942 he started for the first time to reach Tobruck. Equipped for deployment with the necessary instructions by Generalfeldmarschall (German Field Marshal) Rommel'.* Another translation being: *'On July 20th, 1942, he travelled to Tobruk, for the 1st time and got from General Field Marshal Rommel the instructions needed for the action (Einsatz).'*

Regardless of whether Rauff met Rommel or not, and regardless of Rommel's reaction, the fact was that this group had been established by order of the highest authority in Berlin, and had been entrusted with a particular task. This task was not contrary to Nazi policy of the time, and of the assurances given to leading Arab nationalists such as Haj Amin, that the Nazi policy was determined to destroy the Jewish national home in Palestine.

It would be totally understandable if at this crucial time Rommel was pre-occupied. The battle in and around El Alamein had been continuing for several weeks by the time Rauff flew to Tobruk. The remainder of the group meanwhile set out for Athens on 29 July. There they waited for the inevitable Axis victory, at which time they would no doubt collectively make their way to North Africa and become attached to the Axis force and enter into Cairo to begin the fulfilment of the task to which they had been assigned.[17]

17 As there was no victory at El Alamein the men were not sent to Egypt. Later they went to Tunisia and were involved there in the persecution of Jewish people.

Chapter 26

First Battle of El Alamein

Prayer and intercession for victory

While the New Zealand division and parts of the Indian division managed to extricate themselves from near certain annihilation or capture, Rommel, despite the tiredness of his troops, pressed immediately on from Mersa Matruh in order to reach and take El Alamein before the retreating Allied forces had enough time to establish themselves there. This was the most critical time in the North African campaign.

Jewish and Christian people the world over now began to pray and intercede for this critical situation. The Bible College of Wales, based in Swansea prioritised its time to pray about this potential crisis. The College principal, Rees Howells stated on 4 July 1942:

> "Unless God will intervene on behalf of Palestine … there will be no safety there for the Jews. These Bible Lands must be protected, because it is to these lands the Saviour will come back. If I had the choice today, I would say to God, 'Take all I have, but preserve Palestine.' We want to say to God today, 'Unless there is a special reason for Egypt to fall, don't let Alexandria be taken, but give Rommel a setback.' Can I carry the same burden today for Alexandria as I would if Swansea were being attacked?"[1]

The 4th July was a Saturday, so Howells called for a special prayer meeting, and at the conclusion of the following day, he declared, 'I thought he might be allowed to take Egypt … but I know now he will never take Egypt – neither Alexandria nor Cairo will fall.'[2]

These may have been reassuring words from a Bible-believing Christian to his praying students and faculty, but the reality on the ground was that the Jewish people in Egypt and Palestine still feared for their very survival, and many of the Allied soldiers at El Alamein were fully aware that General Rommel might just do it again.

Time was soon to tell if what Rees Howells had discerned was of the Lord or not.

Rommel's basic battle plan

The main object of Rommel's attack was to break through the Allied front line using the 90th Light Infantry Division and the 15th and 21st Panzer Divisions. Once through, the 90th

1 Grubb, N. *Rees Howells, Intercessor*, (Fort Washington, 1952), p. 250.

2 Grubb, N. *Rees Howells, Intercessor*, p. 251. Grubb mentions an interesting story which only came to light after the war of the surrender of 1,100 German soldiers of the 90th Light Division at this period due to them having drunk salt water from the pipeline which the British were constructing to bring water from the Nile to the front line. For further information see, Grubb, ibid, pp. 251-52.

Light Infantry Division was to veer left (northward) and reach the coast, thereby encircling the El Alamein 'box'. The two Panzer divisions were to then veer right (turn south) and encircle the 13th Corps which was centered upon the Bab el Qattara 'box'. One Italian division was to attack the El Alamein 'box' from the west, while another was to follow the 90th Light Infantry Division. The entire 20th Italian Corps was to follow behind the two Panzer divisions of the *Afrika Korps*. Various German reconnaissance units and the Italian *Littoria* Armoured Division were to protect the vulnerable ring flank of the Axis thrust, as the Allies could potentially break out through that position and encircle the attacking Axis force.

Once the two key positions of the El Alamein and Qattara 'boxes' had been encircled and captured, then there was little between Rommel and the Suez Canal.

The battle for the future of the Middle East begins

Early in the morning on 1 July 1942 the 90th Light Infantry Division began moving towards their objective, but in the process they travelled a bit too far north and were heavily engaged by the 1st South African Division on the perimeter of the El Alamein 'box.'

Despite being severely pressed, Rommel kept pushing his 90th Light Infantry Division to break through. This pressure increased after the *Luftwaffe* commander had informed him that the Mediterranean Fleet was leaving from Alexandria. This news, he wrote, '... determined me to go all out for a decision in the next few days. The British no longer seemed to trust their luck and were preparing for a retreat. I was convinced that a break-through over a wide front by my forces would result in complete panic.'[3]

The German forces only managed to break-free in the early afternoon, but then they were heavily bombed by the South African artillery and had to stop and dig in. Their anticipated encirclement of El Alamein on the first day had failed.

Further to the south weather conditions delayed the *Afrika Korps* from setting out on time, and they were then further delayed by heavy bombing from the RAF. When they finally managed to get around the Deir el Abyud position, they were confronted by men of the recently arrived 18th Indian Infantry Brigade (hurriedly brought in from Iraq) who were positioned on the western end of the Ruweisat Ridge and a position known as Deir el Shein.

Auchinleck thrust the 1st Armoured Division forward to assist the Indians, and throughout that first day an intense battle raged around the western end of Ruweisat Ridge. At the end of the day the Panzer Korps managed to capture this position, and capture some 2,000 Indian soldiers in the process. The 1st Armoured Division, however, had managed to knock out many of the German tanks, thereby seriously denting Rommel's plan for an early break through and envelopment of the 30th Corps positions.

This failure, in addition to the failure of the 90th Light Infantry Division to break through to the coast and envelope the El Alamein 'box' meant that by the end of the first day's

3 Rommel, E. *The Rommel Papers*, p. 248.

fighting the offensive had not succeeded as Rommel had anticipated. On this first day the men from South Africa, India and the British armoured units had done the job.

This was a very intense day for all soldiers and their commanders. At one point Rommel, as he often did, went into the front of the attacking force, but he too came under heavy fire, and wrote of this event later:

> Bayerlein and I had to lie out in the open. Suddenly to add to our troubles, a powerful British bomber force came flying up towards us. Fortunately, it was turned back before it reached us by some German fighters who had been escorting a dive-bomber raid.[4]

Failure of an Axis break-out

The failure to break through on the first day of the battle robbed Rommel of his best opportunity of victory at El Alamein. He then had to improvise, and look for another potential weak spot in the Allied line. The following weeks witnessed a very intense war of attrition.

While the South Africans continued to hold at bay the assault of the 90th Light Infantry Division, Rommel decided to halt the projected advance of the *Afrika Korps* south to encircle the Allied 30th Corps, and instead for them to advance and capture Ruweisat Ridge, and then continue on to the coast and thereupon encircle the El Alamein 'box.' Ruweisat Ridge thereafter became one of the main focal points of the battle for El Alamein.

That day the Desert Air Force (DAF) offered invaluable support to the British armoured units and infantry as they fought desperately against the experienced soldiers of the *Afrika Korps*. By the end of 2 July 1942 Rommel's second desperate move towards encircling El Alamein had failed. While he now rearranged his forces in order to throw more troops at Ruweisat Ridge, Auchinleck now went somewhat onto the offensive.

On 3 July he sent the New Zealanders from their position at Bab el Qattara 'box' northward towards Ruweisat Ridge. They succeeded in defeating the *Ariete* Division, and of the survivors, 400 were taken prisoner and the remainder fled. The British 22nd and 4th Armoured Brigades also had more success against the *Afrika Korps*.

This set-back provoked a radical change in Rommel's plans.[5] He had to bring his troops from the southern part of the line to the centre. At that point he decided not to press on offensively any more for the present, but to retain the positions held. His supply lines were being severely hit by the DAF which was flying hundreds of sorties. While in the process of withdrawing some of his front-line troops on 5 July, the Eighth Army counter-attacked, and the Axis force just managed to hold this counter-attack at bay.

4 Rommel, E. *The Rommel Papers*, p. 246.
5 Rommel, E. *The Rommel Papers*, p. 249.

Tel el Eisa and Tel el Makh Khad

The vanguard of the 9th Australian Division arrived at El Alamein on 4 July and went into the El Alamein 'box'. Thomas Derrick and the men of the 2/48th Battalion rolled into El Alamein on 6 July. These seasoned warriors of Tobruk heard the guns and were 'chafing at the bit.' Derrick wrote in his diary, 'A flight of Jerry planes flew over at 15 000 feet, dropping about 16 sticks, casualties 14…' Some of those casualties were from his own company and platoon.[6]

With their arrival Auchinleck and the commanders could consider more offensive actions, now that they had blunted Rommel's initial thrust. One of the main objectives was the capture of Tel el Eisa, which was a forward German observation position, about ten kilometres west of the El Alamein 'box' (or salient), as well as other related positions, and then raid south and west into Axis territory. This assault was due to begin on 10 July, and was entrusted to the 9th Australian Division. Before heading out, Derrick wrote, 'All troops feeling keen and very confident about the show.'[7] The South Africans, with supporting armour, were entrusted with capturing another nearby position, Tel el Makh Khad.

The men had crept forward towards the Axis front line and then charged forward yelling 'Australianos'. The Italian soldiers were mostly caught unawares. Thomas Derrick was like an Aussie version of Charles Upham and inspired his men. The *Sabratha* Division was annihilated, with the survivors either surrendering or fleeing westwards. Apart from capturing well over 1,000 Italians, the 9th Division also captured the German Signals Intercept Company 621, which was an invaluable intelligence gathering unit for Rommel.

The 9th Division men could not rest on their laurels, they had to endure German artillery attacks and *Stuka* dive bombers, then they had to dig in and await the anticipated counter-attack. Once again Rommel found himself pushing German troops into a situation caused by inadequate Italian defence.

Derrick wrote, 'Digging in was a mammoth task, the ground being so rocky; a slight compensation for this was the rather large and appetising meal we had, which was supplied by Mr Gill, who had … scrounged a heap of Itie rations. A few noggins of rum, the gift of L/Cpl Lindsay, who had been doing something similar, was received with open arms (mouths) too.'[8]

They needed that extra food input, as Rommel indeed counter-attacked with everything he had, for if the Eighth Army broke through they would come upon the Axis supply depots. For three days Rommel attacked Tel el Eisa, and throughout those days there were many acts of heroism by the Australians. Thomas Derrick received the Distinguished Conduct Medal for his continuous acts of bravery.[9]

6 Farquhar, M. ibid, p. 95.
7 Farquhar, M. ibid, p. 99.
8 Farquhar, M. ibid, p. 101.
9 Derrick was later to win the Victoria Cross at Sattelberg in New Guinea in 1943.

Rommel attempted a further advance on 13 July, towards the northern section of the line. This assault, however, petered out before it really got going, due, he states to an improper starting position of his troops who were then blasted by the British artillery.[10] It was renewed the following day, and he stated, 'Fierce fighting followed with the Australians, whom we knew only too well from the time of the Tobruk siege, and lasted well into the night.'[11]

One German assault during these intense days of combat resulted in some 600 German casualties, while one Australian assault to capture the strategic Point 24 position resulted in 50% casualties to the attacking force.

From 10 July the Australian and South African infantry had been heavily engaged in the northern sector, but by 16 July somewhat of a stalemate had developed there. Rommel had failed to dislodge these colonial soldiers from the El Alamein salient, so he now had to find another weak spot.

Ruweisat Ridge

One of the numerous key positions along the El Alamein line was Ruweisat Ridge, while just north lay another strategic position, the Miteirya Ridge. Following Rommel's initial thrust, the western end of the Ruweisat Ridge was held by the Axis forces. Auchinleck planned to capture the Axis positions on Ruweisat Ridge. The New Zealanders were entrusted with this task, assisted by the 5th Indian Infantry Brigade.

General Inglis was wary of some aspects of this attack, as he knew there was the potential of facing off against German Panzer formations. If this attack was indeed to proceed then he wanted total assurance of Allied tank support. General 'Strafer' Gott, commander of 13th Corps agreed, albeit somewhat reluctantly, that the 2nd Armoured Brigade would be involved, Despite this assurance Inglis was still wary, partly because there had already been several occasions when the infantry felt they were left unprotected by the armoured forces.

The battle for Ruweisat Ridge began early in the morning of 15 July with the vanguard of the New Zealanders engaging what they thought were the forward Axis lines. They moved along the ridge straight through the Axis lines, and then when the support battalions came, including Upham's 20th Battalion, it was realised that numerous Axis positions remained in-tact on the periphery. These were not advance Axis positions – this was the centre of the Axis position, and now they were springing to life after the surprise early morning assault.

Much hand-to-hand combat took place, and again Upham and the men of the 20th Battalion were in the midst of it. At one point Upham heard the sound of tanks and spoke to Bob May.

'Ours, I suppose,' Charles ventured.

10 Rommel, E. *The Rommel Papers*, p. 255.
11 Rommel, E. *The Rommel Papers*, pp. 255-56.

'Hope so.'

'They'd better be.' Charles said grimly. 'If they're Jerries there'll be trouble in the morning unless they're cleaned out. They'll be in behind us.'[12]

The sound was indeed that of German tanks, and trouble there certainly was in the morning for the New Zealanders, as the German armour came upon them in force. The British armour, unfortunately, did not appear as planned. The entire 22nd New Zealand Battalion was surrounded by German tanks and surrendered. By midday the remainder of the division on Ruweisat Ridge were being heavily bombed, and they had neither tanks nor artillery to fire back with. Still the armour did not appear.

The German counter-attack came in the late afternoon, and despite resolute fighting, the New Zealanders kept losing ground – and men. While Charles Upham continued to fight unceasingly and rally his men, the casualty rate grew by the minute, and the field hospital also came under fire. Then the inevitable happened, Upham was badly shot in the arm. Although his wounds were dressed and he was quite weak – he still returned to his men.

Nearby there was a German 88 artillery gun, and Upham began to disable it so it could not be used again. Nearby were the wounded German gun crew. Everyone knew of Upham's hate for the Nazi regime, whom he saw as being represented by German soldiers. He walked towards them - and his men thought the worst. Then, wrote Sandford, 'Charles was bending over the wounded men, one after another, and was giving them each a long draught from his own water-bottle. The Germans drank gratefully.'[13]

His men were quite surprised, as they knew his deep hatred of the Germans. But perhaps, just perhaps, at this moment Charles Upham saw just ordinary men, ordinary human beings, before him, and was able to make a distinction between them and the evil and racist system which had made them its slaves and brought them to this isolated and barren location in North Africa.

By late afternoon the British armour had still not appeared as promised, and then at 4pm the expected German counter-attack began. Sandford wrote:

> Ruweisat Ridge was drenched with fire. Gone now were our own anti-tank guns, gone any means of defence against the enemy. There was no chance even of skulking below ground, for the men in their sangars lay only inches below the surface.
>
> And as the guns of the tanks swivelled down on to them there was no more to be done, nothing more to be said. The tank commanders stood up in the turrets, waving the men up from the ground.[14]

Upham left the safer confines of the field station where had been forced to return to, and

12 Sandford, K. ibid, p. 162.
13 Sandford, K. ibid, p. 171.
14 Sandford, K. ibid, p. 172.

stumbled towards his men of the 20th Battalion again. When asked what he was doing, he replied, 'If we're going to be cleaned up I'm going to be with the boys,'...[15] A few minutes later he was hit by shrapnel. Wounded in the arm and now the leg, Charles Upham was soon compelled to surrender like hundreds of other gallant New Zealanders. His war in North Africa was now over – but he continued fighting even while being a guest of *der Fuhrer*.

Sometime later Charles Upham's bravery at Ruweisat Ridge was recognized and he was awarded a second Victoria Cross, only the third soldier ever to have achieved this amazing citation. One of the others was Noel Chavasse, whose twin brother Christopher was the Bishop of Rochester in England, and a personal friend of a British general named Bernard Montgomery.[16]

The 2nd Armoured Brigade finally arrived at 18.15, and halted the onward progress of the Panzer division's thrust. It was too late, however, to save the surviving New Zealanders from these battalions, as they were already being moved backwards towards Mersa Matruh, en-route to Germany.

Subsequent battles – Miteirya Ridge and El Mrier

The battle at Ruweisat Ridge did however siphon off German forces, which then enabled the 9th Australian Division to again go onto the offensive, aiming for Miteirya Ridge, which was dubbed Ruin Ridge hereafter by the Australians. Rommel wrote, 'The Australians had attacked from El Alamein again, this time towards the south-west. They had soon penetrated our line in the Trento and Trieste's sectors and had taken a large number of Italian prisoners. Now they were trying to roll up our front to the south.'[17]

After initial success, a concerted Axis counter-attack then drove the Australians back to their starting position, at considerable cost in men. This, and other Allied attacks had a telling effect upon Rommel, as it was a war of attrition on the Panzer Army Africa, and now the Italian authorities were not being fully supportive. Rommel wrote to his wife on 18 July 1942, 'Yesterday was a particularly hard and critical day. We pulled through again. But it can't go on like it for long, otherwise the front will crack. Militarily, this is the most difficult period I've ever been through.'[18]

There was a lull in the fighting for several days, but the quiet ended on 21 July when waves of Allied infantry attacked the positions of the 15th Panzer Division. This they managed to stop, and in the process bagged some 500 Allied prisoners. Shortly afterwards the 9th Australian Division with supporting tanks initiated a diversionary attack upon the Axis lines.

The main Allied attack occurred in the middle of the line by New Zealand and Indian

15 Sandford, K. ibid, p. 172.
16 www.birkenheadrsa.com
17 Rommel, E. *The Rommel Papers*, p. 257.
18 Rommel, E. *The Rommel Papers*, p. 257.

infantry and British armoured units. They broke through and began penetrating behind the Axis line. The situation became so critical that Rommel had to siphon off troops from his southern sector, and these, combined with the 21st Panzer Division's armour not only blunted the Allied assault, but also rolled it back. In the process they bagged another 1,400 Allied prisoners, and destroyed in total some 140 Allied tanks.[19]

This brief but exerted attack all but depleted the ranks of both sides, although the Australians did make another breakout on 26 July, which although initially successful, was then blunted after they incurred heavy casualties and they had to return to the same lines as before. Another attack by the 69th Infantry Brigade also ended in failure around the same time, losing another 1,000 men as prisoners and another 32 invaluable tanks.[20]

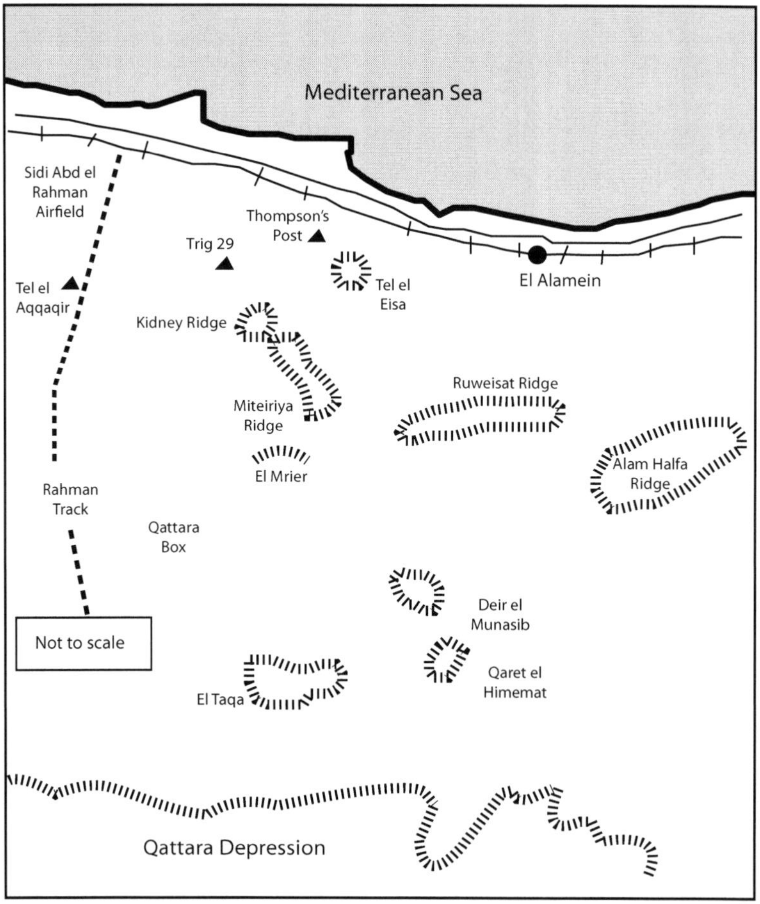

19 Rommel, E. *The Rommel Papers*, p. 258.
20 Rommel, E. *The Rommel Papers*, p. 260.

Consequences of the first battle of El Alamein

Although there were further smaller skirmishes, the major battles connected to the first battle of El Alamein had now ended. When later describing this battle Rommel was quite realistic when he stated:

> But there our attack came to a halt and our strength failed. We were met by greatly superior British armoured formations thrusting against our front. Our chance of overrunning the remainder of the Eighth Army and occupying Eastern Egypt at one stroke was irretrievably gone.[21]

After capturing Tobruk and then pursuing the retreating Eighth Army, Rommel saw an opportunity which would close again very quickly if he did not take hold of it. He went for it with all he had. It certainly was not from lack of trying that the Axis forces were stopped at El Alamein in the first battle.

The Panzer Army Africa had, however, bloodied the nose of the British Empire, as he stated:

> We had, of course, dealt the British severe losses. Between the 26th of May and the 20th of July, 60,000 British, South Africans, Indians, New Zealanders, French and Australians had found their way into our prisoner-of-war camps. My men had destroyed well over 2,000 British tanks and armoured vehicles. The equipment of an entire British offensive army lay destroyed in the desert and thousands upon thousands of their vehicles were now being used by my troops.[22]

However, he was also realistic, and saw that despite his losses being much fewer, he was less able to replenish his force than the Allies were.

21 Rommel, E. *The Rommel Papers*, p. 245.
22 Rommel, E. *The Rommel Papers*, p. 262.

Chapter 27

Roosevelt, Montgomery and Alam Halfa

Time to regroup

Although Rommel wrote that he felt his best chance of getting to the Suez Canal had passed with the failure to break through in the first days of the first battle of El Alamein, he had no choice but to plan for another breakthrough.

He also fully understood that with the entrance of the United States into the war there would be a huge Allied effort made sooner or later against the Axis forces somewhere. If that somewhere would be in North Africa and if he was to succeed in his goal, then he would need to strike quickly, penetrate into Egypt, capture the Suez Canal and defeat Britain.

The Allies had the luxury of time in order to replenish their severely tried forces, but he never had that luxury. In fact Rommel had to struggle against numerous challenges in obtaining sufficient supplies. The amount of material needed in North Africa was never attained, and the ration of those supplies going to the Italians was proportionally much higher than the amount going to the Germans.

One of the worst deficiencies was the lack of sufficient replacement vehicles – tanks, troop-carriers and armoured cars. These were the very materials the Allies were now receiving from the United States.

Roosevelt's assessment

Towards the end of the intense fighting in the first battle of El Alamein, President Roosevelt wrote a Memorandum which he gave to his three delegates Harry Hopkins, General George Marshall and Admiral King as they travelled to London to meet with Churchill and the British military and political leadership to discuss future British and American combined efforts.

Roosevelt was determined to see US troops actively involved somewhere in the European theatre in 1942. Various possibilities had previously been discussed between Churchill and Roosevelt, including a landing in France. It was appearing more unlikely that this would happen in 1942. If not France, then where could such a landing take place?

In point 8 of his Memorandum, Roosevelt stated:

8. The Middle East should be held as strongly as possible whether Russia collapses or not. I want you to take into consideration the effect of losing the Middle East. Such

loss means in series:

(1) Loss of Egypt and the Suez Canal.

(2) Loss of Syria.

(3) Loss of Mosul oil wells.

(4) Loss of the Persian Gulf through attack from the north and west, together with access to all Persian Gulf oil.

(5) Joining hands between Germany and Japan and the probable loss of the Indian Ocean.

(6) The very important probability of German occupation of Tunis, Algiers, Morocco, Dakar, and the cutting of the ferry route through Freetown and Liberia.

(7) Serious danger to all shipping in the South Atlantic and serious danger to Brazil and the whole east coast of South America. I include in the above possibilities the use by the Germans of Spain, Portugal, and their territories.[1]

After having laid out to his three representatives the consequences of the Middle East passing from Allied (i.e. British-led) control to Axis control, Roosevelt then clearly instructs them:

(8) You will determine the best methods of holding the Middle East. These methods include definitely either or both of the following:

(a) Sending aid and ground forces to the Persian Gulf, to Egypt, and to Syria.

(b) A new operation in Morocco and Algeria intended to drive in against the back door of Rommel's armies. The attitude of French Colonial troops is still in doubt.[2]

Roosevelt then stated his opposition to a total US effort to defeat Japan, and saw it as imperative in the first instance to assist Britain in defeating Germany. His representatives, however, were initially not of the same way of thinking as their President, and much depended upon Churchill and his Chiefs of Staff to convince them. All this was to happen at the same time as the heavy fighting at El Alamein was beginning to slow down to a stalemate.

A number of plans and proposals for operations against Nazi Germany had been previously discussed and worked on by separate British and US Chiefs of Staff, operations such as 'Sledgehammer' and 'Round-up'. Now was the time to come to a unified agreement. Any future joint British-US-Canadian operations against the Axis in western European were much reliant upon the outcome of the battle in Russia, which at that point was coming to a climax outside the city of Stalingrad in the south.

The US representatives still desired an initial landing in Brest or Cherborg on the west

1 Memorandum for Hon. Harry L. Hopkins, General Marshall, and Admiral King, Subject: *Instructions for London Conference, July 1942.* 16 July 42, in Churchill, W. *The Hinge of Fate*, pp. 443.

2 Memorandum, ibid, in Churchill, W. *The Hinge of Fate*, p. 443.

coast of France (Operation *Sledgehammer*). The British firmly believed that any operation against the Axis in Europe in 1942 was premature, due to their already stretched resources. They preferred an operation into western Africa (codenamed 'Gymnast'), beginning in Morocco, and then moving eastwards towards Tunis. It was planned that this operation, combined with Auchinleck's move west from Egypt (codenamed 'Acrobat') would move in against the Axis forces from two sides.

Initially the United States representatives and their British counterparts could not agree, as the Americans insisted on persevering with 'Sledgehammer.' This too was what the Russians desired in order to take pressure off their long and intense front. Finally Roosevelt intervened and agreed to forestall the European operation, and he accepted the British proposal of a landing in north-west Africa. At a meeting on 24 July 1942 a new name was given for this forthcoming operation – *Torch,* due to begin before 30 October 1942.[3]

Churchill's plans

With this new agreement with the United States, Churchill was in the best position he had been for some time, especially after the crushing loss of Cyrenaica, Tobruk, Sollum and Mersa Matruh. He now set out to re-establish the strategic imperative, first by visiting Cairo and meeting with Auchinleck, and then by continuing on to Moscow to discuss the recent British-US accord with Stalin.

On 31 July Auchinleck had telegrammed Churchill and stated that after conferring with his Corps commanders that they would need to retain a purely defensive position until the middle of September.[4] This position seemed to irk Churchill.

Churchill arrived in Cairo on 4 August, and had General Smuts come up from South Africa and Wavell to come over from India to meet together. His main decision was whether Auchinleck had lost the confidence of the army to lead them. Also present at a special meeting was Casey, General Sir Alan Brooke (the CIGS), Admiral Harwood and Air Marshall Tedder.

Churchill visited the El Alamein front on 5 August, and met with as many Corps and Divisional commanders as he was able, including with General Leslie Morshead, the real hero of the siege of Tobruk in 1941. He particularly wanted to meet Lieutenant-General William Gott, to determine if this man was suitable for leading the Eighth Army at this crucial period of time. Although he was tired, Gott consented to accept any responsibility entrusted to him.

Change of Structure

On 6 August 1942 Churchill sent recommendations to the War Cabinet for a change of structure. It was already abundantly clear to all that the area entitled Middle East Command was far too large for one man to oversee. This region was now divided into

3 Churchill, W. *The Hinge of Fate*, pp. 447-8.
4 Churchill, W. *The Hinge of Fate*, p. 455.

two, these being (a) Near East Command, and including Egypt, Palestine and Syria and based in Cairo, and which would oversee the Eighth and Ninth Armies; (b) Middle East Command, comprising Persia (Iran) and Iraq, based in either Basra or Baghdad and which would oversee the Tenth Army.

The proposal was for Auchinleck to become Commander-in-Chief of Middle East Command, and General Sir Harold Alexander (until then designated as the British commander of *Torch*) to become Commander-in-Chief of Near East Command. Alexander's position in Operation *Torch* would be taken by General Bernard Montgomery.

Churchill also expressed that a victory over Rommel 'may have a decisive effect upon the attitude of the French in Vichy controlled North Africa when "Torch" begins.'[5] The Cabinet agreed to most of Churchill's proposals, except the division of the Middle East Command. Churchill then prevailed upon them on this matter, and they reluctantly agreed, albeit with a name adjustment.[6] The name Middle East Command for Alexander's new position would remain as before. In all this readjustment General Auchinleck was perhaps unfairly treated, but he accepted it as part of the job.

General Gott killed and replaced by General Montgomery

Except for this name adjustment, Churchill was now reassured that his changes could take immediate effect, and that he could proceed on to Moscow. Such however was not to be. On 7 August General Gott was killed as he was flying down to Cairo. Suddenly all of Churchill's neat plans seemed to be falling down.

Churchill, together with Brooke and Smuts, agreed that the only possible replacement was to be Lieutenant-General Bernard Montgomery. Churchill later received the consent of the Cabinet, and by the morning of 8 August Montgomery was informed of his new command. That same day, General Bernard Montgomery was on his way to a new command, back in the region where he had previously served, this time however in a completely different set of circumstances from 1937.

By 10 August both Alexander as C-in-C and Montgomery as commander of the Eighth Army were taking up their new positions. Churchill instructed Alexander:

> "Your prime and main duty will be to take or destroy at the earliest opportunity the German-Italian Army commanded by Field-Marshall Rommel, together with all its supplies and establishments in Egypt and Libya..."[7]

Malta relieved

While Churchill was in Moscow discussing the Anglo-American plans with Stalin, another attempt was made to break the Malta blockade. A large flotilla which included several

5 Churchill to deputy Prime Minister, 6 August, 1942, in Churchill, W. *The Hinge of Fate*, pp. 460-1.
6 Churchill, W. *The Hinge of Fate*, pp. 462-3.
7 Churchill to Alexander, in Churchill, W. *The Hinge of Fate*, p. 471.

aircraft carriers and other warships was off the coast near Algiers on 11 August and was initially attacked by a U-boat. The carrier *Eagle* was sunk. Worse followed in the following days as other warships and numerous of the convoy ships bringing much needed supplies to the beleaguered island garrison, were sunk or damaged.

Ultimately only five of the original fourteen convoy ships arrived in Malta, and altogether some three hundred and fifty men of the Merchant Navy and Royal Navy died. The result though meant that the blockade was broken and provided a much needed morale boost to the people and garrison on the island.

The German commanders were very disappointed that this convoy managed to break through their blockade, as they knew that ultimate success in the North African campaign depended upon a clear passage from Italy to Tunis, Benghazi and Tobruk of their supplies and reinforcements.

This bold initiative by the Merchant Navy and Royal Navy again revealed that there needed to be a combination of all three services if there was to be ultimate victory. The Royal Air Force, with its Australian, New Zealand and South African components, again proved its invaluable contribution to the war effort.

Montgomery and Rommel face off

Montgomery with Alexander's support set about restructuring and reinvigorating the Eighth Army. There were three Corps, the 13th Corps commanded by General Horrocks, the 30th Corps commanded by General Ramsden and the 10th Corps commanded by General Lumsden.

Shortly after he arrived and having ascertained the lay of the land, Montgomery established where he believed Rommel would attack, a matter greatly assisted by the British intelligence unit, known as Ultra, breaking the German code. He was therefore aware that Rommel anticipated breaking in through the mine field south of the Bab el Qattara 'box', and just south of where the New Zealand Division was located, and then intended coming in behind the Allied forward line and aiming for Alam Halfa Ridge, which once taken would enable him to cut off the Allied forces from retreating.

Montgomery left the region south of the Bab el Qattara 'box' open, except for extensive minefields, but positioned much of the three armoured divisions and artillery adjacent to Alam Halfa Ridge ready to pounce on the Axis armour when it swung north and was aiming towards the coast. The 7th, 10th and 23rd Armoured Divisions were all stationed behind the front lines in readiness.

While Montgomery prepared for his first battle of the campaign his opposite number, the now Field Marshal Rommel, was battling chronic fatigue and other stress related symptoms and needed to return to Germany for treatment. He desired for General Guderian to temporarily replace him, but when this was not possible, he had no choice but to remain at his post.

The end of August provided Rommel with the last opportunity for an assault with the moon full. He had to press on, despite not having the supplies that he needed. He wrote to his wife on 30 August, 'To-day has dawned at last. It's been a long wait worrying all the time whether I should get everything I needed together to enable me to take the brakes off again. Many of my worries have been by no means satisfactorily settled and we have some very grave shortages. But I've taken the risk…[8]

The Battle of Alam Halfa

During the evening of 30 August 1942 Rommel sent the *Afrika Korps* as well as the 90th Light Infantry Division and the 20th Italian Corps to the south, at the supposed weak link between Deir el Munassib and Qaret el Himeimat. There were diversionary attacks along the line further north against the 9th Australian Division, 1st South African Division and 5th Indian Division.[9]

The *Afrika Korps* advance was seriously held up penetrating through the Allied minefield and as a result they lost that key element of surprise. At this point Rommel was in two minds about breaking off the engagement or continuing. General Bayerlein recommended continuing.

Once through the minefield, the Axis force wheeled left and headed due north towards the strategic Alam Halfa Ridge, where they ran into the Eighth Army armoured divisions and artillery. A savage battle now took place in and around the Alam Halfa Ridge in which both sides lost many of their prized possessions – tanks.

During 31 August Rommel's forces were also severely harassed by the DAF and suffering from lack of fuel, he had no choice but to slow down his thrust. Field Marshal Kesselring assisted with fuel from the *Luftwaffe*, which helped.

Such help, however, was not enough and it came too late. Rommel ordered a general withdrawal, which began on 2 September. On 3 September the 7th Armoured Division (the 'Desert Rats), began to attack the retreating columns, and, Montgomery stated 'the weight of our air attacks was stepped up to its maximum.'[10] Then during the night and into the following day, New Zealand infantry and some recently arrived British infantry attempted to cut off the withdrawal. Montgomery wrote that:

> The reaction was fierce. Bitter fighting took place, and the enemy launched heavy and repeated counter attacks on 4 September to repel our attempts to bottle him in. We did not succeed in cutting him off, but he was forced slowly and relentlessly back throughout 4 and 5 September.[11]

8 Rommel, E. *The Rommel Papers*, p. 275.
9 Montgomery, B. *El Alamein to the River Sangro,* p. 6.
10 Montgomery, B. ibid, p. 8.
11 Montgomery, B. ibid, p. 9.

Rommel's retreat was completed by 6 September, and his forces returned to virtually the same positions from where they had begun. Montgomery called off the battle at 0700 on 7 September. He wrote:

> The victory at Alam Halfa had a profound effect on the Eighth Army. The morale of the soldiers became outstanding. Rommel had been defeated in his purpose, and had suffered severe casualties. The confidence of the troops in the higher command was re-established...[12]

This defeat induced a very philosophical comment from Rommel, who wrote:

> With the failure of the offensive our last chance of gaining the Suez Canal had gone. We could now expect that the full production of British industry and, more important, the enormous industrial potential of America, which, consequent on our declaration of war, was now fully harnessed to the enemy cause, would finally turn the tide against us.[13]

This was a very sobering assessment, considering his earlier optimism of victory. This optimism is possibly best revealed through a sketch he made of how he planned to move on to Alexandria and Cairo after victory. His son Manfred later wrote that Rommel drew this sketch before the battle of Alam Halfa, in anticipation of defeating Montgomery's force.

Apparently there was a logistical problem with the lack of pontoon bridges with which to cross the Nile. Rommel anticipated capturing several bridges before they could be destroyed by the British. He intended, wrote Manfred:

> ... to throw his reconnaissance units and paratroopers forward to a lightning attack on the Nile bridges ... By means of this operation, he not only intended to secure the bridges, but wanted to undermine the 8th Army's power of resistance with the news that "the Germans have reached the Nile." It was my father's view that there was small likelihood of the British having prepared the bridges for demolition at this time. It was also planned that the moment the first German paratroopers and reconnaissance units appeared in and around Cairo and Alexandria, the Egyptians would be called upon to support the Axis forces. It was known from Egyptian officers who were in touch with the Germans that such a revolt was contemplated.[14]

Rommel's plan did not come to fruition.

Although the Axis lost more men that the Allies, the Allies lost more tanks in this battle

12 Montgomery, B. ibid, p. 9.
13 Rommel, E. *The Rommel Papers,* p. 283.
14 Rommel, E. *The Rommel Papers*, Appendix.

than did the Axis. Yet the ability of the Allies to replenish their supply was now better than the Axis.

This battle was Montgomery's first major offensive as commander and he had triumphed. As resilient as Rommel's resolve and soldiers had been, the resolve and fighting abilities of the men from New Zealand, Australia, South Africa, Britain, India and other Allied nations, had again saved the situation. In addition, there was now tangible evidence of the new nation involved on the Allied side – the United States. They may not have had any soldiers there, but their provision of supplies had played a decisive role in the Allied victory.

CHAPTER 28

THE INTERLUDE

Following the battle of Alam Halfa both the Allied and Axis armies went into a period of recuperation and regrouping. The Eighth Army was now in a more dominant position. The Axis had suffered large losses at Alam Halfa; Rommel was exhausted; the continued existence of the Malta garrison hindered the Axis supply line; and the promised reinforcements from Britain as well as new materials, especially Sherman and Grant tanks from the US, were arriving.

Another factor of immense importance was the growing strength of the Desert Air Force, under the command of Air Marshal Coningham and the overall command of Air Marshal Tedder. By September 1942 the air-force had some 550 aircraft. Together with planes stationed in Malta and United States planes in the region, the Allied air strength numbered some 1200.[1]

Rommel's sick leave and strategy

Whereas both Alexander and Montgomery were relevantly fresh and new to the region, Rommel by September had been in North Africa for about eighteen months and was desperately in need of a break. Hitler finally agreed. He left for Germany on 23 September, handing over command to General Georg Stumme.

Prior to his departure Rommel set in motion his plan for the upcoming campaign. He fully understood the bigger picture involving a German victory in Russia, which was the main focal point of the German High Command. Rommel tried to convince the German High Command that the overall strategy should incorporate a two way German movement, from Russia southwards over the Caucasus and into the Middle East, and linking up with the Panzer Army Africa which would be moving eastwards from Egypt, over the Suez Canal and into Syria.

A German victory in Stalingrad was of the utmost importance as it would then cause the British to siphon off some of its manpower for the garrison duties of the Ninth and Tenth Armies, and some of these would need to come from the region of the Eighth Army. He thereby established a very firm defence line opposite the Allied forces, also running from the Mediterranean at Tel el Eisa through to the Qattara Depression. There he anticipated waiting either for the anticipated Allied assault, or for the German victory at Stalingrad.

A major part of his defensive line involved the laying of almost half a million mines.

1 Churchill, W. *The Hinge of Fate*, p. 587.

The Axis position

The battle of Greece was lost before it began due to German aerial superiority over the Allies. Now Allied aerial superiority began to heap huge losses upon the Axis before the big battle began. In the months of September and October between 30-40% of the Axis shipping was destroyed, mostly by the RAF. This was a huge blow to their aspirations. However, as had been proved previously, the Axis forces and especially the Germans, were an extremely resilient foe, and such set-backs were no guarantee of an Allied victory.

In his later assessment of the upcoming battle Rommel already admitted that the Axis force was so disadvantaged that 'there was practically no hope of our coming out of it victorious.'[2] Not only were his forces undermanned but they were seriously under-provisioned.

These aspects he tried to impress upon his superiors when he met with Mussolini on 24 September and then with Hitler several days later. He reiterated to both of the Axis leaders the problems which Panzer Army Africa faced, which was primarily one of lack of supplies, and a stronger Allied air-force. Both leaders, as well as their adjutants promised extra support, but in reality little extra went to North Africa, let alone to the front-line.

Einsatzkommando Egypt and Arab-German Battalion depart from Greece

As a result of there being no breakthrough at El Alamein the *Einsatzkommando* Egypt was withdrawn from the region. This specialized murder squad had been in Athens since July waiting for the anticipated Axis victory at El Alamein before venturing into the war zone. But when victory eluded the Axis, this unit was withdrawn back to Germany in September.[3]

The unit was not disbanded, and awaited a potential future deployment to the region. Unfortunately that opportunity arose in early 1943, when they were redeployed to carry out their murderous acts on the innocent Jewish community in Tunisia.[4]

Haj Amin and the former Iraqi Prime Minister Rashid Ali al-Gaylani had been quite active during this period in Europe. Haj Amin had been keeping up his pro-Axis and anti-Allied propaganda, and had been expecting to be involved in the liberation of Palestine. A major part of his work involved working with Rashid Ali to recruit Arab volunteers for the Arab-German Battalion that General Felmy was training in Greece.

While there was a stalemate in North Africa, the German High Command was anticipating a clear victory on its Eastern Front, and expected to defeat the Soviet forces blocking the route to the oil fields of Baku and the Caucasus Mountains. It would only be a matter of time, so they believed, before they reached the Middle East. The two key Arab personalities in Germany at that time were Haj Amin and Rashid Ali, and it was

2 Rommel, E. *The Rommel Papers*, p. 302.

3 Mallman and Cuppers, ibid, p. 157.

4 This is outside the scope of this book, but is presented in Mallman and Cuppers, *Nazi Palestine*.

anticipated that these two would then become more actively involved in the Eastern sphere of operations – a sphere of operations which Germany did not have to share with the Italians.

It was within this context that the Arab-German Battalion was transferred from Greece to the Eastern Front - without consultation with Haj Amin. Haj Amin opposed this move, believing this battalion should be ready for involvement in the North African theatre of war, once the Axis forces finally broke out of El Alamein.[5]

It would appear that the German leadership had greater hopes of entering into the Middle East via the Caucasus than via El Alamein. To enter the Middle East via the Caucasus, however, would require a significant victory against the Soviet forces. At that very juncture the Germans had just launched a major offensive to capture Stalingrad, the city which controlled the passageway over the Volga River, and which blocked the route to the oil fields further south at Baku, and the passage over the Caucasus Mountains. Two battles were now in process at the same time – Stalingrad and El Alamein.

Timing of Operations *Lightfoot* and *Torch*

Churchill was anxious to know the date that Alexander and Montgomery had agreed upon to attack the Axis line at El Alamein. Such an understanding was imperative for Churchill, as he was also involved with the planning of Operation *Torch* in northwest Africa, scheduled to begin in early November. Both attacks needed to be closely integrated, as the whole purpose was to crush the Axis forces in a pincer movement, the Eighth Army moving from the east from Egypt, and the mostly United States forces moving from the west, from Morocco and Algeria.

Alexander informed Churchill that the beginning of Operation *Lightfoot* was scheduled for the full moon period around 24 October. Alexander had taken into account the beginning of Operation *Torch* and calculated to begin his operation some thirteen days prior to the beginning of the western offensive.[6] Churchill later responded to Alexander:

> Events are moving in our favour both in North Africa and Vichy France, and "Torch" goes forward steadily and punctually. But all our hopes are centred upon the battle you and Montgomery are going to fight. It may well be the key to the future ...[7]

Churchill's concluding words here were so relevant. The battle of El Alamein was indeed to be a key to the future. It was a key not just to an Allied military victory, but it was also a key to Jewish security in the region and especially in the land of Israel. Perhaps though we could expand Churchill's statement and include the joint battles of Stalingrad and El Alamein as being the key to the future.

5 See Mallman and Cuppers, *Nazi Palestine*.

6 Churchill, W. *The Hinge of Fate*, pp. 587-8.

7 Churchill to Alexander, 20 October 1942, in Churchill, W. *The Hinge of Fate*, p. 588.

The Allied Battle formation

The Allied forces forming the Eighth Army were:

30th Corps commanded by General Oliver Leese, comprised of the

- 9th Australian Division
- 51st Highland Division
- 2nd New Zealand Division
- 1st South African Division

13th Corps commanded by General Horrocks, and comprised of the

- 4th Indian Division
- 50th British Division
- 44th British Division
- Greek Brigade
- Free French Brigade

10th Corps under General Herbert Lumsden were in reserve, and was comprised of the 1st Armoured Division, the 7th Armoured Division and the 10th Armoured Division.

Montgomery's plan was for the four infantry divisions of the 30th Infantry Corps to move forward along a sixteen mile (twenty-six kilometre) line, and in the process cut two corridors through the extensive Axis minefields, thereby allowing the armour of 10th Corps to move through and attack the Axis armour. This initial thrust was to be called Operation *Lightfoot.* The thrust of the 10th Corps through the corridor was to be the crucial breakthrough, and Montgomery named it Operation *Supercharge.* A special mine detector invented by a Pole was to be used in this operation. The men of the 13th Corps on the south of the line were to make diversionary attacks aimed at distracting the Axis forces from the operations of 30th Corps, and particularly by drawing away the 21st Panzer Division. Montgomery also used a number of ruses to trick the Axis forces, in what became known as Operation *Bertram.*

Possible consequences from the upcoming battle

Much was at stake with the outcome of the two major battles at Stalingrad and El Alamein. If the German-led Army was victorious in both locations, then there was little to stop the hate-filled Nazi regime from completing their goal of annihilating all eleven million Jewish people in Europe – and countless millions of other so-called 'undesirables.'

If the Germans were victorious in both places then was a very strong likelihood that the Holocaust would have been introduced into the Middle East and that the Jewish national home in Palestine would have been devastated.

The outcome of the battle would probably make little difference upon the average Arab or Egyptian. In both countries, however, there were those who cooperated with the

British. If the Axis forces won at El Alamein then they would either have to leave or their lives could potentially be endangered.

Among the Arab and Egyptian peoples though there were many who were decidedly pro-German, pro-Nazi and pro-Axis. These people may have been Axis sympathizers because they understood and agreed with the Nazi ideology or because they saw the German-led Axis forces as being the vehicle to bring their vengeance against both the British (or even the French as far as Syria was concerned) and the Jews.

The world now waited to see the outcome of the two battles which would be the key for the future.

CHAPTER 29

SECOND BATTLE OF EL ALAMEIN

Preparing for battle

Everyone knew that the upcoming second battle at El Alamein would be the decisive battle of the entire Middle East theatre of operations. Montgomery and his staff had worked tirelessly on their plan, of which he wrote:

> An essential feature of my plan was that every commander in the Army, down to the rank of Lieutenant-Colonel, should know from me personally how I proposed to fight the battle, what issues depended on it, and what were the main difficulties we were likely to encounter. I toured the Army addressing the officers.
>
> On 21 and 22 October, the battle was explained to the troops by their officers.
>
> I was determined that the soldiers should go into battle having been worked up into a great state of enthusiasm, and realizing fully what was expected of them.[1]

The period leading up to the battle was the Jewish High Holidays season, a time for reflection, repentance and celebration. On the front line a meal was arranged for the *Rosh HaShanah* (Jewish New Year), and over 300 Jewish soldiers attended – Jewish soldiers from Palestine, South Africa, other nations, and even one veteran of the 'Jewish Legion' from the First World War. Mosenson wrote:

> ... there was not a great deal of gaiety in the program arranged for the evening. Uppermost at this celebration was our anguish at the suffering of European Jews and our fears for the fate of Palestine.[2]

While anticipating the opening of the battle Thomas Derrick wrote :

> This is a moment in history.[3]

During the morning of 23 October Montgomery's personal message to the troops was read out to all:

> The Battle which is now about to begin will be one of the decisive battles of history. It will be the turning point of the war...

1 Field Marshal The Viscount Montgomery of El Alamein, *El Alamein to the River Sangro,* (London, 1948), p. 16.
2 Mosenson, M. *Letters from the Desert,* p. 129.
3 Farquhar, M. *Diary of Thomas Derrick*, p. 113.

The Lord mighty in battle will give us the victory.[4]

On the eve of the battle Brigadier Howard Kippenberger, a veteran of Greece, Crete and numerous North African battles, addressed his men from New Zealand:

> I told them that this was the turn of the war and the greatest moment of their lives: they had the duty and honour of breaking in, on which everything depended: our hats were in the ring and I expected them to do it no matter what the cost …[5]

Somewhere else along that long line, Mosenson wrote to his beloved wife in Palestine. Mosenson realized that if the battle was lost, they the soldiers would be interned in a POW camp. The same fate probably would not befall his wife and family on Kibbutz Na'an. He wrote:

> The sun has set and the world is sunk in darkness. I'll finish now. I don't know when I'll be able to write again – and perhaps not at all. This is a hallowed moment. In another three and a half hours the attack will begin and my own fate may be decided one way or another. In the shadow of death that is hovering over the very hills on the horizon that we may conquer by tomorrow the heart clings to its dear ones, to its dear and distant home …[6]

'There was tension and excitement at Headquarters' recalls Blyth. '… the 8th Army was going to make an attack along the whole front. Somebody said we had 900 guns ahead of us, almost wheel to wheel, and there was going to be the biggest gun barrage ever heard in the Middle East.'[7]

The battle begins

The Second Battle at El Alamein began at 9.40 pm on 23 October 1942 when some 1000 Allied artillery guns opened up fire on the Axis lines.[8] After twenty minutes the firing then concentrated upon the forward Axis positions to facilitate the assault by the infantry divisions of the 30th Corps (9th Australian, 51st Highland, 2nd New Zealand, 1st South African) and 13th Corps (4th Indian, Greek Brigade, 50th British, 44th British, Free French Brigade).

The infantry were to advance over the length of their line aiming at the main Axis defensive line. The engineers were to follow the 30th Corps infantry and clear the mines

4 Montgomery, *El Alamein to the River Sangro*, p. 16.

5 Kippenberger, H. *Infantry Brigadier,* (Oxford, 1961), p. 225 & 228.

6 Mosenson, M. *Letters from the Desert,* pp. 134-135.

7 Blyth, J. *Soldiering On*, p. 65.

8 The numbers vary, with Montgomery himself stating there were over a thousand 'field and medium guns'. See Montgomery, *El Alamein to the River Sangro*, p. 16.

and prepare two corridors for the 1st and 10th Armoured Divisions of 10th Corps to then pass through and then come in behind the Axis line.

The 9th Australian and 51st Highland Divisions were to force a northern corridor, while the 1st South African and 2nd New Zealand Divisions were to force open a south-west corridor.

Although the infantry reached their objectives, the planned major break-through did not happen as the Axis minefields were found to be deeper than expected. The dust thrown up for the 400 or so tanks also hindered visibility.

The diversionary attack along the south of the line which was carried out by 13th Corps (which included the 'Desert Rats' – the 7th Armoured Division), failed to obtain all of its objective due to very strong Axis resistance.

By the morning of 24 October Montgomery's initial objectives had not been completely met. The failure to obtain all of the anticipated objectives resulted in twelve days of intense attrition warfare, as the Allied forces tried to wear down the Axis forces.

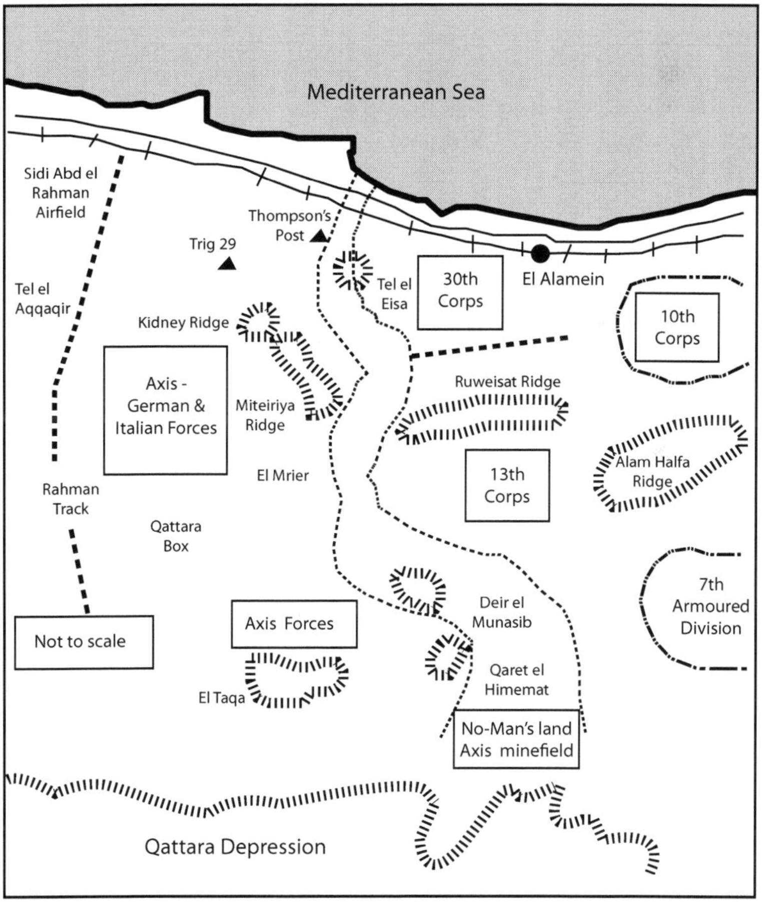

Rommel returns

One unexpected development of the battle was that General Stumme was missing in action. He was later found dead, probably from natural causes.

On 24 October Field Marshal Keitel, the Supreme Head of the Armed Forces (OKW) informed Rommel who was undergoing treatment in Austria of the situation and asked if he was willing to return to duty. Later Hitler asked him to return.

Rommel left immediately, stopping at Rome where he asked the *Comando Supremo* to ensure sufficient supplies, especially of fuel, was despatched to the battlefield. By dusk on 25 October Rommel was back at the front line, and was incensed at the state of the battle.

Northern assaults - Trig 29 (Hill 28) and Kidney Ridge

Considerable gains were made by the Allied force during 24/25 October. The South African, New Zealand and Indian Divisions had all played a part in gaining and retaining the Miteiriya Ridge, and the armoured brigades had moved through the corridors and had taken up defensive positions in order to draw the Axis armour to them.

Montgomery had originally intended advancing south west from Miteiriya Ridge with the New Zealanders, but then he realized this would be too costly. He now refocussed his attention upon capturing several strategic positions in the northern part of 30th Corps sector, west of Tel el Eisa, namely Kidney Ridge and Point (Trig) 29 (known as Hill 28 by Rommel and the Germans). The 51st Highlander Division would attack Kidney Ridge and the Australians would assault the Trig 29 position. He called this his 'crumbling' action, of slowly wearing down the Axis infantry, while at the same time ensuring his armoured brigades were keeping the Axis armour occupied, both in the 30th and 13th Corps sectors.

The Trig 29 position was of particular importance as the Axis artillery was utilising this high point for precision shelling of the Allied positions. Although not all that high, Trig 29 was going to feel like Mount Everest to those who fought there over the following days. The ultimate fate of the battle rested much upon the seizure and ongoing control of that small hill. Ken Beamish of the 2/7th Field Regiment told Craig Beech that 'it was but a small rise in the land on this vast battlefield yet became the most sought after vantage point in the battle of El Alamein.'[9]

Early in the evening of 25 October men from the two divisions began moving to their objectives. The main thrust for Trig 29 was entrusted to two Tobruk stalwarts, the 2/24th and 2/48th Battalions, including Thomas 'Diver' Derrick. Jack Ralla recalled the role that 8 Platoon A Company 2/48th Battalion played that night:

> It was damn dark. Jerry woke up. He mortared and shelled hell out of us. Ten of our supply trucks went up ... Behind the assault waves was a raging inferno. Night became day. Oddly it took some pressure off the attack as salvo after salvo crashed

9 Beech, C. *Greater love has no man than this* .... (Perth, 2012), p. 35. Craig's father, Frank Beech served alongside Beamish at both Tobruk and El Alamein.

> into the blaze. Not one driver or his mate survived. Lit up or not, it was no use going to ground. Diver kept shouting, 'Keep going! Keep going!' And straightened the line. Others did the same ... So we just went on. It was hideous. We were silhouetted. As much as you felt like going to ground, you just kept plugging on. I kept thinking the next shell could have my number on it.'[10]

The fighting was extremely intense but the Australian soldiers captured their objective. As with the fighting right down the line there were many acts of individual bravery, including that of Private Percy Gratwick who was posthumously awarded the Victoria Cross.

The casualties were high, and after some hours hundreds of German soldiers lay dead and hundreds more were captured. The Highlanders also suffered terrible casualties in their fighting around Kidney Ridge.

Now the captors had to quickly dig in before the anticipated Axis counter-attack. Having just returned to the frontline and while attempting to come to grips with the battle situation, Rommel was very perturbed that these prime positions had been lost. He was determined to recapture them, and subsequently transferred the 21st Panzer Division from the south to this sector, and during the following days he also poured other reinforcements into the battle to recapture them. In his attempts to regain this strategic position Rommel in turn presented weaknesses in other parts of his line. It was all to no avail, and Rommel recorded:

> Unfortunately, the attack gained ground very slowly. The British resisted desperately. Rivers of blood were poured out over miserable strips of land which, in normal times, not even the poorest Arab would have bothered his head about.[11]

During those several days there were again numerous acts of bravery, with 'Diver' Derrick in the midst of it. On one occasion he did an Upham and single handedly silenced three German machine-gun posts. During these horrendous days of non-stop fighting the 2/24th and 2/48th Battalions lost over 400 men each.

The casualties incurred by the 51st Highland Division were also high. For several days intense fighting took place in and around two positions north and south of Kidney Ridge known as 'Woodcock' and 'Snipe'. The fighting here, and especially around Snipe was on a par with that taking place at Trig 29, and Lieutenant-Colonel Victor Turner received the Victoria Cross for bravery in this action.

Regrouping

Despite the capture of Hill 29, and other Allied gains, and despite the lack of fuel and

10 Farquhar, M. ibid, p. 117.
11 Rommel, E. *The Rommel Papers*, p. 306.

ammunition on the Axis side,[12] Montgomery too had suffered many casualties and attrition upon his own forces and thereupon readapted his overall plan.[13] He wrote:

> By evening of 26 October I had decided to regroup, in order to create fresh reserves for further offensive action. The next phase would be in the north again, as I had been impressed with the results of the Australian attack on the night of 25/26 October. If I could get behind the enemy holding the coastal salient, I would annihilate or capture a strong force of Germans and perhaps open up the operation along the coastal axis. The first stage of the regrouping was the reversion of 2 New Zealand Division into reserve ...[14]

On 28 October the 9th Australian Division and 23rd Armoured Brigade began their attack. These units sustained heavy casualties and many Allied tanks were lost as the Axis forces were fully aware of the implications if this strategic area was lost. A key Axis position was the area which the Allies named Thompsons Post.

Ground was won, and despite repeated Axis counter-attacks the 9th Division infantry were not going to relinquish it. The casualty rate continued to mount. One important aspect of this assault was alluded to by Montgomery:

> During 29 October, and again early on 30 October, repeated counter attacks by tanks and infantry were hurled against the Australians in the wedge, but they held on and retained the ground won.
>
> I learnt during the morning of 29 October that 90 Light Division had moved into the Sidi Abd el Rahman area. This was very significant, for it showed that Rommel was reacting to the threat in the north and had properly guessed my intention of striking west along the coast road and rail axis.[15]

The strain of battle was by now beginning to have its effect upon Rommel. The lack of fuel and essential supplies was critical. His letters to his wife during these days reveal a man caught between reality and duty. On 29 October he wrote, 'The situation continues very grave. By the time this letter arrives, it will no doubt have been decided whether we can hold on or not. I haven't much hope left.'[16]

Special meeting in Britain

On 29 October 1942 a special meeting took place at Albert Hall in London, led by Anglican Archbishop William Temple. It was convened by Christian and Jewish leaders to call

12 The RAF had just sunk a large fuel carrying ship in Tobruk harbour, denying the Axis valuable fuel supplies.
13 Editorial comment by Liddell-Hart, in Rommel, E. *The Rommel Papers*, p. 307.
14 Montgomery, ibid, p. 20.
15 Montgomery, ibid, p. 22.
16 Rommel, E. *The Rommel Papers*, p. 312.

attention to the murder of Jewish people in Europe. News by this time had come through of the systematic annihilation of the Jewish people and other so-called undesirables, in the death camps of Auschwitz-Birkenau; Treblinka, Sobibor, Chelmno, Belzec and others.

Although by this stage the full extent of the 'Final Solution to the Jewish Problem' was not known, enough was known for people to understand that a human tragedy of the highest order was being perpetrated – and it had to be stopped.

Like the soldiers fighting at El Alamein these people too were probably unaware that the German High Command had set in place a plan to introduce this 'Final Solution to the Jewish Problem' into the Middle East as well. Whether or not this plan ever came into Egypt would depend upon the battle now being fought at El Alamein – and even at Stalingrad. This was certainly a timely gathering of Christian and Jewish people.

Montgomery prepares for Operation *Supercharge*

Montgomery had pulled the New Zealanders out of the front line in order to prepare them for the ultimate break-out – Operation *Supercharge*. Freyberg was unsure about this move due to their depleted numbers (they had lost some 1200 men at Ruweisat Ridge in July). Montgomery compensated by placing other British units under them, as well as 7th Armoured Regiment.

With more Axis troops now flooding into the area opposite where the Australians were attacking, Montgomery revised his plans, now intending to breakout in the area just north of Kidney Ridge. The success of Operation *Supercharge* depended upon as many Axis forces as possible being relocated to the very northern part of 30th Corps sector.

In order to achieve this goal Montgomery called for yet another offensive by the Australians, from the area they had captured, towards the coast – thereby cutting off the Axis forces within the salient. This would require the taking of Thompson's Post.

It is somewhat ironic that at this crucial period of the battle, political activities were taking place to have the 9th Australian Division pulled out and sent immediately back for home defence. General Morshead was caught between the demands and desires of General Macarthur, Supreme Allied Commander in the Pacific and the Australian Government on one side, and the reality of the battle situation on the other. He was probably very relieved when Montgomery flatly overruled and stated that they needed to remain.[17]

To obtain their objectives the 9th Division men had to cross the railway line which was enfiladed by German machine guns. Jack Ralla recalled of this time, 'One minute you'd be with chaps, next you would look around and they were gone. They were knocked off like flies.'[18] Ralla also mentioned that there was one constant during this time - Thomas Derrick was always there urging his men to 'Keep going.' Wally Fennell wrote, 'Those two days, the 30th and 31st, were really rough. So few of us got through.'[19]

17 Farquhar, M. ibid, p. 119-120.
18 Farquhar, M. ibid, p. 120.
19 Farquhar, M. ibid, p. 121.

One of those casualties was Sgt. William Kibby who showed exceptional courage on several occasions during the course of the battle. He was also posthumously awarded the Victoria Cross.[20]

The cost was high, but the diversion worked. New Zealander Jim Blyth, wrote:

> Something had to break the stalemate, and it was the Australians who did it. Ninth Australian Division out on the coast ... made the spectacular advance in their sector which created a serious bulge in the enemies defences which Montgomery was quick to exploit. It was the beginning of the end.[21]

Operation *Supercharge*

The initial aerial and artillery barrage for Operation *Supercharge* began in the afternoon of 1 November, aimed mostly at the Axis positions in and around Tel el Aqqaqir and Sidi El Rahman. Then at 01.00 in the morning of 2 November 1942 the New Zealand Division began moving forward, steering a course just north of Kidney Ridge and aiming towards Tel el Aqqaqir. The engineers then followed the infantry and cleared a route for the leading armoured cars of the Royal Dragoons to go through.

The way was now open for the 9th Armoured Brigade to break right through, engage and destroy the Axis armoured units in the area. This they basically did, but in the process they sustained a 75% casualty rate upon tanks and personnel. The 2nd and 8th Armoured Brigades then followed through the gap won by the 9th Armoured Brigade.[22] A major tank battle took place in the vicinity of Tel el Aqqaqir.

Rommel's plight

Although the Allied breakthrough had not yet resulted in a complete encirclement, Rommel realized that unless he pulled his forces back then they would be completely destroyed. If it was withdrawn, it could re-organize and then fight again from a position of strength. He withdrew his HQ back to Fuka.

Rommel informed Hitler on 3 November 1942 of the dire situation, and requested permission to break off the engagement and withdraw. Permission was denied, as revealed in Hitler's telegram to him:

> It is with trusting confidence in your leadership and the courage of the German-Italian troops under your command that the German people and I are following the heroic struggle in Egypt. In the situation in which you find yourself there can be no other thought but to stand fast, yield not a yard of ground and throw every gun and every man into the battle. Considerable air force reinforcements are being sent to C-in-C. South.

20 Derrick received the DCM and later received the Victoria Cross at Sattelberg in New Guinea.
21 Blyth, J. *Soldiering On,* pp. 66-67.
22 Editorial comment by Liddell-Hart in Rommel, E. *The Rommel Papers*, p. 319.

The Duce and the Comando Supremo are also making the utmost efforts to send you the means to continue the fight. Your enemy, despite his superiority, must also be at the end of his strength. It would not be the first time in history that a strong will has triumphed over the bigger battalions. As to your troops, you can show them no other road than to victory or death.[23]

This order was not what Rommel expected, and he wrote of it, 'This order demanded the impossible … We were completely stunned, and for the first time during the African campaign I did not know what to do. A kind of apathy took hold of us as we issued orders for all existing positions to be on instructions from the highest authority. I forced myself to this action, as I had always demanded unconditional obedience from others and, consequently wished to apply the same principle to myself … this first instance of interference by higher authority in the tactical conduct of the African war came as a considerable shock.'[24]

The Axis position continued to deteriorate. Rommel was caught in a moral bind: he could see the inevitable, but Hitler and the Nazi leadership could not envision a German retreat, which was tantamount to defeat. Rommel was also bound by his personal oath of allegiance to Hitler.

Victory at El Alamein

Had Rommel withdrawn to Fuka on 3 November he could have saved a greater part of his army. But he could not. Then on 4 November, Montgomery's encirclement began taking full effect, with the *Ariete* Division being the first to be engulfed at 15.30 on 4 November.

When this news reached him, Rommel then gave orders for immediate withdrawal, so that what could be saved of Panzer Army Africa could be saved. The withdrawal though was heavily bombed by the Desert Air Force which was relentless in its attack. Those who were left behind, which included thousands of Italian infantry, were quickly overtaken by the pursuing British armour and New Zealand infantry, and then by the other units following them.

With Rommel's withdrawal the Battle of El Alamein was over. The Allies had won.[25]

Great relief - and sorrow

People the world over received the news with great joy – and trepidation. Once the dust of battle had settled, the casualty figures began to be released. Many Allied families were to mourn for lost loved ones, as too were many German and Italian families.

Several Allied units were particularly hard hit, including the 9th Australian Division.

23 Rommel, E. *The Rommel Papers*, p. 321.

24 Rommel, E. *The Rommel Papers*, pp. 321-22.

25 The Australians, however, would not be part of Operation *Supercharge.* Since 23 October their Division had sustained 2,694 men killed, wounded or missing. After pursuing the retreating Axis forces to El Daba, they received the call to return home to Australia to fight the Japanese.

Murray Farquhar recorded of Thomas 'Diver' Derrick's company in 2/48th Battalion, 'Precisely eighty men had marched into battle; three officers and sixty-seven other ranks had been killed or wounded.'[26]

The Jewish community in Palestine was also elated at the news of the victory, but also deeply sorrowful at the terrible loss of life. The late Uzi Narkiss was the Israeli general who commanded the capture of the Old City of Jerusalem in 1967, and in his career also witnessed the loss of many young men in combat. Narkiss understood the significance of this victory:

> Thanks to the British and the Australians and the New Zealanders and all the others present here, the German Army was stopped at El Alamein. Montgomery then counter-attacked. But as far as we are concerned, we were rescued by the British Empire that included all those mentioned armies. [27]

One surviving soldier from El Alamein, Moses Mosenson wrote to his young daughter on 5 November:

> We are pursuing the German armies who are fleeing before us ... We have pushed them far away from the place where they threatened our country. That danger is now over. But the job is not finished yet...
>
> ... We went out to war so that our children, when they grow up, will not have to go through this horror a second time. We went out to war in order to defend our country and our work, to free our people from the dreadful fate which the Nazis have forced upon them ....
>
> ... And after we clean Africa up we will go and fight them in their own country, until we wipe out this Nazi-Fascist plague completely. Then, my daughter, we will go home again.[28]

Plight of Jewish communities in Libya

Later in the campaign as the Eighth Army subdued all of Cyrenaica, it was the time of the Jewish festival of *Hanukah*. *Hanukah* is usually a time of rejoicing, of triumph of good over evil, of the Jewish people over their enemies.

Such was not to be the case for the Jewish soldiers in North Africa in 1942. At the *Hanukah* party the rabbi remorsefully informed them of the welfare of the Jewish communities in Cyrenaica. All the Jewish men had been commandeered into road-building (which was basically slave labour). Some 2,000 Jewish residents of Libya were taken away,

26 Farquhar, M. ibid, p. 123.

27 Interview with the late General (Res) Uzi Narkiss, as shown on *The Battle for Zion* documentary.

28 Mosenson, M. *Letters from the Desert,* pp. 136-137.

and more than one in five of them perished.[29]

The remaining families from the Jewish communities in Cyrenaica, especially Benghazi, had been killed or taken away by the German-led forces. The fate of some of these people is recorded by a Dutch Jewish lady, Miriam Bolle, who was incarcerated at Bergen Belsen concentration camp. Bolle wrote in her dairy on 31 January 1945:

> Tonight eighty-three Jews arrived, coming from Benghazi, Derna and Tula ... They have already been in seven camps. [30]

The Ben Dusa family, who had invited young Australians to their Purim party in 1941 and had invited Mosenson for a Shabbat meal a week later, suffered terribly. Mosenson wrote to his wife:

> ... the young daughter of the Ben Dusa family, whose guest I was, was carried off by the Italian army; the mother was raped by drunken Italians and was then stabbed to death and the rest of the family were taken to labor battalions and no one knows how they met their death.[31]

Again a few days later he wrote to his wife on 15 December 1942:

> When we appeared in Libya for the first time and went in a group to the synagogue, the Jewish quarter hummed with joy and happiness. They believed, innocently, that we had the keys to Palestine. Now they are beaten and wretched, and we have no word of hope for them. Think of the feelings of a Jewish soldier who goes to battle in order to save his people, but is completely helpless when he meets them, crushed and miserable.[32]

This dour description of the plight of the Jewish people in Libya provides further evidence of the potential fate of the Jewish communities east of El Alamein - had the Axis forces won there.

Americans arrive and Australians return home

While the battered and bruised Eighth Army continued to pursue Rommel's equally battered and bruised forces westwards across North Africa the first United States troops entered into the European theatre of war. They landed in Morocco and Algeria on 8 November 1942 signalling the beginning of Operation *Torch*. Ultimately the two armies

29 *The Jewish people in Libya*, www.wikipedia

30 Bolle, M. *Ik zal je beschrijven hoe een dag er hier uitziet,* ('I Will Describe for you what a day here is like') Amsterdam, 2003, p. 210. The Jerusalem Post wrote on 10 April 2011 under the title *Libyan Jews divided over bid to rebuild Tripoli temple*, 'During World War Two they were interned by the Italians, and some were sent to concentration camps in Europe'.

31 Mosenson, M. *Letters from the Desert,* pp. 145-146.

32 Mosenson, M. *Letters from the Desert,* p. 149.

met in Tunisia in 1943 and finally defeated the Axis forces in North Africa. Field Marshal Rommel, however, had previously left and returned to Europe.[33]

One Allied division did not pursue Rommel westward. The 9th Australian Division was required back home to help stop the Japanese threat. The survivors made their way back to their camps in Palestine, arriving there on 7 December 1942. After several days leave tours were arranged for them to be taken to Jerusalem, Tel Aviv, Haifa and elsewhere where weary and aching bodies could be restored.

They then partook of perhaps the biggest military ceremony in Palestine during the war, at the Gaza airfield on 22 December 1942. The Commander-in-Chief of the Middle East forces, General Sir Harold Alexander, then addressed and saluted these men before they departed. One of those who witnessed this parade, Major-General Edward Spears, wrote:

> ... The men, I was told, had taken immense pains to be drill-perfect, for they regarded this parade as a message, a token of sorrow and respect to all those Australian soldiers whom they left behind, buried on the soil of the Levant.[34]

These men represented not just the Australians but the tens of thousands of young Allied soldiers from all the nations who had served and died in this region between 1940-1942. Their service and sacrifice halted the Axis forces and associated Nazi ideology from entering into Egypt east of El Alamein, and into Palestine itself.

33 Rommel was later implicated in the assassination attempt against Hitler in July 1944, and was forced to commit suicide in October 1944.

34 Quoted in Laffin, J. *Greece, Crete and Syria,* p. 162.

CONCLUSION

EL ALAMEIN – KEY TO THE FUTURE?

At the end of the War the leadership of the Jewish people in Palestine (the *Vaad Leumi*), presented General Montgomery, the commander of the Eighth Army with a gift of gratitude – the 'Montgomery Bible.'

What is significant is not so much the actual Bible, but the words which accompanied it. Those few words really do say much about the significance of this battle, which ran from July to November 1942, and indeed the entire 1940-1942 Middle East campaign.

During those years the very same forces of darkness which covered Europe and were snuffing out all pockets of light, were attempting to do the same in the Middle East.

Within that context let us look at those profound words which accompanied the Bible. The actual words are in italics:

(To) *Field Marshal Viscount Montgomery …*
Montgomery was a representative British military leader from the campaign. Despite any faults and mistakes made, they collectively kept the Axis forces at bay during this period. Perhaps then we should read, 'General Wavell, General O'Connor, Admiral Cunningham, General Neame, General Auchinleck, Air Marshal Tedder, General Ritchie, General Cunningham, General Alexander … and Field Marshal Viscount Montgomery.'

Then there are the numerous Corps and Divisional commanders who played very significant roles in the campaign, particularly 'General Morshead, General Freyberg and General Gott.'

In addition there are certain political leaders who showed vision, fortitude and faith during these years, especially Winston Churchill, who despite some mis-judgments (including, perhaps, the Greek campaign and the sacking of Auchinleck) never stopped supporting the Middle East theatre even at the expense of home defence. There were also the leaders of the nations who volunteered to send their men to the Middle East and who supported their presence there, even when danger was threatening back home, particularly Prime Ministers Savage and Menzies and General Smuts.

… the gallant leader of the victorious British forces …
These words are again representative, as it was the men of the land, sea and air services from Britain, India, Australia, New Zealand, South Africa, France, Poland, Greece, Palestine, Belgium, the Netherlands and elsewhere, such as Charles Upham, Bob Holt, Arthur Leggett, Ron Turrel and Thomas Derrick, who ultimately brought about the victory.

Not all these men were heroes like 'Jock' Campbell, Charles Upham and Thomas Derrick, but they all had one thing in common: they desired to preserve justice, protect freedom and to keep the light burning. Deep down they understood the severe consequences for their home nations if Nazi Germany and Fascist Italy triumphed; and they were willing to lay down their lives to stop the spread of totalitarian regimes.

Although outside the remit of this book, honour must also be given to all those brave people in Germany who also attempted to keep the light burning, such as Neimoller (who survived) and Bonhoffer (who died) and the many others.

… by whose hand God …

Throughout these troubling years Christian and Jewish people prayed ceaselessly for victory over the forces of darkness as represented in the Nazi system. People such as Rees Howells, Derek Prince and General Montgomery knew that if they humbled themselves and confessed their own inadequacies, then the God of Israel would fight for them – and prevail.

None of the Allied leaders were immune from making mistakes. Those words point to a higher authority in whom is found all wisdom and all knowledge.

… has placed salvation in Zion in the days of El Alamein.

The historical record as presented in the previous pages (albeit briefly), and to which others especially Mallman and Cuppers, have also testified, seems to strongly indicate that if German forces had become actively involved in Iraq, Syria, Egypt and Palestine, then they would have tried to destroy the Jewish people, just as they did in Greece.

In the Middle East there was the potential (and even real) union between the forces of radical Islam and Arab nationalism (as represented by Haj Amin). We do not know to what extent the Holocaust would have entered into the Middle East if Rommel had broken through any time after July 1942, but the mechanisms were there for it to have been introduced.

In the bigger perspective the Jewish people in Zion were saved by the combined victories at El Alamein and Stalingrad. And, I hasten to add, it was not only the Jewish people who were potentially saved by these two victories, for despite the darkness that the Soviet system then imposed upon Eastern Europe, western freedom itself owed much to those two victories.

It is almost as if the two, the survival of the Jewish people and the preservation of western democracy, are somehow closely connected.

Some challenges for the future

As I draw this narrative to a close I am challenged by an over-arching question:

'If it happened then, could it happen again?'

This question has four sub-questions:

1. 'Could so many nations of the world again be locked in conflict in that region?'
2. 'If a civilized nation like Germany in the 1930's could be bewitched by Adolf Hitler and the hate ridden and racist Nazi ideology, and if Nazi Germany could so easily link up with radical Islam and Arab nationalism as espoused then by Haj Amin, could it happen again?'
3. 'Could there ever again be such a concerted effort to switch off the light, not just in Europe, but anywhere, especially within the western world?'
4. 'Are there ideologies out there today with a similar agenda to that of the Nazis?'

The short answer to these questions would have to be: 'Yes, it could happen again.'

The reason it could happen again is because of man's propensity to be deceived, and because the foundational principles of Hitler's ideology (of the supremacy of his people over all others and the associated aspects of hate and racism), are still very much alive and with us today. Additionally, the strategic significance of that coveted piece of territory, particularly the Suez Canal and the land of Israel, have ever since 1942 continued to be a source of world attention and agitation.

Perhaps Churchill was right when he stated to General Alexander that the battle of El Alamein was the key to the future. But in what ways though was it a key?

It could be that similar geo-political dynamics which drew the Germans towards the oil fields of Mosul and the Suez Canal will again become factors. It may also be that the very presence of the Jewish people in the land of Israel will of itself provoke those same forces of darkness to attempt to destroy them – just as Hitler desired to.

Such forces of darkness, though, will not just be attempting to destroy the people of Israel, they will also be attempting to switch off the light of justice, freedom and democracy, just as Nazism did. The challenge before us will be to spot those signs, and ensure that we will not be easily deceived as were most of the people in Germany at that time.

In conclusion then, perhaps the real legacy of El Alamein is that it revealed how brave and insightful people fought to preserve freedom and justice - and in the process also halted the Holocaust from entering into the Middle East.

'Behold, he that keepeth Israel shall neither slumber nor sleep.' (Psalm 121: 4. King James Version)

Selected Bibliography

Books

Antonius, G. *The Arab Awakening,* Beirut, 1936.

Badman, Peter. *North Africa 1940-1942. The Desert War*, Sydney, 1988.

Barnett, Correlli. *The Desert Generals*, London.

Beech, C. *Great Love has no man than this…* Perth, 2012.

Bethell, Nicholas. *The Palestine Triangle*, London, 1979.

Blyth, J. *Soldiering On. A Soldiers War in North Africa and Italy*, Auckland, 1989.

Bolle, M. *Ik zal je beschrijven hoe een dag er hier uitziet,* ('I Will Describe for you what a day here is like') Amsterdam, 2003.

Churchill, W. *The Gathering Storm,* Boston, 1948.

Their Finest Hour, ibid.

The Grand Alliance, ibid.

The Hinge of Fate, ibid.

Triumph and Tragedy, ibid.

Davin, D.M. *Battle of Crete,* In *Purnell's History of the Second World War.* Volume 5, Paulton, 1967.

Dayan, Moshe, *Story of My Life,* New York, 1977.

Documents on German Foreign Policy, Her Majesty's Stationery Office, London, 1962, Volumes X,XI,XII,XIII.

Ebery, S. *Weary,* Castle Hill, 1994.

Farquhar, M. *Derrick V.C.* Adelaide, 1982.

Fitzsimmons, P. *Tobruk,* Sydney, 2006.

Foley, J. *Tobruk Survives.* In Purnells *History of the Second World War,* Vol. 2, Paulton, 1967.

Gabriel, M. *Islam and the Jews,* Lake Mary, Florida, 2003.

Gilbert, M. *Churchill and the Jews,* London, 2007.

Glen, J. *Tobruk to Tarakan,* Adelaide, 1960.

Goodrich-Clarke, N. *The Occult Roots of Nazism,* London, 1985.

Grubb, N. *Rees Howells Intercessor*, Fort Washington, 1952.

HaCohen, D. *Time to Tell*, New York, 1985.

Hill, M. *Diggers and Greeks,* Sydney, 2010.

Hitler, A. *Mein Kampf,* English translation, London, 1969.

Holt Bob, *From Ingleburn to Aitape*, Brookvale, 1981.

Horne, A & Montgomery, D. *Monty,* London, 1944.

Hourani, A. *Syria and Lebanon,* Oxford, 1946.

Israel Pocket Library. *Zionism*, Jerusalem, 1973.

Israel Pocket Library. *History from 1880*, Jerusalem, 1973.

Johnston, M & Stanley, P. *Alamein – The Australian Story*, Melbourne, 2002.

King, M. *New Zealanders at War*, Auckland, 1981.

Kinross, Lord. *Between two Seas.* New York, 1969.

Kippinger, Lieut-Col. H. *Infantry Brigadier*, 1949.

Kirk, G. *The Middle East in the War*, London, 1953.

Laffin, J. *Anzacs at War*, London, New York, Toronto, 1965.

Laffin, J. *Greece, Crete and Syria*, Sydney, 1989.

Leggett, A. *Don't Cry for Me,* Oldbury, 2006.

Lewis, B. *The Middle East and the West*, New York, 1964.

Lossin, Yigal. *Pillar of Fire*, Jerusalem, 1983.

Lowenthal, M. *The Diaries of Theodor Herzl,* New York, 1956.

Mallmann, K & Cuppers, M. *Nazi Palestine*, New York, 2010.

Manning, Olivier, *The Flap*, In *Purnell's History of the Second World War*, London, 1967.

McCullough, C. *Roden Cutler, VC.* Sydney, 1998.

McCleod, G. *Anzacs*, North Ryde, 1985

Montgomery, B. *El Alamein to the River Sangro,* London, 1948.

Monson, J. *The Land in Between,* Jerusalem, 1983.

Mosenson, M. *Letters from the Desert*, New York, 1945.

Parkes, J. *Whose Land?* Britain, 1970.

Pearlman, M. *The Mufti of Jerusalem*, London, 1947.

Reich, C. *Australia and Israel,* Carlton South, 2002.

Reuth, R. *Rommel, The End of a Legend,* London, 2005.

Roland, P. *The Nazis and the Occult,* London, 2007.

Rommel, E. *The Rommel Papers*, New York, 1953.

Sacher, H. *A History of Israel*, New York, 1976.

Sandford, K. *Mark of the Lion,* London, 1962.

Sinclair, K. *A History of New Zealand*, Auckland, 1959.

Shirer, William, L. *The Rise and Fall of the Third Reich*, New York, 1960.

Slater, R. *Rabin of Israel*, London, 1996.

Snyder, T. Bloodlands, London, 2011.

Stein, L. *The Balfour Declaration*, London, 1961.

Stockings, C. *Bardia,* Sydney, 2009.

Taylor, Capt R.J. *Kiwis in the Desert*, New Zealand Defence Force, 1992.

Teveth, S. *Ben Gurion: The Burning Ground, 1886-1948*, Boston, 1997.

Teveth, S. *Moshe Dayan*, New York, 1972.

Turrell, R. *It's Only Me,* Durban, 1980.

Vader, J. *Anzac*, Britain, 1972.

Wallach, J. *Germany and the Middle East 1835-1939,* Tel Aviv, 1975.

Weizmann, C. *Trial and Error: 2 Volumes*, Philadelphia, 1949.

Other Sources

Shraga Elam and Dennis Whitehead, *In the service of the Jewish State,* Ha'aretz newspaper, 31 March 2007, www.haaretz.com/weekend/magazine/in-the-service-of-the-jewish-state.

Shraga Elam and Dennis Whitehead, *Rauff vs. The Yishuv,* 29 March 2007, *Haaretz* Daily newspaper, www.haaretz.com/weekend/magazine/rauff-vs-the-yishuv.

Hansard, Speech of Neville Chamberlain, 14 December 1939, Vol. 335, cc 1342.

Jerusalem Post, Jerusalem. May 23, 1990; December 4, 1992; November 13, 1994; December 15, 1978; October 23, 1992; 10 April 2011.

Journal of the Australian War Memorial. April, 1984; October 1983; April 1991.

Palestine Post, Jerusalem. Numerous articles during period of 1940-1942.

www.wikipedia.com. (Used on numerous occasions)

www.kooriweb.org/foley/essays/essay.

www.ess.uwe.ac.uk; Dr. S. Stein, *Statements by Hitler and Senior Nazis concerning Jews and Judaism.*

www.aso.gov.au; *Menzies Speech: Declaration of War.*

www.balkananalysis.com/2005/11/30/the-holocaust-in-greece-1941-1944; Savich, C. *TheHolocaust in Greece, 1941-1944.*

www.historyplace.com/worldwar2/holocaust/h-wannsse; *Minutes of Wannsee Conference.*

www.virtuallibrary.org.

Archives, Libraries, War Memorials, etc.

Australian War Memorial, Canberra.

British Library, London.

Bundesarchiv (German Federal Archive), Berlin.

Central Zionist Archives, Jerusalem.

Imperial War Museum, London.

Jabotinsky Institute, Tel Aviv.

National Archives, Kew, London.

Queen Elizabeth II War Memorial, Waioru, New Zealand.

Other Materials

Various interviews and conversation, particularly with Prime Minister Mr. Yitzak Rabin (z.l) and General Uzi Narkiss (z.l.)

For further information about Genocide prevention

Genocide Prevention Centre, www.genocidewatch.org

Jerusalem Centre for Genocide Prevention, www.jc4gp.org